HEALTHY FATS

FOR LIFE

Preventing and Treating

Common Health Problems

with Essential Fatty Acids

Lorna R. Vanderhaeghe, B.Sc.

Karlene Karst, B.Sc., R.D.

QUARRY
HEALTH
BOOKS

The publisher acknowledges the support of the Government of Canada, Department of Canadian Heritage, Book Publishing Industry Development Program, and the Government of Ontario, Ontario Media Development Corporation, Book Initiative Program.

ISBN 1-55082-330-2

Cover Design : Rachael Roulston & Susan Hannah
Text Design & Imaging: Tanja Hutter
Photo Credits: front cover, (left to right): evening primrose courtesy of Siegfried Gursche, *alive* magazine; borage courtesy of Bioriginal Food & Science Corporation; salmon courtesy of Gilbert van Ryckevorsel/www.salmonphotos.com; flax courtesy of Bioriginal Food & Science Corporation. Back cover photo of Lorna R. Vanderhaeghe by Donna Newman; Karlene Karst by Jerry Humeny/Black Box Images.

Printed and bound in Canada.
Quarry Health Books
PO Box 1061
Kingston, Ontario
K7L 4Y5 Canada

HEALTHY FATS

FOR LIFE

CONTENTS

Lorna R. Vanderhaeghe, B.Sc.

Lorna Vanderhaeghe is a medical journalist who has been researching and writing on the subject of nutritional medicine for over 20 years. Her list of accomplishments include: working at the *Journal of Orthomolecular Medicine* at the Canadian Schizophrenia Foundation; past editor-in-chief of *Healthy Living Guide*; senior editor of the *Encyclopedia of Natural Healing* (winner of the prestigious Benjamin Franklin Award in 1998).

She is currently an associate editor for *Total Health* magazine in the United States and *alive* magazine in Canada. Lorna is co-author of the award-winning, best-selling book *The Immune System Cure* now published in six countries and translated into French, Dutch and German and author of the Canadian bestseller *Healthy Immunity, Scientifically Proven Natural Treatments for Conditions from A-Z*, released in September 2001. Her most recent co-authored book, *No More HRT: Menopause Treat the Cause*, was released in September 2002. An internationally-known lecturer, she believes in empowering people with health knowledge so they can achieve optimal wellness. You can contact her through www.hormonehelp.com.

Karlene Karst, R.D.

Karlene Karst holds a Bachelor of Science degree in Nutrition and is a Registered Dietitian. She provides technical and regulatory advice on essential fatty acids, as well as giving educational seminars, lectures and presentations to the public on the role of EFAs in nutrition and health. She previously worked as a clinical dietitian, teaching classes and providing counseling for nutrition, diabetes, and cardiovascular health. Karlene is currently the Clinical Research and Education Coordinator at Bioriginal Food and Science Corporation, the world's leading supplier of essential fatty acids. She can be contacted at www.fatsforhealth.com.

ACKNOWLEDGEMENTS

To the pioneers in fats and oils research, we thank you. Without your dedication to introduce new theories on healthy fats in our diet we would not have had the research upon which to build this book.

My love goes to my co-author Karlene Karst for her youth, enthusiasm, knowledge and commitment to this book. Tanja Hutter I honor you. For without your sleepless nights this book might not have been. Deane Parkes, a kindred spirit, your words of encouragement I cherish. My dear friend Udo Erasmus, the fat man, I thank you for the endless hours spent discussing fats. To Siegfried Gursche for introducing the first cold pressed nut and seed oils to Canada. My family has been eating healthy oils for over a decade because of you and Udo. To Shelagh Jamieson, we have shared laughter, trust and camaraderie. I love working with smart women.

My greatest accomplishment in life has been raising my children Crystal, Kevin, Kyle and Caitlyn. Your unconditional love and support deeply touches my heart. To my grandsons Matthew and Hayden your little hands and wet kisses help me remember the simple things in life and to Hayden for drinking flax oil right out of the bottle. Mom, thank you for the instilling in me the drive to make a difference. I remember the days when you championed for the poor, a woman, speaking out in the days when women did not.

Thank you to the readers of my books. Your shared stories and my desire to ensure that no woman or man has to endure so much needless physical suffering —when the answers are so easily found in nature—fuel my passion for writing.

Lorna Vanderhaeghe

To my dad, who passed away eight years ago after a courageous battle with cancer. His hard work, determination and strength have given me the drive to succeed in everything I do. The courage he showed me during his illness will never be forgotten and it truly made me into the person that I am today. To mom, you have blessed me with so many wonderful gifts. Thank you for your continued support, love, faith in my abilities and most importantly, your prayers. God has blessed me with a mom like you, I love you.

To Tim, you have been a pillar of strength, love and continued support during the writing of this book, thank you. To my sister Kristin, you are so special to me, thanks for being there to listen—you're the best. To my brother Trenton, you are an important person in my life who shares so many similar qualities with me. You never cease to amaze me with your continued drive to do bigger and better things.

Thank you to Bioriginal Food & Science Corp. for supplying the world with high quality essential fatty acid oils, so that we can continue to reap the health benefits they provide, and strive to become a healthier society. Thank you for this opportunity, to help me reach my dreams. You have shown so much faith and trust in me and my abilities during the writing of this book, thank you for this opportunity! To Shelagh Jamieson, your organization, skills and devotion to Healthy Fats For Life are appreciated by all, especially me. Thank you for believing in me, and for your mentorship.

A special thank you goes to Janice McColl, pharmacist, master herbalist and director of R&D for a company specializing in herbal extracts. Thanks for taking the time out of your very busy schedule to use your technical expertise to review this book and make it more complete. Rakesh Kapoor and Janice McColl, you have taught me everything I know about essential fats. The breadth and depth of your scientific knowledge is amazing. You are both such inspirations to me, and without you, I would not have been able to publish this book.

My appreciation goes out to my co-author Lorna who continues to do amazing things for people everywhere by sharing her knowledge and expertise about nutrition and disease. Your love and passion for making people healthy is an inspiration to me. Lorna, you are my role model and mentor, and I look forward to a continued friendship and our next "project" together. And last but not least, Tanja Hutter for burning the midnight oil to complete this book. Your knowledge, skills, and experience are what made this all possible.

Karlene Karst

This book is dedicated to all those who have been misguided with the message that "low fat, no fat" diets are healthy. *Healthy Fats for Life* will ensure you acquire a healthy oil change!

INTRODUCTION

We have been consistently told that fat is bad for us and we should reduce or eliminate its consumption. Yet low fat, no fat diets with their dangerous transfatty acids are killing us. So pervasive are fat-reduced foods that if we look closely at the labels on the foods we purchase we might be surprised at how many low fat or fat-free foods we put into our grocery cart each week. Over the last decade North American food manufacturers have delivered well over 15,000 reduced-fat foods from low fat cookies to low-fat salad dressings married with the message of lose weight by cutting or reducing fat in the diet. Yet with the focus on no fat, low fat foods we have skyrocketing rates of obesity, diabetes, heart disease and cancer.

Research into the 'right fat' diet has been conflicting. We have been told that margarine is better than butter. Then some scientists did a complete about face and we were advised that we should eat butter instead of margarine. Many of us stopped eating eggs because doctors told us they added to our high cholesterol. Then a decade later nutritionists said we made a mistake, "Eggs are good for you and have little effect on cholesterol." Fats are bad for us is another myth perpetuated by those who fail to understand how all the different types of fats affect the body. Lumping all fat into the same category has caused the disease scales to rise.

Thousands of studies worldwide, many of them quoted in this book, provide the evidence that certain fats are not bad for us but essential for life. Extra virgin olive oil, organic flax seed oil, coconut butter, borage, evening primrose, fish oils, butter and CLA provide amazing healing properties. These marvelous healing fats reduce our risk of heart disease and diabetes, help us burn fat, oil arthritic joints, prevent depression, manufacture our hormones, improve our skin, boost our immune system and so much more.

Advances in medicine are often thought of in terms of pharmaceutical drugs, gene therapies, diagnostic or surgical techniques, yet simply making healthier food choices would give us the biggest breakthrough in preventing and treating the illnesses of our affluence. Diseases of inadequate nutrition affect up to 80% of North Americans. We are the most overfed, undernourished group of people in the world filling our bodies with empty calories and toxic foods with very dangerous side effects.

A return to a diet consisting of fresh, organically grown fruits and vegetables, wild fish, free-range chickens and eggs, grassland fed beef, and nuts, seeds and grains in their whole form could solve most of our health problems. But alas convenience of shopping weekly at the grocery store and our busy schedules send us packing the freezer with frozen foods and our pantry with processed foods that last for weeks without spoilage. This book assumes that you know you should not smoke, that exercise is important, that junk food is dangerous and that you must limit your intake of alcohol, so we won't remind you of this. We also wanted to focus solely on fats and oils so we did not encumber the book with information on vitamins and minerals. Lorna's other books and other authors have thoroughly covered that area.

Healthy Fats for Life provides you with an overview of all the healing fats and how you can incorporate them into your diet. It also exposes the deadly fats and advises which foods they are lurking in. We have explained how nutritional supplement manufacturers make quality oils in capsule or liquid form. It is important to use oils of the highest quality. The days of eating rancid cod liver oil every day are thankfully a thing of the past. Most importantly, we help you to understand how to use these oils to prevent or treat certain disease conditions.

Our goal with this book is to ensure that you and your loved ones consume the best fats to prevent disease. We also want you to achieve optimal health and vitality by changing the bad fats in your diet to the healthy fats. Thankfully it takes a very short time to reverse the damage done by eating bad fats. Simply start your new fat diet today and soon you will notice your energy and vigor return.

Chapter 1

THE ABCS OF EFAS

Many of us have been brainwashed into thinking all fats are bad. This is simply not the case. In fact, a lack of certain fats in the diet can be detrimental to our health. The low-fat, no-fat diet that has been avidly promoted over recent years not only strips away the "bad" fat from our diet, but deprives us of the "good" fats that are essential to our health. In addition, most people eagerly reducing their fat intake will eat more high carbohydrate items such as pasta, muffins and bread rather than increase the amount and variety of complex carbohydrates including vegetables and fruits. Instead of seeing a decrease in diabetes, heart disease and weight gain, we have witnessed an unprecedented increase in these conditions. Nutritional researchers would like us to know that "good fats" are essential for maintaining health.

The focus of this book is to explain why fats, especially essential fatty acids (EFAs) are crucial to our health and how they help alleviate specific conditions. However, good fats are one of many groups of nutrients required for health. They do not replace the need for a well-balanced diet, drinking plenty of water, and getting adequate sleep and exercise. Even though the research presented in this book will focus primarily on the positive health benefits of good fats, we do not mean to imply that they are more important than vitamins, minerals, protein and carbohydrates but rather, that they are equal in importance. It is our intention to demonstrate how good fats can easily become a part of your daily diet.

This chapter provides a solid overview of the different fats and the science behind them. You can read this chapter for a thorough understanding or skip to the specific health condition of your choice.

IN THE BEGINNING

Four million years ago our ancestors' diets consisted mainly of wild meat, fish, plants, nuts, seeds and berries. Grain products and concentrated sugars were absent from human nutrition until the development of agriculture 10,000 years ago. The nature of an agrarian society encouraged humans to settle down, to produce gardens and crops, and domesticate animals. The meat of more sedentary domesticated animals has more fat than those of wild animals. This point in our history marks the initial increase in our fat consumption. The Industrial Revolution sparked another huge change in nutrition as more people left the farms to work in factories, thus increasing the need for store-bought food for those without access or time to produce their own. Reliance on grocers to provide food, and the grocer's financial concern to keep wasted food down to a minimum, paved the way for the highly processed and preserved foodstuffs you find on North American supermarket shelves today.

The changes over the past 100 years in the human environment have happened too quickly for evolution to keep up. We are nearly genetically identical to our hunter-gatherer ancestors, yet we live in overcrowded and polluted cities, have frequent contact with harsh chemicals, and consume processed foods that are relatively deficient in essential nutrients. In comparison to our ancestors, we eat hundreds of times more transfatty acids (harmful, man-made fat that is linked to many diseases, including cancer and heart disease) and ten times more saturated fats. Some scientists have suggested that the key to our health is to adapt some aspects of the pre-agricultural diet of our ancestors. By changing the type and balance of fatty acids in our diet, we may actually prevent some of today's modern diseases.

UNDERSTANDING FATS: HEALTHY FATS FOR A HEALTHY BODY

There are fats that can kill you. Most of us eat them every day. However, there are some fats that are necessary for the body to function and you should be including them in your diet. Bad fats are associated with cancer, heart disease, diabetes and arthritis, but good fats can reduce inflammation, burn unwanted fat, stabilize blood sugar levels and lower blood pressure. It is important to understand which fats you should be leaving out of your meals and which should be going in. There are two main groups of fats—saturated and unsaturated.

Saturated Fats:
The Good, The Bad and the Not-so Bad

Saturated fats are semi-solid at room temperature and are found in animal products, such as red meat, pork, lamb, lard and dairy products like milk, cheese and butter, as well as in processed foods. They are generally considered "bad" fats, as they can contribute to heart disease; therefore, most health authorities recommend a reduction of saturated fats in the diet.

However, not all saturated fats are created equally. There are three subgroups of saturated fats based on their fat chain length: short-chain, medium-chain and long-chain.

THE GOOD

Short-chain saturates, found in butter, coconut oil and palm kernel oil, do not clog arteries, nor do they cause heart disease. Rather, they are easily digested and a source of fuel for energy. As well, short-chain saturates do not contain as many calories as the longer chain fatty acids. Butter is only 80% fat and margarine is 100% fat, so one pound of butter has 8 fewer calories than a pound of margarine made with seed oils.

THE NOT-SO-BAD

Medium-chain saturates are found in several different foods, but the highest content (just as in short-chain saturates) is also found in palm kernel and coconut oils, and they are not associated with increasing cholesterol levels or the occurrence of heart disease. Medium chain triglycerides oils (MCT oils) are used in special medical formulas for people who need energy from fat but have trouble digesting it from regular dietary sources, and for athletes and dieters looking to convert fat into energy rather than store it as fat.

THE BAD

Long-chain saturates are the "bad" fats associated with raising LDL (the bad cholesterol), lowering HDL (the good cholesterol) and the increasing risk of heart disease. The bad saturated fats are those found in meat. Long-chain saturates are also a by-product of hydrogenation, a process that turns a liquid fat (at room temperature) into a solid and is employed in the manufacture of most margarines and shortening. Long-chain saturates are also abundantly present in restaurant fried foods, junkfood, packaged baked goods and processed foods. Hydrogenation or partial hydrogenation also distorts the fatty acids into a more poisonous form.

NO MORE TRANSFATTY ACIDS

McDonald's took the leap first, announcing in September 2002 that it will switch cooking oils to reduce the amount of transfatty acids in its food by almost half. Frito-Lay has followed, with plans to eliminate transfats from Doritos™, Tostitos™ and Cheetos™ early in 2003. Science and the media have continued to scrutinize food manufacturers for the use of transfats in their food. Are transfats really that bad? The simple answer—they are deadly.

Numerous research studies have shown that transfats are more damaging to the heart than saturated fats, and in fact, the Institute of Medicine, a division of the National Academy of Science, released a report in July 2002 on transfats. It is a strongly worded report declaring there are no safe levels of transfats and the consumption should be reduced as much as possible. The institute declined to declare any upper limits on transfats.

Transfatty acids are man-made. Our bodies cannot recognize them as nutrients and therefore are not able to process them. While there has been much debate over whether saturated or transfats are worse, harmful transfats are not naturally occurring while saturated fats are. The Harvard School of Public Health has declared transfats dangerous to our health. While saturated fats in high levels are not healthy for the body either, they are still a source of energy that our bodies can use. Transfats are truly junkfood and should be avoided. Looking for hydrogenated or partially hydrogenated oils in food-product ingredient lists is one clue to the presence of transfats. Clearly we should avoid them.

The U.S. Food and Drug Administration is moving to require the listing of transfats on labels based on the recently released Institute of Medicine report. This mandatory labeling is critical to help consumers avoid foods that contain transfats, although eating some transfats may be unavoidable. The FDA has estimated that listing transfatty acids on food labels would save between 2,000 and 5,600 lives per year due to people choosing healthier foods. When the FDA ruling comes through for the mandatory labeling of transfats, you won't have to look too far to recognize this nutrition demon.

Operation: Covert Transfatty Acids

As you shop for your usual grocery items, read the label and add up the percentages of fat. There is a good chance that they will not equal 100%. The missing percentage could be poison—the transfatty acid content.

THE TRUTH ABOUT COCONUT OIL

We would like to expand on coconut oil a little more because it has been wrongly branded as a nutritional evil for so long. In the 1960s, data collected from research was misinterpreted, concluding that coconut oil raised blood cholesterol levels. In fact, it was the omission of essential fatty acids in the experimental diet that caused the observed health problems, not the inclusion of the coconut oil.

As we mentioned earlier, coconut oil is a short-chain fat that is easily digested and used by the body. More recent subject groups studied in the South Pacific for their regular use of coconut oil in the diet exhibited low incidences of coronary artery disease and low serum cholesterol levels. Little or no change is evident in serum cholesterol levels when an EFA-rich diet contains non-hydrogenated saturated fats. Coconut oil is naturally saturated, so it does not need to go through hydrogenation. Other benefits of coconut oil are that it is slightly lower in calories than most other fats and oils, and you don't need to use as much coconut oil as you would others when cooking or baking.

Coconut-Flaxseed Spread Recipe*

Place 1/2 cup (125 mL) of flaxseed oil in freezer for two hours or more. Melt 1 cup of coconut butter on low temperature. Remove from heat. Add frozen flaxseed oil. Blend and keep in the refrigerator for up to six weeks. Store in an opaque container to prolong life. Not for cooking or baking. Makes 1-1/2 cups (375 mL).

BUTTER IS BETTER

The great debate over whether butter is better than margarine still exists and it is a travesty that butter has been unfairly demonized. We are not alone in our belief that butter is better. Fats and oils experts, such as Mary Enig, author of *Know Your Fats*, also believes that butter is an important fat and one that should not be replaced by hydrogenated fats like margarine.

Recipe originally appeared in Healthy Immunity

Butter contains many healthful components, including lecithin, which aids the body to break down cholesterol. It is also a rich source of vitamin A, which is necessary for the healthy functioning of the adrenal and thyroid glands. The vitamins A and E and the mineral selenium in butter also serve as important antioxidants in protecting against free radical damage that can destroy tissues and weaken artery walls.

If you look at the fat component of butter, it is made from cream and contains a wide range of short- and medium-chain fatty acids, as well as monounsaturated and some polyunsaturated fatty acids. The dangers of butter's saturated fat components have been blown out of proportion; however, as we described a little earlier, not all saturated fats are equal.

Natural saturated fatty acids like coconut oil and butter have vital and protective properties. While it is important to limit excess consumption of saturated fats, especially the long-chain ones found in red meat (they clog arteries), a balanced diet should contain the beneficial saturated fats such as those found in butter and coconut oil.

Butter is one of the few foods available in our supermarkets that still contains natural conjugated linoleic acid (an essential fatty acid with fat-burning and cancer-fighting properties; for more information, see Chapters 2 and 8). However, butter is relatively void of the other essential fats, such as linoleic acid and alpha-linolenic acid, which you will learn about shortly. Try Lorna's Better Butter recipe to ensure you are getting all the essential fats your body craves. Make the switch from margarine to butter—your body will thank you!

Better Butter Recipe*

Cut 1 lb of unsalted butter into eight pieces. Put butter and 1 cup (250 mL) of a high quality EFA-rich oil into the food processor and blend until smooth. Spoon into covered container and refrigerate. Not only will you have better butter, but it will remain soft even though refrigerated. Makes 2 cups (500 mL).

Ghee, You're Terrific

Ghee is clarified butter and has been used for centuries, especially in India. A clear gold liquid, it is resistant to bacteria and rancidity because the milk solids and water have been removed. It doesn't burn at high temperatures and keeps indefinitely. Ghee is used for sautéeing, but you should be able to use less of it.

Recipe originally appeared in Healthy Immunity

Ghee-lightful Recipe*

To make your own ghee, melt unsalted butter over low heat. The milk solids, or curds, will fall to the bottom. Skim the foam off the top and pour the remains through muslin or mesh. The remaining clear oil is the ghee. Do not let the ghee come into contact with water.

Unsaturated Fats: Looking for Liquid Gold

Unsaturated fats are liquid at room temperature and are generally considered to be "good" fats. Typically the more liquid a fat is, the healthier it is. Unsaturated fats can be further classified as either monounsaturated or polyunsaturated. Monounsaturated fats remain liquid at room temperature but solidify in colder temperatures. Sources of these fatty acids are olive, canola and peanut oils. These fatty acids are associated with the good cholesterol.

Polyunsaturated fats remain liquid at room temperature and remain in liquid form even in colder temperatures. Sources of polyunsaturated fats include black currant, borage, corn, flaxseed, safflower, sesame, soy, sunflower, evening primrose oils and fatty fish.

Unsaturated fats can be further classified into three major classes: omega-3, omega-6 and omega-9. The omega-3s and omega-6s are polyunsaturated—and they are essential because the body cannot make them. The omega-9s are monounsaturated and non-essential because the body can make them from other fatty acids.

UNDERSTANDING EFAS: WHY ESSENTIAL FATS ARE SO ESSENTIAL

Essential fatty acids are polyunsaturated fats that include:

- the omega-6 fatty acid – linoleic acid (LA), and its by-products, gamma-linolenic acid (GLA) and arachidonic acid (AA)
- the omega-3 fatty acid – alpha-linolenic acid (ALA) and its by-products, eicosapentaenoic acid (EPA) and docosahexaenoic acid (DHA)

Theoretically, only LA and ALA are absolutely essential. However, the fatty acids derived from them are also generally considered essential. Deficiencies in EFAs are common today for three reasons: modern dietary and lifestyle choices, environmental pollution, and for some people it is because they have trouble

Recipe courtesy of Lorna Vanderhaeghe

converting LA and ALA to their by-products that are responsible for hormone production. EFA deficiency is a serious health concern that can eventually lead to disease and even death.

In 1929 two scientists, George and Mildred Burr, were the first to recognize the effects of EFA deficiency in lab animals. They found that animals deprived of certain fats (later pinpointed as EFAs) developed growth retardation, skin lesions, impaired fertility and many other problems that eventually resulted in death. Researchers now know that EFAs are required for the proper structure and function of every cell in the body, and are critical for optimal health. EFAs increase the absorption of vitamins and minerals; nourish the skin, hair and nails; promote proper nerve functioning; help produce hormones; ensure normal growth and development; and prevent and treat disease. There are over 45 essential nutrients, including EFAs, vitamins, minerals and amino acids, that must be supplied by the diet. Improper nutrition and, more specifically, an imbalance of dietary fats, have had a significant impact on the development of modern diseases.

Research on both animals and humans has demonstrated a wide range of symptoms that can result from an EFA deficiency. Symptoms can vary in each individual, but generally include dry scaly skin and other skin problems, fatigue, impaired growth and fertility, cell death, losses in visual acuity, neuropathies (problems with the nervous system), organ damage and failure, failure to thrive, increased illness and occurrences of death.

Functions of EFAs

The three main functions of EFAs are to regulate cellular processes, influence membrane function and integrity, and produce hormones.

CELL PROCESSES
The cellular processes that fatty acids regulate include:
- Regulation of enzymes
- Regulation of cell signaling pathways
- Attachment of proteins to fatty acids
- Regulation of gene expression
- Gene activation
- Receptor function and activation
- Membrane permeability

- Ion channels (the transport system for potassium and sodium)
- Transport properties
- Oxidation of fats
- Communication from the cell membrane to the nucleus of the cell
- Lipid signaling

CELL MEMBRANE INTEGRITY

EFAs are integral components of cell membranes, determining fluidity and other physical properties as well as affecting the structural functions such as the maintenance of enzyme activity. Cell membranes built with EFAs are less rigid and more fluid (as opposed to membranes built with saturated fats). Fluid cells are extremely important as they allow the transport of valuable nutrients into the cells; help keep toxins out of the cells; elasticize tissue; expand blood vessel walls to reduce heart workload; and improve the overall function of organs.

Early researchers believed that all the benefits of EFAs were attributed to their role in maintaining the cellular processes and the integrity and function of the cell membrane. It was decades later in the early 1970s, when scientists learned that the body also uses EFAs to produce a family of powerful hormone-like compounds.

THE POWER OF HORMONES

Some of the most potent effects of essential fatty acids are related to their conversion into a series of eicosanoids, or hormones. These agents of intracellular communication control the balance of virtually every system in the body, including the mechanisms for inflammation, blood clotting and blood vessel dilation. They include, but are not limited to, anti-inflammatory and inflammatory prostaglandins (PGE series 1, 2, 3), and other immune system responders, such as thromboxanes, leukotrienes and hydroxy fatty acids.

Linoleic Acid: The Omega-6 Parent

EFAs control the break down and use of hormones through a metabolic pathway in our body. Under optimal conditions, the body processes linoleic acid, one of the two primary essential fatty acids needed for health, through a series of steps that eventually leads to the production of hormones. The following diagram, The Metabolic Pathway of LA, shows how LA produces GLA with the help of the delta-6-desaturase, or D6D enzyme. Another enzyme, elongase, creates

The Metabolic Pathway for LA

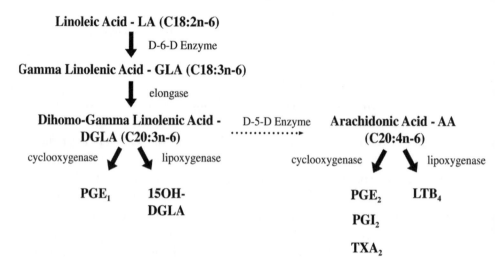

Linoleic Acid - LA (C18:2n-6)

↓ D-6-D Enzyme

Gamma Linolenic Acid - GLA (C18:3n-6)

↓ elongase

Dihomo-Gamma Linolenic Acid -   D-5-D Enzyme   **Arachidonic Acid - AA**
DGLA (C20:3n-6) ·············▶   **(C20:4n-6)**

cyclooxygenase ↙ ↘ lipoxygenase   cyclooxygenase ↙ ↘ lipoxygenase

PGE₁   **15OH-**   **PGE₂**   **LTB₄**
     DGLA

                                                      PGI₂

                                                      TXA₂

dihomo-gamma linolenic acid (DGLA). After one more reaction, the end result is PGE1 and 15-hydroxy DGLA, the hormones that reduce inflammation, dilate blood vessels and inhibit blood clotting. Their strong anti-inflammatory properties help the body recover from injury by reducing pain, swelling and redness.

DGLA also has the potential to produce arachidonic acid with the help of the delta-5-desaturase enzyme. The hormones resulting from arachidonic acid work completely opposite from those of DGLA, although they are both part of the omega-6 family. Arachidonic acid produces PGE2, which is pro-inflammatory, constricts blood vessels, and encourages blood clotting. These properties are important when the body suffers from a wound or an injury because without them you would bleed to death from a cut. However, an excess of the hormones from arachidonic acid can be harmful and may even contribute to disease. The amount of arachidonic acid produced depends on a variety of dietary and lifestyle factors. North Americans tend to consume too much arachidonic acid from red meat and eggs, whereas those who follow a vegetarian diet will have more healthy, more moderate levels of arachidonic acid.

Alpha-linolenic Acid: The Omega-3 Parent

The body processes alpha-linolenic acid in much the same way as it does linoleic acid, as you can see from the following diagram, The Metabolic Pathway of

ALA. However, the D6D enzyme has a higher attraction for ALA than LA—it will convert ALA into its by-products before it will break down LA. From ALA, the D6D enzyme creates stearidonic acid. In turn, the elongase enzyme creates eicosatetraenoic acid. Following that, D5D creates eicosapentaenoic acid, or EPA. EPA can be elongated into docosahexaenoic acid (DHA), or it can react with two more enzymes and create more beneficial hormones.

There are three families of hormones that are derived from EPA, AA and DGLA. LA and ALA do not directly produce hormones but are still important as they have other beneficial properties not related to hormone-production. Hormones from EPA are a mixed bag—some work to dilate blood vessels while others constrict them. Their ability to decrease inflammation and inhibit blood clotting is weak. In general, EPA hormones are useful as defense mechanisms against trauma and infection. DHA is critical for the nervous system and brain function, i.e., infant brain development, prevention of depression, stress reduction, eye function and so on.

Most of us do not have a healthy balance of these dietary fats, and this good fat deficiency can lead to many diseases like breast cancer and heart disease. The typical North American diet contains too much saturated fat, transfats, and arachidonic acid found in red meat and processed foods, but is deficient in healthy GLA, EPA and DHA fats. This problem is further compounded when the

The Metabolic Pathway for ALA

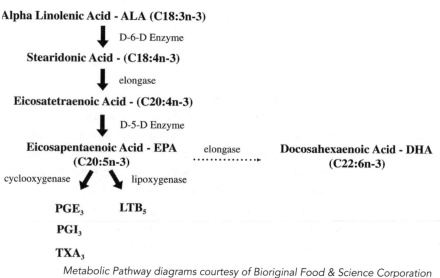

Alpha Linolenic Acid - ALA (C18:3n-3)
↓ D-6-D Enzyme
Stearidonic Acid - (C18:4n-3)
↓ elongase
Eicosatetraenoic Acid - (C20:4n-3)
↓ D-5-D Enzyme
Eicosapentaenoic Acid - EPA   elongase   **Docosahexaenoic Acid - DHA**
(C20:5n-3)   ·············▶   **(C22:6n-3)**
cyclooxygenase ↙ ↘ lipoxygenase

PGE₃   LTB₅

PGI₃

TXA₃

Metabolic Pathway diagrams courtesy of Bioriginal Food & Science Corporation

D6D enzyme is impaired and can't produce all the GLA, EPA and DHA it should from the dietary sources supplied.

When Good Fats are Good for Nothing: Enzyme Impairment

Both linoleic acid (omega-6) and alpha-linolenic acid (omega-3) require the D6D enzyme to begin the first step in the reaction, a slow step known as the "rate limiting step." Without the action of the D6D enzyme the pathway is blocked and the production of good hormones is altered. There are numerous lifestyle and environmental factors that can impair the D6D enzyme, including:

- a high intake of saturated fat and transfatty acids
- a high intake of LA (from refined, grocery store vegetable oils such as corn, canola, sunflower, safflower)
- some pharmaceutical drugs and food additives
- excess alcohol consumption
- smoking
- stress
- advancing age (as we grow older the enzyme becomes less effective)
- infant prematurity (D6D enzyme does not become very efficient until about 6 months of age)
- allergy-related eczema
- diabetes
- cancer
- viral infections

A deficiency of the D6D enzyme results in a hormonal imbalance which can have serious health effects. Inflammation, blood vessel constriction, increased allergic response, impaired immune response, and abnormal cell function may result. In fact, an overwhelming number of diseases that are affecting us today are associated with this imbalance: arthritis, diabetic nerve damage, heart attacks, high blood pressure, atherosclerosis, allergies and skin inflammations.

How can we overcome impaired enzymes to prevent hormonal imbalances? Impaired enzymes cannot be fixed but they can be "bypassed" by supplementing the diet with EFAs that do not require the D6D enzyme for processing. For example, a diet high in fatty fish would supply the body with EPA without having to follow the reaction process to receive the beneficial hormones.

Because a constant dietary intake of EFAs is needed to maintain integrity and function of cell membranes, and to regulate cellular processes and produce hormones, supplementation may be required if the diet is deficient.

GOOD FOODS WITH GOOD FATS

Healthy fats are easily consumed from a variety of delicious sources. Avocados, dark green vegetables, fatty fish, nuts and seeds, olives, and unrefined cold-pressed oils are rich in essential fatty acids and can protect you from cancer, diabetes, heart disease and excess weight. Flaxseed is rich in essential fats but should be combined with a good omega-6 source such as unrefined organic sunflower or sesame oil to balance the essential fats. (See page 18 for more on getting the right balance of omega-3 and omega-6 fats.)

EFAs and Their Sources

There are plenty of ways to get the good fats that you need to keep healthy.

Linoleic Acid (LA): Present in many vegetable oils—safflower (79%), evening primrose seed (72%), sunflower (65–75%), corn (57%), hemp (57%), pumpkin (55%), peanut (31%), borage (starflower) oil (20–30%), canola (19–26%) and olive (8%). LA is abundant in our food supply, so there is no need to supplement.

Gamma-linolenic Acid (GLA): The richest sources of GLA are borage oil (20–24%), black currant oil (15–17%), and evening primrose oil (8–10%). GLA is present in small amounts in human breast milk and some foods, but not in high enough amounts that we can maintain our nutritional needs through diet alone.

Arachidonic Acid (AA): Found in high amounts in eggs, fish and meat. AA is abundant in the food supply and supplementation is not usually necessary. Too much arachidonic acid can actually be harmful, leading to inflammation and blood clots.

Alpha-linolenic Acid (ALA): ALA is found in perilla oil (54–64%), flaxseed oil (50–60%), flaxseed (18–22%) and hemp oil (19%) and, in small amounts, some nuts, green leafy vegetables, wheat germ and black current seeds.

Eicosapentaenoic Acid (EPA) and Docosahexaenoic Acid (DHA): Fatty fish like salmon, mackerel and tuna are common sources. Depending on the source, fish and fish oils vary in the amount of EPA and DHA they provide. Fish oil supplements often contain 18% EPA and 12% DHA, with more concentrated oils containing 30% EPA and 20% DHA. Algal sources of EPA and DHA are also widely available.

Other less common sources of essential fatty acids are found in plants such as echium and lunaria, in fish such as krill, and in fungi.

Concentrates

Oil concentrates are produced through various processing and purifying techniques to maximize the key ingredients. For example, regular fish oil with a 30% omega-3 concentration usually contains 18% EPA and 12% DHA. An oil that has been concentrated can have a total omega-3 content of as little as 30% and as high as 95%. Fish oil concentrates are used when higher doses of EPA and DHA are required, and would be difficult to receive from eating fish regularly or taking oil supplements.

Concentrates come in different forms, including ethyl ester, natural triglyceride and a reconstituted triglyceride form. Ethyl esters and natural triglycerides are good forms of concentrates and are commonly available. While reconstituted triglyceride concentrates offer enhanced bioavailability and potency over ethyl esters and natural triglycerides, they may be difficult to find in the marketplace and are probably more expensive. Concentrates in general will cost more than regular supplements due to the state-of-the-art technology required for processing.

Plant-based concentrates from borage and primrose oil are also available with GLA concentrations ranging from 25–40%.

ESSENTIAL FATTY ACID PROFILE OF DIFFERENT OILS

Oil	Omega-3	Omega-6	Omega-9	Saturated Fat
Flaxseed (500-600 mg ALA, 200 mg LA)	50-60% ALA	10-20% LA	13%	7%
Perilla oil (540-650 mg ALA, 200 mg LA)	54-65% ALA	14-20%-Omega-3	13-21%	19%
Tuna (50 mg EPA, 250 mg DHA)	5% EPA, 25% DHA	N/A	N/A	28%
Salmon (60 mg EPA, 90 mg DHA)	6% EPA, 12% DHA	N/A	N/A	27%
Mixed fish 18/12 (180 mg EPA, 120 mg DHA)	18% EPA, 12% DHA	N/A	N/A	27%
Borage (200-240 mg GLA, 300 mg LA)	N/A	20-24% GLA,30% LA	8%	12%
Evening Primrose (80-100 mg GLA, 650 mg LA)	N/A	8-10% GLA, 65% LA	5%	7%
Black Currant (100-120 mg ALA, 150-170 mg GLA, 80-140 mg LA)	10-12% ALA	15-17% GLA	8-14%	8%
Coconut	N/A	N/A	7%	91%
Hazelnut	14%	N/A	77%	8%
Olive	1%	9% LA	75%	15%
Peanut	N/A	33% LA	48%	19%
Pistachio	N/A	30%	54%	16%
Pumpkin (550 mg LA, 250 mg OA)	N/A	55%	25%	20%
Safflower	N/A	78%	12%	10%
Sunflower	N/A	71%	16%	12%

Chart courtesy of Bioriginal Food & Science Corporation

HOW TO USE EFAS EFFECTIVELY IN YOUR DIET

Just as there are good and bad fats, there are good and bad methods of preparing them and consuming them in suitable quantities. This last section will help lift the fog on what to choose and how to use them.

The Great Forms of Flax

To receive the numerous health benefits flax has to offer, it can be added to the diet in many different ways. There are different forms of flax, including whole seed, milled/ground seed, defatted ground flax (for example, LignaMax®), bottled oil, and soft gels, which are all convenient and healthful options.

Milled flaxseed has become a popular dietary supplement providing omega-3s, lignans and protein. Whole flaxseeds contain an outer layer that is very difficult to digest unless the seeds are thoroughly chewed. Therefore, when whole flaxseeds are consumed, they pass through the digestive system relatively intact. Milling (grinding) the seed makes it more digestible. It can be readily absorbed by the body, providing the full range of nutrition that flax has to offer. If whole flaxseeds are purchased, they can be ground with a coffee grinder prior to being consumed.

Defatted ground flax is a relatively new form of flax recommended primarily for its fiber and lignan profile. Defatted ground flax is sometimes referred to as meal, powder or flour because it is finely ground and has the majority of the oil removed. Gram per gram, defatted ground flax offers a higher lignan, protein and fiber content and a lower calorie profile. It can be incorporated into foods in the same way as traditional milled flax, with the added benefit that it can be used in cooking and baking. Defatted ground flax can also be used as an alternative to conventional fiber supplements.

Flax oil is a rich source of ALA. Flax oil can be taken by the spoonful or added to salad dressings, blender drinks, yogurt and cereal, but cannot be used for cooking, as the high heat will destroy the omega-3 fats. Many flax lovers enjoy the light nutty taste that natural flax oil has to offer, but for those who don't, flax oil is also available in easy to swallow soft gel capsules.

It is important to remember that the fiber, protein and lignans will not be found in the oil, but only in the milled seed and defatted ground flax. However, some manufacturers offer a high-lignan flax oil, in which the particulate matter containing lignans has been added back into the oil. If consumers are specifically interested in the benefits of lignans, milled seed or defatted ground flax contain significantly higher levels of lignans than high-lignan flax oil.

Safety of EFAs

EFAs have been consumed in large amounts (as much as 50 g per day) in thousands of studies performed worldwide with no serious side-effects or harmful drug interactions reported. Occasional minor side effects may include bloating, nausea, burping, upset stomach and loose stools. These side effects often lessen with continued use and occur more often at higher doses.

To minimize side effects it is a good idea to take your EFA supplements with food, divide the daily doses into smaller portions and increase the dose gradually over several weeks. Persons on anticoagulant or blood thinning medications should consult a health care practitioner before taking EFA supplements from fish since they can thin the blood. Long-term studies of EFA supplementation have not been performed; therefore, more data is needed to safely recommend high doses long term.

As with any nutritional or herbal supplement, patients should consult their health care practitioner when starting EFA supplementation, especially if taking other pharmaceutical drugs.

Hot Topic in Nutrition: The Omega-6 Debate

One of the hottest topics in nutrition today is the omega-6 debate. There is a misconception that we get too much omega-6 in our diet and therefore we don't need to eat as much of it. If you walk away from this book having learned only one thing, let it be this: not all omega-6s are the same. We mentioned this earlier and it bears repeating.

Linoleic acid, gamma linolenic acid and arachidonic acid are all omega-6s, but they each have very different effects and they each appear in our diet in different quantities. Linoleic acid is very plentiful in our diet, and while it is a good fat that has an important job as the parent omega-6 (see page 9), we get enough in our diet so there is no need for extra supplementation, as is the case with arachidonic acid. What we are missing is an adequate supply of GLA.

You are familiar with the saying, "everything in moderation?" GLA is required to act as a counterpoint to arachidonic acid. We need the inflammatory and blood-clotting properties of arachidonic acid to alert us to injury and prevent us from bleeding to death. But without GLA to calm the system down once the danger is over, the body is left to cope with the continuous "warning cry" that eventually wears it down, leaving us susceptible to arthritis, psoriasis and heart disease.

It is GLA's importance to our healthy function that we want to impress upon you.

Hotter Topic in Nutrition: How to Balance Your EFA Intake

Optimal fat ratios are important to increase the omega-3 and omega-6 (good fat) content of our body tissues. Increasing the good fat in our body will help to decrease the "bad" saturated fats linked to disease. While all essential fatty acids are crucial for our diet, it is important to ensure that we have a balance of the omega-3s and omega-6s, and even a further balance between the different types of omega-6s. For example, someone who frequently gets their omega-3s by using flaxseed or oil in their meal preparation but does not have a source of GLA-rich omega-6s (as found in evening primrose oil or borage) may become deficient in GLA, even though the food they eat gives them enough of the other omega-6s, linoleic acid and arachidonic acid.

To make matters more complicated, there is a wide range of opinions on what is the "optimal" ratio of fats. Health Canada, for example, adopts a conservative position by recommending an intake of omega-6 to omega-3 of 4 to 1; in other words, you should be eating four times as much of the omega-6 fats as you do omega-3. In theory this is easy to achieve due to the spreads and oils we consume on a daily basis that are high in omega-6s. However, Health Canada's recommendations are rather simplified; they do not go far enough to explain or account for the different types of omega-6s or highlight that GLA is typically deficient in the North American diet.

Popular nutrition experts advocate a higher intake of omega-3 oil and so there will be other ratios, 2 to 1 or even 1 to 2, for example, heralded as "optimal." Their position is that the ability of omega-3 fats to convert to the beneficial by-products of hormones can be impeded by any number of factors, and that to counteract those influences, higher omega-3 intake is required.

To ensure you are receiving enough omega-3s in your diet, fill your plate with fatty fish. Add nuts, seeds and seed oils like flaxseed oil and hemp seed oil to your salads, cereals, stir-frys and sauces. If your diet consistently lacks these omega-3 rich foods, then you should consider supplementing with an omega-3 oil like flaxseed oil or fish oil.

HOW TO STORE GOOD OILS

Healthy oils are essential to our health, but they are more temperamental than the inferior oils you see on the supermarket shelf. Light, air and heat can destroy them. Nature packages these oils in seeds, and left intact, these oils will sometimes keep for years without spoiling.

When we extract the oil from such seeds, we need to make sure that the oil is shielded from the destructive elements before pressing and until the oil is opened. Special care needs to be taken in processing, packaging, and storing oils rich in essential fats to prevent the oil from turning rancid. Rancid oil has a scratchy, bitter, fishy, or paint-like taste, and may be accompanied by a characteristic unpleasant smell. When oil has turned rancid, dozens of by-products form with toxic or unknown effects on our body's functions.

Fresh, EFA-rich oils should be pressed and packaged in the dark, in the absence of oxygen, and with minimal heat, then stored in opaque bottles to prevent exposure to light.

At home, once you've opened a bottle of good oil, it should be stored in the refrigerator and protect it from turning rancid. Prior to opening, the oil is safe in a bottle on a shelf at room temperature; this is because during the packaging process, the oil was packaged in the absence of the destructive elements and then sealed tightly. Be sure to keep your healthy oils away from the stove and do not leave them on top of the fridge or microwave.

There are many quality brands in both Canada and the U.S. that have been pressed and packaged using these ultimate procedures. For more information on the quality of your oils and companies providing quality products, see Chapter 13 and the Resource Guide at the back.

Good Cooking with Good Fats

Now that you know which fats and oils to use, how do you use them to maximize their goodness? When you can, buy organic, cold-pressed, unrefined oils and store them properly (see previous section). Heating oils changes the structure of the fat molecules, making them toxic and unusable by the body, so it is important to use the right oil under the right conditions. See the chart How to Use Good Oils to match oils with their uses.

To minimize the damage caused by heat, cook with as little oil as possible. Never fry with any of the healthy oils that we recommend, because to do so would destroy their healing ingredients. They must be added after cooking, and after the pot has been removed from heat. The addition of these oils will give your food the satisfying flavor and texture that we crave. With the exception of extra-virgin olive oil, supermarket oils should never be consumed, especially processed corn and canola oil.

Several tablespoons of water or vegetable stock can be substituted for low-heat sautéeing. Cover the bottom of the pan with the ingredients you wish to sauté and slowly add more liquid until cooked to prevent sticking and stir often. This method of sautéeing keeps the temperature inside the pan at a safe level of 212°F (100°C).

HOW TO USE GOOD OILS

No Heat 120°F/49°C	Low Heat 212°F/100°C	Medium Heat 325°F/165°C	High Heat 375°F/190°C
Condiments Salad Dressings	Sauces Baking	Light sautéeing or add after cooking	Higher Heat
• Flaxseed oil	• Safflower oil	• Almond oil	• Coconut oil
• Borage oil	• Sunflower oil	• Hazelnut oil	• Ghee
• Canola oil	• Pumpkin oil	• Olive oil	
• Hemp seed oil		• Pistachio oil	
• Soy oil		• Sesame oil	
• Walnut oil			

Chart courtesy of Healthy Immunity

What We Learned In This Chapter:

- Essential fatty acids are required for optimal functioning of cellular processes, maintaining the integrity and function of cellular membranes and producing hormones.

- The North American diet typically contains too many bad fats, such as those found in meat, processed foods and junkfood; and contains too little of the good fats found in fresh produce (avocados, dark leafy vegetables), grains (flaxseed), nuts and seeds (sunflower, hazelnut, walnut) and herbs (evening primrose and borage).

- When consuming good fats, we have to ensure we're getting the right balance of omega-6 and omega-3 and we need to increase our GLA-rich omega-6 supplementation.

- EFA deficiency can lead to ailments like heart disease, diabetes, joint problems, learning disorders, skin problems, and inflammatory diseases, PMS and certain cancers.

The decades of villainizing fat are over. Recognition of the importance of EFAs is a major nutritional breakthrough that has generated substantial scientific research around the world. In a perfect world, you would receive all your good fats from your diet. Begin by incorporating nut and seed oils into your recipes and use appropriate oils for cooking. However, if you can't always get what you need from your diet, you should consider taking a quality supplement.

Now that we have presented a general overview of fats and oils, the following chapters will explain how important they are for specific health conditions.

Chapter 2

WIN THE WAR
AGAINST WEIGHT

North Americans are obsessed with their weight. We spend more than $33 million U.S. annually to find our magic weight loss pill. We are spending more money to lose weight and yet we are more overweight than ever. Every day a new miracle diet promises to help us lose weight in record time ("Wipe out 30 years of bad habits in just 10 days!"). Poor nutrition, specifically dietary fat, bears most of the blame for the surge in overweight individuals. Manufacturers of weight loss products capitalize on the latest and greatest diet craze promoting high protein/low protein, high carbohydrate/low carbohydrate, herbal miracles and liquid diets. Fad products and diets don't work—they lead to binge eating, repeated cycles of weight gain and loss, and are emotionally and physically destructive due to their restrictive nature; in short, they are harmful to your health.

Reports show that one to two thirds of weight lost is usually regained within one year and almost all weight is regained within five years. Diets are only considered a success if weight loss is maintained without damaging your overall health. They should satisfy all nutritional needs, meet individual tastes and habits, minimize hunger and boost energy. The cornerstone to successful weight loss is enjoying a moderate lifestyle—every day. Eat healthily when you can, and get plenty of rest and exercise. Drink water throughout the day, take supplements if you need extra help in meeting your nutritional needs and don't beat yourself up for having the occasional treat.

Obesity is considered to be the most common nutritional disorder in the industrialized world today. Data from the U.S. between 1990 and 2000 shows a 65% increase in obesity and 25% increase in overweight individuals, resulting in 34% of the population being overweight and another 27% obese. This means that more than 60% of the entire U.S. population has what can be defined as a weight problem. The picture is much the same in Canada with data between 1990 and 2001 showing a 63% increase in obese individuals and a 9% increase in overweight individuals in the same time period, resulting in 48% of the population being overweight and 15% being obese.

This rise in the prevalence of excess weight and obesity is now recognized as a worldwide problem with numerous health implications and public health costs. The direct and indirect costs of treating obesity are USD$99.2 billion in the U.S. and CDN$3.2 billion in Canada. This epidemic is a "time bomb" for future explosions as manifested in the frequency of cardiovascular disease, type 2 diabetes and their many complications.

ARE YOU OVERWEIGHT?
THE BODY MASS INDEX EXPLAINED

Techniques for measuring excess fat have varied over the years. Underwater weighing is considered the gold standard for assessing total body fat, but in large human studies and clinical practice, it is most typically estimated by body mass index, commonly referred to as BMI. BMI is one of the most accurate ways to determine when extra pounds translate into health risks.

A healthy BMI is considered to be 24 or less. The United States Department of Health and Human Services and the World Health Organization have defined being overweight as a BMI of 25 to 30, and obesity as a BMI greater than 30.

The higher the BMI, the greater the risk of developing additional health problems; however, one variable BMI fails to consider is lean body mass (tissue, bone and muscle) which weighs significantly more than fat does. It is possible for a healthy, muscular individual to be classified as obese using the BMI formula. If you are a trained athlete, your weight based on a measured percentage of body fat would be a better indicator of what you should weigh. A normal healthy man should not exceed 15% body fat, while the healthy limit for a woman is 15–22%.

How to Calculate Your BMI:

Technically, BMI is calculated by dividing your weight in kilograms by the square of your height in meters; however, the vast majority of North Americans know their measurements in pounds and inches so check the table provided. Find your height in inches (remember there are 12 inches in a foot) along the left-hand side. Move along to the column with your weight in pounds. At the top of the table is your BMI.

THE OBESITY EPIDEMIC

Now that you have established what range your body mass index falls into, for those in the overweight or obese range it is critical to understand what is causing it. It would be extremely rare for only one factor to be the culprit. More than likely it is a combination of genetics, little or no physical activity, eating too many foods with a high glycemic index (carbohydrates that enter the bloodstream too quickly and encourage fat storage), and poor dietary choices. North American culture encourages reliance on convenience foods and excess sugar consumption covertly found in packaged and processed foods and overtly found in alcohol, baked goods and junkfood. Few people eat five to ten servings of fresh fruit and vegetables and 25 g of fiber every day... and it only makes sense that dietary fat should be linked to fatness, right? No.

Nutrition researchers are extremely frustrated with the "eat fat, get fat" chant. Why? Because it ignores the science that has proven that bad fats are bad for your health, whereas good fats are good for your health. It is an important distinction and yet that message is rarely broadcast. Good fats such as borage oil and evening primrose oil promote the use of stored fat for energy and rev up your metabolism. At first, this concept of supplementing with fat may seem contradictory or eccentric, but you will soon see the light.

Fat Metabolism

When we consume fat, the gastrointestinal tract breaks fat in the triglyceride form down into free fatty acids by enzymes known as lipases. The fatty acids are absorbed by the intestinal cells where the lymphatic system and the liver produce fatty complexes to transport these fatty acids throughout the body. The fatty acids derived from saturated fats found in red meat and dairy products, like milk and cheese, are the main source of energy production and fat storage in the body. When we eat too much saturated fat, and couple it with an inactive lifestyle, we will gain weight. When our diets contain higher amounts of the good polyunsaturated fats found in healthy oils such as flaxseed, hemp, sunflower, safflower, evening primrose and borage, it discourages fat storage and encourages fat burning.

BMI CALCULATIONS

(Table adapted from the National Institutes of Health)

BMI H (in)	19	20	21	22	23	24	25	26	27	28	29	30	31	32	33	34	35	36	37	38	39	40	41	42	43	44	45
												Weight (lbs)															
58	91	96	100	105	110	115	119	124	129	134	138	143	148	153	158	162	167	172	177	181	186	191	196	201	205	210	215
59	94	99	104	109	114	119	124	128	133	138	143	148	153	158	163	168	173	178	183	188	193	198	203	208	212	217	222
60	97	102	107	112	118	123	128	133	138	143	148	153	158	163	168	174	179	184	189	194	199	204	209	215	220	225	230
61	100	106	111	116	122	127	132	137	143	148	153	158	164	169	174	180	185	190	195	201	206	211	217	222	227	232	238
62	104	109	115	120	126	131	136	142	147	153	158	164	169	175	180	186	191	196	202	207	213	218	224	229	235	240	246
63	107	113	118	124	130	135	141	146	152	158	163	169	175	180	186	191	197	203	208	214	220	225	231	237	242	248	254
64	110	116	122	128	134	140	145	151	157	163	169	174	180	186	192	197	204	209	215	221	227	232	238	244	250	256	262
65	114	120	126	132	138	144	150	156	162	168	174	180	186	192	198	204	210	216	222	228	234	240	246	252	258	264	270
66	118	124	130	136	142	148	155	161	167	173	179	186	192	198	204	210	216	223	229	235	241	247	253	260	266	272	278
67	121	127	134	140	146	153	159	166	172	178	185	191	198	204	211	217	223	230	236	242	249	255	261	268	274	280	287
68	125	131	138	144	151	158	164	171	177	184	190	197	203	210	216	223	230	236	243	249	256	262	269	276	282	289	295
69	128	135	142	149	155	162	169	176	182	189	196	203	209	216	223	230	236	243	250	257	263	270	277	284	291	297	304
70	132	139	146	153	160	167	174	181	188	195	202	209	216	222	229	236	243	250	257	264	271	278	285	292	299	306	313
71	136	143	150	157	165	172	179	186	193	200	208	215	222	229	236	243	250	257	265	272	279	286	293	301	308	315	322
72	140	147	154	162	169	177	184	191	199	206	213	221	228	235	242	250	258	265	272	279	287	294	302	309	316	324	331
73	144	151	159	166	174	182	189	197	204	212	219	227	235	242	250	257	265	272	280	288	295	302	310	318	325	333	340
74	148	155	163	171	179	186	194	202	210	218	225	233	241	249	256	264	272	280	287	295	303	311	319	326	334	342	350
75	152	160	168	176	184	192	200	208	216	224	232	240	248	256	264	272	279	287	295	303	311	319	327	335	343	351	359
76	156	164	172	180	189	197	205	213	221	230	238	246	254	263	271	279	287	295	304	312	320	328	336	344	353	361	369

Fat Burning

Thermogenesis, white fat, brown fat—have you heard these terms before? Probably not. Thermogenesis is the scientific term used to describe the creation of heat in the body. The food we eat provides us energy that is measured in calories. When the body burns calories (regardless of whether it is from sleeping or running a marathon), heat is produced. Brown fat is metabolically active fat that surrounds our organs, cushioning the blood vessels and spinal column. You can't see brown fat on you, but this is the type of fat that is burned in the body to create heat, not the kind that stores calories. So another way to look at it is, thermogenesis describes the activity of brown fat. White fat is the insulating layer of fat just beneath the skin that buffers us from the cold and stores calories. This is the type of fat we so desperately try to get rid of.

Thermogenesis is important for two functions: to burn calories and adapt to cold. The ability of some animals to hibernate during the winter is due to thermogenesis. Their bodies burn brown fat to create heat. The heat, in addition to keeping them warm, burns the white fat for energy (to "feed" the body even though they haven't eaten). You may have noticed after eating a large meal that you start to sweat. This is called diet-induced thermogenesis. A portion of the food we eat is converted into heat, and the rest is metabolized, absorbed and stored. This process burns calories and eating the meal stimulates an increase in heat production ranging from 10–40%.

Thermogenesis and brown fat activity explain why it appears as if one person can eat all day without gaining an ounce while another person can gain weight just thinking about food. Thin people have activated brown fat, while overweight individuals have dormant brown fat.

Identifying the mechanism that stimulates brown fat will be a major scientific breakthrough. Some research has suggested that EFAs, such as borage oil or evening primrose oil, can stimulate brown fat activity.

The Gene Link

If you recall in Chapter 1, we mentioned that fatty acids can regulate hundreds of cellular processes, including the regulation of gene expression and gene activation. This function of EFAs may be the critical link to weight loss. Dr. Alan Shuldiner, Professor and Head of the Division of Endocrinology, Diabetes and Nutrition at the University of Maryland, has researched obesity extensively and believes its susceptibility to associated conditions, such as type 2 diabetes, hypertension, and high cholesterol, are the result of a complex interaction between genes and our environment. There is increasing evidence of genetic factors leading to obesity, but the exact genes involved have not been defined. Gene mutations, such as leptin, leptin receptor and PPAR gamma, have been found as causes of a few syndromes of obesity. One study published in the *New England Journal of Medicine* examined this hypothesis. The study found that of the 121 obese subjects studied, four had a mutation in the gene PPAR gamma compared with none of the 237 subjects of normal weight, confirming gene mutations may be potential causes of obesity.

Polyunsaturated fats have a demonstrated effect on genes that lead to increased metabolism and decreased fat storage, thus helping to prevent weight gain. Fatty acids released into the blood from fat stores or from dietary sources are metabolized in two compartments within the cell. These are peroxisomes and mitochondria. Peroxisomes are found in all tissues, but are particularly abundant in liver and kidney. Mitochondria are more complex and contain genetic information. Peroxisomes primarily break down fats of carbon chain lengths between 12 and 16. They are metabolized for energy inside the peroxisome (a sac within the cell membrane that helps to break down fat). Peroxisomes place more effort on creating heat, rather than storing fat. Polyunsaturated fats are also activators of peroxisomes by increasing the activity of the peroxisomes.

FATS FOR FAT LOSS

Omega-6: Why GLA Aids in Weight Loss

As mentioned in Chapter 1, GLA is an omega-6 fatty acid found primarily in borage and evening primrose oil. Numerous research studies have examined the role of GLA for improving health, specifically in the area of weight loss. Above we discussed the importance of burning brown fat and how certain gene mutations can affect weight loss. Research is demonstrating that both of these occurrences may be linked to GLA.

Animal studies conducted by Dr. Takahashi from the National Food Research Institute in Ibaraki, Japan has demonstrated that GLA from borage oil causes less body fat to accumulate, as well as increasing brown fat activity. Scientists such as Dr. M.A. Mir, a researcher and consultant at the Welsh National School of Medicine in Cardiff, Wales, have shown GLA from evening primrose and borage oils activates a metabolic process that can burn close to 50% of the body's total calories. In one GLA study, individuals lost from 9.6 to 11.4 pounds over a six-week period.

Dr. Horrobin, a former professor of medicine at the University of Montreal, identified a calorie-burning mechanism that evening primrose oil helps to regulate. Evening primrose oil makes underactive brown fat in overweight people more active; thus it helps to burn more calories. Dr. Horrobin described evening primrose oil as "a safe, non-drug way to stimulate the body's metabolic activity and burn off fat."

More recently published animal studies have demonstrated that obesity is linked to low GLA levels. With supplementation, these levels are normalized, the obese animals reduce their food intake and weight gain is prevented. Japanese research published in *The Journal of Nutrition* in 1994 confirmed that dietary GLA could reduce body fat by increasing brown fat activity and that GLA may affect enzymes involved in the metabolism of fat, as well as glucose.

Although studies are still in their early stages, GLA, like other fatty acids, is suspected to have the potential to elevate levels of serotonin, a brain chemical that contributes to feeling of fullness. Elevated serotonin levels would make you feel satisfied sooner, eat less, and be less tempted to overindulge.

> *Recommended Dosage:* The average dose of GLA is 250–500 mg per day for general health. To obtain this level of GLA, take three to five 1,000 mg capsules of evening primrose oil or one to two 1,000 mg capsule of borage oil.

> *Recommended Products:* Swanson's EFAOmegaTru™ Borage Oil; Health From The Sun's Total EFA; Herbal Select's Borage Oil; Preferred Nutrition's FemmEssentials FemmOmega™.

Omega-3: Why ALA Aids in Weight Loss

The omega-3 fatty acids (ALA, EPA and DHA), primarily found in flaxseed and fish are also associated with reduced fat storage and a decrease in heart disease (see Chapter 4 for more information). Recent research conducted by the Center for Human Nutrition at the University of Colorado Health Sciences Center examined the role of omega-3 and omega-6 polyunsaturated fats in improving metabolic fitness in moderately obese, hypertensive subjects. The study results showed that omega-3 fatty acids were more effective for losing fat and noticed a trend that omega-3s could further enhance insulin sensitivity.

Omega-3 fatty acids are involved in fat burning by increasing the body's metabolic rate. Ann Louise Gittleman, one of the premier nutritionists in the U.S. and author of *Eat Fat, Lose Weight* and *The Fat Flush Plan,* has seen tremendous weight loss results in her clients who use flax oil. Ann Louise recommends "the addition of omega-3 oils to the diets of all individuals who are suffering from obesity, diabetes and high blood pressure."

Recent research shows that essential fatty acid deficiency is related to low leptin levels. Leptin is a hormone that regulates appetite, brown fat thermogenesis and body fat. Supplementation with EFAs may increase leptin levels, serving to decrease appetite and burn more fat.

> *Recommended Dosage:* The average dose of ALA is 1.1 g per day for women and 1.6 g per day for men for general health. To obtain this level of ALA, two to three capsules of organic flaxseed oil, or 1/2 to 1 teaspoon of organic flaxseed oil would be required.

Conjugated Linoleic Acid for Lean Bodies

A chapter on weight loss would not be complete without discussing the latest substantiated health and fat loss benefits of CLA. First discovered in the 1930s,

TAHINI SAUCE

1 cup (250 mL) tahini
1/2 cup (125 mL) freshly-squeezed lemon juice
1/2–1 cup (125-250 mL) purified water
4 garlic cloves
1 T organic and wheat-free tamari
4 T extra-virgin olive oil
Combine all ingredients in a blender and process until smooth. Refrigerate. Makes 1-1/2 cups (375 mL). It's a delicious veggie dip or can be used as a sauce with Mediterranean-style food such as chicken, olives, spinach pie and Greek salad.

Recipe originally appeared in Healthy Immunity

CLA is considered to be necessary for both cell growth and as a building block of cell membranes. CLA occurs naturally in dairy foods and grass-fed beef and lamb; it is produced by the intestinal bacteria of these animals when they convert omega-6 linoleic acid into CLA. Humans cannot convert linoleic acid into CLA so we are completely reliant on the foods we eat or supplementation to acquire the necessary amount of CLA. Unfortunately, the CLA content of dairy and meat products has declined over the last few decades due to increased antibiotic use in cattle and changes in the cattle's food supply from grass to grain.

Luckily, CLA* is available today as a convenient dietary supplement, made by converting the high linoleic acid content of either sunflower or safflower oils into CLA. To date there are over 500 published research studies supporting CLA's ability to exert positive effects on fat loss, prevent and control type 2 diabetes, protect against heart disease, reduce the risk of atherosclerosis and modulate immune response. It may also inhibit the growth of certain kinds of cancers such as breast, prostate and colon cancer.

CLA: REDUCES FAT, IMPROVES MUSCLE MASS

Early animal research in 1951 paved the way for further groundbreaking research on CLA and fat loss in humans. The first human clinical trial using CLA was conducted in 1997 in Norway and published in *The Journal of Nutrition* in 2000.

MOM'S PIECRUST

4 cups (1 L) unbleached white flour
1 tsp sea salt
1 1/2 cups (375 mL) coconut butter
2 tsp apple cider vinegar
1 cup (250 mL) ice water

Mix flour and salt in a large bowl. Cut in coconut butter with a pastry knife until crumbly. Add vinegar to water. Stir in two-thirds of water and vinegar to flour mixture. Add in the remaining water and vinegar mixture until dough forms a ball and is not sticky. Refrigerate one hour before rolling into a piecrust. Keeps up to one week in the fridge or freezer. Makes 2 double-crust pies.

Recipe originally appeared in Healthy Immunity

* A number of patents have been issued relating to CLA, including the use of CLA to reduce body fat. For example, see U.S. Patent No. 5,554,646 issued to Cook et al.

This study is, to date, the largest scientific evidence published showing CLA's effects on human fat tissue.

The 90-day double-blind, randomized, placebo-controlled study investigated the effects of different doses of CLA. Control groups were compared to those receiving 1.7 g to 6.8 g per day. Results showed that 3.4 g of CLA per day is enough to obtain all the beneficial effects on body fat, while the group given the highest dose of 6.8 g of CLA per day also experienced the increase in lean body mass. In fact, a remarkable 20% decrease in body fat, with an average loss of seven pounds of fat in the CLA group (in comparison to the placebo group) was seen without changing their diet. These results support previous observations that CLA is quite effective as a fat-fighting supplement and a producer of lean muscle mass.

CLA: STOPS FAT FROM COMING BACK

In August of 2000, Dr. Pariza presented the long-awaited results of a clinical trial which was designed to assess the effects of CLA on the body composition of obese men and women. Eighty overweight people took part in the six-month study in which they dieted and exercised. As expected, most initially lost weight but once their diets ended, many regained some of their weight. The participants who were not given CLA put pounds back in a fat to lean muscle mass ratio of 75 to 25, which is typical for most people. For those subjects taking CLA regularly, less fat was regained and more muscle mass retained, with an impressive, statistically significant ratio of 50 to 50. The results also showed the CLA made it easier for the participants to stay on their diets.

CLA & EXERCISE: LOSE FAT MORE QUICKLY

The next logical question for those studying CLA would be: does CLA influence the effects of exercise? A Norwegian study published in 2001 in *The Journal of International Medical Research* says: yes, it does. This double-blind, randomized, placebo-controlled trial focused on 20 healthy volunteers recruited from a physical fitness center where they participated in regular physical training consisting of 90 minutes of strenuous exercise, three times a week. The volunteers did not make any changes to their lifestyle or diet during this trial.

The study shows those participants who ingested 1.8 g of CLA per day for 12 weeks experienced significant body fat reduction versus the control group. The control group continued to exercise but were given a fake pill instead of CLA. As seen in previous clinical trials, CLA reduced body fat, but because the lean muscle mass was increased, there was no change in actual body weight.

What We Learned In This Chapter:

- Good fats are essential in weight management, a key component in maintaining health.
- Healthy oils, such as flaxseed, hemp, evening primrose and borage, discourage fat storage and encourage fat burning.
- CLA content in dietary sources has been depleted, but concentrated supplementation can provide the added benefits to accelerate fat loss.

In the next chapter we discuss diabetes, a condition that is often associated with obesity, and how healthy fats can prevent its onset and complications.

Chapter 3

TYPE 2 DIABETES: YOU MAY BE AT RISK

In Chapter 2 we discussed the growing rate of obesity and excess weight. Excess weight is one contributing factor in type 2 diabetes, so the rise in obesity has been closely followed with a rise in diabetes. In Canada, diabetes affects 1.5 million Canadians and another 750,000 are undiagnosed. Diabetes is the 7th leading cause of death in Canada, with an annual cost of $5 to 6 billion CDN. In the U.S., there are currently 16 million Americans with type 2 diabetes (11.1 million diagnosed, 5.9 million undiagnosed) and 1 million new cases of diabetes are discovered every year. Total costs related to diabetes and its complications is $98 billion USD.

Type 2 diabetes, also known as adult-onset or non-insulin dependent diabetes, is the most common type of diabetes, occurring in 90% of all diabetic cases (the remainder are type 1, or juvenile diabetes, as well as 2–4% of all pregnancies are affected by gestational diabetes). The condition occurs when the pancreas does not produce enough insulin or when the body does not effectively use the insulin provided. Symptoms include insatiable appetite and thirst, frequent urination, lightheadedness, blurred vision, numbness or tingling in the hands and toes, deep fatigue, irritability, depression and recurring vaginal or bladder infections. Type 2 diabetes usually begins around the age of 40 in people who are over-weight, although the rate is rising in overweight children. Take a moment to complete the "Diabetes: Are You at Risk?" quiz to find out if you or someone you know are susceptible to this illness. The earlier you know, the sooner you can take steps to prevent it.

Several population studies have demonstrated the link between the increased risk for type 2 diabetes and a high body mass index (the accepted measurement of excess weight and obesity—see page 24 for more information). In a report from the Nurses' Health Study, patients with a low BMI of 22 were observed to be at risk of diabetes. Women with a BMI in the average range of 24–24.9 had an elevated risk up to five times more than the women with a BMI of 22. The risk of diabetes in patients with a BMI of 31 was 40 times greater. The study also reported that changes in body weight could be a strong predictor of risk for diabetes. When compared with women of stable weight, women who gained 20 kg (44 lbs) or more during adulthood were at risk more than 12 times than the control group. In contrast, women who lost more than 20 kg (44 lbs) lowered their risk by nine times.

Tight blood sugar control is essential for diabetics and those predisposed to the condition, and two factors that can have a significant impact in this area are diet and exercise. Consuming a balanced diet of carbohydrate, protein and good fats can stimulate weight loss and keep blood sugars within a healthy range. Exercise, in addition to losing weight, is also beneficial in helping to lower blood sugar levels and improve insulin's effectiveness.

DIABETES QUIZ: ARE YOU AT RISK?

Check each symptom if it applies to you.

☐ being age 45 or over

☐ being overweight (especially if you carry weight around your middle)

☐ being a member of a high risk group (Aboriginal peoples, Hispanics, Asian or African descent)

☐ having a parent, brother or sister with diabetes

☐ having gestational diabetes, or having given birth to a baby that weighed over 4 kg (9 lbs) at birth

☐ having high cholesterol or other fats in the blood

☐ have higher than normal blood glucose levels

☐ have high blood pressure or heart disease

Chart courtesy of Canadian Diabetes Association

DIABETES: DANGEROUS COMPLICATIONS

Diabetes increases the risk for developing more severe complications. Regulating blood glucose levels, keeping within a healthy weight range, and consuming a healthy diet can help prevent or delay their onset. However, approximately 40% of diabetics will go on to develop related complications. The three main categories are:

- Small blood vessel damage, such as retinopathy, the impairment or loss of vision due to damaged blood vessels in the eyes; nephropathy, kidney disease and failure; and neuropathy-nerve damage, numbness and pain in the hands, feet or legs. Diabetes is the leading cause of adult blindness, and accounts for 28% of all new cases of serious kidney disease.

- Large blood vessel damage, such as heart problems and hypertension. Heart disease is up to four times more common in people with diabetes than without.

- Other complications include infections of the mouth, gums and urinary tract; impotence; and problem pregnancies.

All diabetes-related complications are serious; however, 40–50% of diabetics will have to cope with neuropathy-nerve damage. Caused by a prolonged imbalance in blood glucose levels, neuropathy not only results in numbness and pain in the extremities, but it can also affect internal organs, such as the digestive tract, heart and sexual organs, leading to symptoms of diarrhea, constipation, indigestion, dizziness and bladder infections. Neuropathy can also lead to impotence, which afflicts approximately 9% of all diabetic men.

In severe cases, neuropathy will lead to lower limb amputations, and is the leading cause of all non-accident related amputations. Each year, more than 56,000 amputations are performed among people with diabetes. Lower extremity amputation is 11 times more frequent for people with diabetes than people without diabetes. There is no pharmaceutical drug treatment for diabetic neuropathy.

While diet and exercise are important for diabetes, physicians recommend close regulation of blood sugar levels as the best way to prevent these complications since chronic high blood sugar levels accelerate the development of complications. In theory, close blood sugar monitoring and improved control of blood sugar levels is the best way to prevent the onset of neuropathy—but in practice it is very difficult for diabetics to achieve. Even the most conscientious diabetics experience considerable fluctuations of blood sugar levels.

The Beneficial Omega-6s

GLA-RICH OMEGA-6: TREATS NEUROPATHY

There is hope. Although there is an absence of pharmaceutical drug treatments for neuropathy, certain natural products have been proven successful in moderating the complications of diabetes and neuropathy. Omega-6 essential fatty acids rich in GLA is one of them.

As mentioned in Chapter 1, a healthy body can convert the omega-6 linoleic acid into GLA. The body can then use GLA for building nerve structure. Diabetics, however, often have an impairment in the process that converts linoleic acid to GLA. The result is a lower level of GLA and its by-products, the healthy hormones. The key to improving diabetes and neuropathy is to restore GLA to normal levels through dietary supplementation.

Human clinical studies have concluded that GLA has a beneficial effect on the course of diabetic neuropathy. Trials began in 1986, when a group of researchers conducted a double-blind, placebo-controlled study with 22 patients. The treatment group received 360 mg of GLA per day for six months. All tested variables, including peripheral nerve function, nerve conduction speed, and nerve capillary blood flow, improved in the treatment group and worsened in the control group.

With these positive results, additional research was pursued. Two subsequent multi-center studies, including more than 400 patients, obtained consistently positive results. The first included 111 patients in seven centers, while the second included 293 patients in 10 centers. The patients received 480 mg of GLA daily for one year. The researchers measured 16 variables in all, including nerve conduction strength and speed, hot and cold thresholds, sensation, reflexes, and muscle strength. After a full year of treatment, all 16 variables showed favorable improvement as compared to the control group.

Now laboratory research indicates that recovery of patients may be even more complete when GLA is used in conjunction with antioxidants. Alpha-lipoic acid is a powerful anti-oxidant found in such foods as potatoes, red meat and spinach. It plays an important role in the body's ability to burn blood sugar, which, in turn, helps to sustain normal blood sugar levels. An animal study combining GLA with alpha-lipoic acid showed that subjects had great improvements in the motor skills and blood flow deficits associated with neuropathy. Researchers noted this synergistic combination far outweighed the effects of each supplement used separately.

Recommended Dosage: Clinical research indicates that a dosage of 500 mg GLA per day is effective for treating diabetic neuropathy. To obtain this level, 4 g of evening primrose oil or 2 g of borage oil would be required daily.

Recommended Products: Herbal Select's Borage Oil; Swanson's EFA OmegaTru™ Borage Oil; Preferred Nutrition's FemmEssentials FemmOmega™; and Health From The Sun's EFA Glucose Formula.

CLA: IMPROVES INSULIN SENSITIVITY

We learned in Chapter 2 that conjugated linoleic acid helps to reduce body fat, which will in turn improve insulin resistance, but in several animal studies CLA has demonstrated an outstanding ability to prevent and control adult onset diabetes by sensitizing insulin. Researchers from Purdue University in Indiana reported a dramatic improvement in serum insulin response in patients taking 6 g of CLA daily. The eight-week clinical trial involved 22 subjects. Over 64% of the patients experienced an improvement in their leptin levels—a hormone that regulates both insulin and weight gain. These results suggest that CLA can help prevent or delay the onset of diabetes.

The Beneficial Omega-3s

FLAXSEED: SUPER FOOD TO THE RESCUE!

Flaxseed is gaining stature among health and nutrition experts as well as becoming well-known to consumers. Flaxseed offers a high content of alpha-linolenic acid (ALA) and large quantities of soluble and insoluble fiber, a protein profile similar to soy, and is the richest known source of lignans. Because flaxseed contains so many valuable nutritional components it is often difficult to determine which component is providing the beneficial health effect. Some researchers feel it is a combination of these powerful nutrients, others feel it is a result of the individual components. Either way, you can't deny it—flaxseed is a super food that provides numerous health benefits.

Flaxseed has potential benefits for diabetes that are most likely attributed to the slowed absorption of carbohydrates due to the soluble fiber it contains and other flaxseed components that may slow down the digestion of starch. Slowing carbohydrate absorption is important to reduce blood glucose levels, insulin, and blood fat levels, which in turn reduces the risk for heart disease and possibly diabetes. Enriching foods or supplementing your diet with flaxseed may be a useful way to delay carbohydrate absorption. There are a few human studies and numerous animal studies showing flaxseed's tremendous potential in diabetes prevention and treatment.

Animal research, published in the *Journal of Laboratory and Clinical Medicine* in 2001, suggests a specific lignan found in flaxseed may retard the development of diabetes. The rats were either left untreated or given the lignan from flaxseed. At the 72-day mark the incidence of diabetes in the untreated group was 100% but only 20% in the treated rats still had diabetes. Most of the remaining treated rats (all but 10%) developed diabetes between 72 and 99 days. The lignan delayed the development of diabetes by 80%. In addition, the treated rats did not show an increase in total cholesterol levels, unlike the untreated group which showed cholesterol increases.

FOCACCIA BREAD

2 T dry yeast	4 T fresh oregano, finely chopped
2 T honey	2 T chopped garlic
3/4 (185 mL) cup warm water	5 T olive oil, divided
5 cups (1.25 L) unbleached flour	1–1 1/2 cups (250-375 mL) warm water
3/4 cup (185 mL) LignaMax®, fine	1 cup (250 mL) chopped red peppers
1 T salt	Coarse salt
4 T fresh basil, finely chopped	Makes one large, flat loaf

Dissolve yeast and sugar in warm water, let cool. Mix flour, Lignamax®, salt and dried herbs in a large bowl. Add the dissolved yeast mixture, garlic, 2 T olive oil, and enough additional warm water to make a soft dough. Mix in stand mixer with dough hook 3 to 5 minutes until smooth and resilient, or 100 strokes by hand with a wooden spoon. Turn out onto a floured surface or place in an oiled bowl and cover. Let rest from 10 minutes to an hour.

Roll or pat bread dough out on a greased baking sheet, cover and leave to rise 30 minutes. Preheat oven to 400°F. When ready to bake, uncover dough and press fingers all over to make little dimples. Stir peppers and remaining 3 T olive oil together and pat into dough. Sprinkle with salt. Reduce oven temperature to 350°F and bake around 40 minutes or until quite golden and crusty and bread sounds hollow when tapped.

Recipe courtesy of the Bioriginal Food & Science Corporation

New research presented in April 2002 at the American Physiological Society's annual meeting suggests that diets rich in flaxseed have positive results in controlling weight and diabetes. In this particular animal study, researchers fed lean and obese rats diets containing either 20% casein (isolated soy protein) or flaxseed meal for 26 weeks to both. The obese rats exhibited symptoms of type 2 diabetes prior to beginning the experiment. The results showed that flaxseed decreased total cholesterol and triglycerides in both lean and obese rats, but in the obese rats it significantly decreased the bad cholesterol as well as lowering blood sugar levels. The researchers concluded that flaxseed had greater effects on the variables than soy, and therefore could potentially benefit humans who suffer from excess weight and/or diabetes.

Recommended Dosage: A daily dose of 1.1 g of ALA for women and 1.6 g for men is recommended for general health maintenance, while higher doses may be indicated for disease treatment. To achieve a health maintenance level, consume two to three 1,000 mg flaxseed oil soft gels, 1 teaspoon of flax oil, or to obtain the other nutritional benefits found in the seed, such as the fibers and lignans, consume 1 to 2 tablespoons of milled flaxseed daily.

FISH OIL: REDUCES FATTY SUBSTANCES IN THE BLOOD

The longest and largest placebo-controlled, double-blind, crossover trial of the effect of omega-3 fatty acids on type 2 diabetes gave patients 6 g of omega-3 fatty acids (EPA and DHA) for six months in addition to their usual oral therapy (e.g., Metformin, Glyburide). Fasting blood glucose concentrations increased by 11% during the omega-3 fatty acid phase and by 8% during the "fake pill" phase, showing a non-significant net increase of 3%. However, fasting triacylglycerol (a fatty substance linked to heart disease) decreased by an impressive 43%, which is a highly significant change.

Numerous animal studies have shown the positive effects of fish oil supplementation on reducing blood pressure, platelet aggregation, and even increasing insulin sensitivity. It has been advised that patients with type 2 diabetes may benefit from small/moderate amounts of fish oil for these situations.

FISH OIL: COMBAT CHOLESTEROL IN DIABETICS

People with type 2 diabetes often have high levels of the bad LDL cholesterol, as well as lower levels of the good HDL cholesterol. The beneficial effects of fish oil supplementation on cholesterol levels in type 2 diabetes was suggested when researchers treated these patients for 28 days with 1.7 g of EPA and 1.15 g DHA. Results were encouraging with a demonstrated strong decrease in triglyceride levels, and an increase in the good HDL cholesterol levels.

The findings of a recent clinical trial published in *Diabetes Care* 2002 suggested that diabetics could partially correct their cholesterol abnormalities with the addition of fish oil to their diet. The study involved 42 adults with type 2 diabetes who were randomized to take either 4 g of fish oil containing both EPA and DHA or a fake pill of corn oil for eight weeks. Researchers found that those who took the fish oil supplement for eight weeks lowered their triacylglycerol levels; as well, both of the subtypes of good cholesterol rose in comparison to the corn oil group. The ratio of bad cholesterol to good cholesterol fell by nearly 1% among patients taking fish oil supplements and rose by 4% among those taking the corn oil. Although the fish oil supplements did not alter the bad LDL cholesterol, the researchers still concluded that fish oil supplementation would benefit diabetic patients with cholesterol abnormalities.

FISH OIL: FRIEND OR FOE?

Men and women with type 2 diabetes die from heart disease at three to five times the rate of the non-diabetic population. A combination of high blood fats, high blood pressure and blood clotting in association with insulin resistance may explain the higher risk. Numerous studies have been conducted on the effects of omega-3 fatty acids from fish in patients with type 2 diabetes. In most studies, fish oil consumption lowered blood triglyceride concentrations significantly, but some studies have reported that blood glucose levels rose, so diabetics are cautioned to keep their dosages lower. However, in many of these studies, the number of subjects was small, the dose of omega-3s were greater than 3 g per day and controls were lacking.

Aboriginal peoples living in Greenland exhibit negligible occurrences of heart disease and diabetes. If research points to the lower rate of heart disease as a result of a fatty fish diet (not to mention it is widely accepted that fatty fish diets are good for overall health), then presumably it should explain the lower rate of diabetes. The native Alaskan population, with high intakes of omega-3 fatty acids from fish oil, also shows a reduced risk of developing type 2 diabetes. Because of all the positive effects of omega-3 fatty acids from fish, like reduced blood pressure, reduced cholesterol and even increased insulin sensitivity in animals, it has been advised that patients with type 2 diabetes would benefit from small dose supplements (1 g EPA and DHA) of fish oil, and daily consumption of fish oil may aid in the prevention of type 2 diabetes.

Dr. Barry Sears, author of the *Omega Zone*, has observed powerful benefits of fish oil for diabetic patients in his own research and in fact, has seen changes in insulin and triglyceride levels similar to what can be seen with any drug. However, other clinical trials have found mixed results showing that fish oil won't worsen or improve the blood sugar levels of diabetics. These reports claiming that diabetics need to be cautious about fish intake are somewhat controversial, considering all the powerful benefits of omega-3s that have been documented in populations consuming high fish diets while exhibiting virtually no diabetes or heart disease.

Other clinical research published in the *American Journal of Clinical Nutrition* in November of 2002 has suggested that fish oil may have adverse effects on blood glucose control in diabetic patients with high blood pressure. A total of 51 subjects were randomly assigned to consume daily 4 g of EPA and DHA or a fake pill containing olive oil for six weeks in addition to their regular diets. The results showed fasting glucose levels in the EPA and DHA groups increased, although blood triglyceride levels decreased. Again, this study can be criticized for the dosages consumed by the type 2 diabetic patients, as they were simply too high, almost four times the recommended level. This is why we stress that type 2 diabetics will find benefit with small doses of fish oil (1 g of EPA and DHA), especially to improve triglyceride levels and reduce blood pressure, two complications that diabetics often suffer from.

FISH OIL: POTENTIAL TREATMENT FOR NEUROPATHY

Not only has fish oil been shown to improve certain heart-related complications in type 2 diabetic patients, but it has also been suggested to prevent diabetic neuropathy similar to GLA. Diabetic neuropathy has been associated with a decrease in nerve conduction velocity, and blood damage to the nerve. One particular animal study examined the potential role of fish oil on the sciatic nerve of diabetic rats. The results showed that after eight weeks of fish oil supplementation, nerve conduction velocity was improved, suggesting that fish oil therapy may be effective in the prevention of diabetic neuropathy. Another good reason to ensure adequate fish oil supplementation.

Recommended Dosage: Recent recommendations from the Institute of Medicine have suggested approximately 110 mg and 160 mg of EPA and DHA for general health maintenance. This recommendation has been criticized by various organizations including the Council for Responsible Nutrition, who feels the recommendation is far below what clinical research shows as efficacious, and is below the guidelines set forth by the American Heart Association to consume two fatty fish meals per week.

It is highly recognized that to receive the therapeutic benefits that would be required for diabetes prevention, a much higher dose of the individual fatty acids is required, and clinical research has used dosages of a high quality fish oil around 10 fish oil 18/12 capsules per day or higher which would provide 1.8 g EPA and 1.2 g DHA.

What We Learned In This Chapter:

- Weight loss and exercise help control blood sugar fluctuations and boost insulin sensitivity.
- GLA-rich sources of omega-6 fats are useful in treating diabetic neuropathy.
- CLA can improve insulin sensitivity.
- Flaxseed, rich in lignans and ALA, is a super food that not only works to control glucose levels and insulin, but may delay the development of diabetes and reduce the heart-related complications that can arise.
- Diets high in fatty fish correspond with lower levels of diabetes and heart disease.

Now that you understand why obesity and diabetes go hand in hand, in the next chapter we will look at how obesity and glucose levels can affect the cardiovascular system and cause heart disease.

Chapter 4

HEART HEALTH:
HAVE A LOVE AFFAIR WITH FAT

If you have been reading these chapters in order, you are probably getting a good picture of how interrelated the body's systems are, and how a malfunction in one system can have an impact on another. Weight gain and diabetes have a strong association with heart disease. In spite of the "manly" reputation that heart disease has, women are actually more affected by it than men. The *1999 Statistics Canada Report* attributed 35% of all male deaths and 37% of all female deaths to heart disease. The picture is similar in the U.S., where the American Heart Association states that depending on ethnicity, about 40–42% of death among women is due to heart disease. Postmenopausal women are especially at risk because of the declining estrogen levels which increase the risk of heart disease.

In addition to the higher risk of diabetes, people carrying excess weight (especially around the middle) are susceptible to developing hypertension (high blood pressure), high cholesterol and stroke. Stroke is the result of reduced blood flow to the brain. Excess body weight is associated with increases in mortality from all causes especially heart disease. Heart disease is a term that applies to many diseases or injuries to the cardiovascular system: the heart, the blood vessels of the heart, and the system of blood vessels (veins and arteries) throughout the body and within the brain.

The exact number of Canadians who have heart disease is unknown, although it is generally accepted that one in four Canadians has some form of it or another. If this estimate is accurate, it translates into affecting eight million Canadians. About 60 million Americans suffer from heart disease with 2,600 people dying each day. The economical impact in Canada accounted for over CDN$18 billion in 1994. Heart disease is the largest cost category among all diseases and is the leading cause of death. There are over 200 risk factors that have been identified for heart disease; common risk factors include high stress, high cholesterol, high blood pressure, high triglycerides, sedentary lifestyle, smoking, poor diet, obesity, diabetes and dietary fat imbalances.

THE OBESITY LINK

The association between obesity and heart disease is well documented. Data from the National Health and Nutrition Examination Study (which was designed to assess the health and nutrition of adults and children living in the U.S. based on interviews and direct physical examinations) showed that the prevalence of hypertension increases as body mass index increases in both men and women (see page 24 to calculate your BMI). In adults with a BMI greater than 30 the prevalence of high blood pressure was 38% in men and 32% in women, as compared with 18% in men and 16% in women with a BMI less than 25. Similar data has been reported from the Nurses' Health Study. The mechanism for the association between obesity and hypertension is related to increased blood volume, increased cardiac output, and increased insulin resistance, and so it is well known that weight loss is associated with a beneficial decrease in blood pressure in obese patients.

High cholesterol is common among obese people and is characterized by elevated fasting plasma total cholesterol, triglycerides and bad LDL cholesterol and lower good HDL cholesterol. Obesity and high insulin levels with insulin resistance are thought to cause an excess production of the bad LDL cholesterol.

CHOLESTEROL CRAZY

Cholesterol is the most misunderstood subject in nutrition among the public. Cholesterol is a heart disease risk factor that has received the most attention over any other heart-related factors, and we are usually left with the impression that we need to get rid of the cholesterol foods in our diet. But did you know that cholesterol does not just come from our food? Our body makes cholesterol as well. Dietary cholesterol has been given a bad rap and is now known to have less of an impact on total blood cholesterol levels than previously thought. In fact, cholesterol is actually good for you and is essential for your body.

The old "cholesterol hypothesis" suggested that elevated cholesterol in the blood increases the risk of coronary heart disease and that high intake of saturated fat increases this cholesterol. This theory is now thought to be too simplistic.

It is true that numerous human trials have proven that high blood cholesterol levels are linked to heart disease. For example, data from the Framingham Heart Study and the Multiple Risk Factor Intervention Trial (MRFIT) confirmed a relationship between blood cholesterol and heart disease mortality back in 1971. However, it is not necessarily cholesterol in the diet that is causing an increase in these levels; it may actually be more related to saturated fat and transfatty acid intake. Let's take a little closer look at what cholesterol is.

Cholesterol is found within the bloodstream and in every cell in your body. Cholesterol is used to form cell membranes and is needed to produce sex hormones such as estrogen, androgen, progesterone, adrenocorticoid hormones, as well as manufacture vitamin D. Of the cholesterol in the blood, 75% is produced by the liver. Most people have a feedback mechanism that moderates their cholesterol levels. If we eat too much cholesterol, the liver makes less and if we eat too little, the liver makes more. For a very small group of people, however, their cholesterol regulating system in the liver is dysfunctional and their cholesterol levels must be maintained

ACCEPTED GUIDELINES FOR CHOLESTEROL*
Total Cholesterol:
Desirable: less than 200 mg/dl
Borderline to high: 200-239 mg/dl
High: 240 mg/dl or higher
HDL:
higher than 35 mg/dl
LDL:
Desirable: less than 140 mg/dl
Borderline to high: 130-159 mg/dl
High:160 mg/dl or higher
Triglycerides:
Less than 150 mg/dl

*Courtesy of the NHLBI

by making changes in the diet and taking nutritional supplements. Although we hear plenty about high cholesterol, many are not aware that very low cholesterol levels can be an indicator of other health concerns. Cholesterol levels below the normal range are often associated with cancer, but are also common in those who are very thin and rarely exercise.

Cholesterol is transported in the blood in various protein components known as lipoproteins, including low density lipoproteins (LDL), high density lipoproteins (HDL), intermediate density lipoproteins (IDL) and very low density lipoproteins (VLDL). These transport proteins vary in their effects on the body.

If too much LDL cholesterol circulates in the blood, it can slowly build up in the walls of the arteries, which can form plaque, a thick, hard deposit that can clog arteries. This condition is known as atherosclerosis (hardening of the arteries). A clot that forms near this plaque can block the blood flow to part of the heart muscle and cause a heart attack. This is why LDL cholesterol is called the "bad" cholesterol.

On the other hand, research shows that HDL cholesterol tends to carry cholesterol away from the arteries and back to the liver for disposal. Some experts believe HDL removes excess cholesterol from plaques and thus slows their growth. HDL cholesterol is known as "good" cholesterol because a high HDL level seems to protect against heart attacks.

It is easy to see that not all types of cholesterol are associated with the same risk. Research has shown that low HDL seems to be a particularly important risk factor in women and the elderly.

Symptoms of high cholesterol may include angina or chest pain. A fatty tissue buildup under the skin, especially on the eyelids, indicates poor cholesterol metabolism. In severe cases pain in the legs may occur when walking. See the previous page for the accepted guidelines for determining your level of risk.

FABULOUS FAT: NATURE'S PREVENTATIVE

GLA for the Heart

The major risk factors of heart disease include high blood pressure, high cholesterol, obesity, diabetes and smoking. Research in both animals and humans has shown that GLA can correct blood cholesterol levels, lower blood pressure and inhibit the formation of plaque in the arteries.

CHOLESTEROL

In 1994, a placebo-controlled human trial conducted in Chile demonstrated the positive effects of evening primrose oil supplementation on cholesterol levels. The study included 12 men with increased levels of bad LDL cholesterol and with a known family history of coronary artery disease. The patients received 240 mg of GLA daily from evening primrose oil. After two months of supplementation, the average bad LDL cholesterol level in the treatment group had fallen to a healthy 125 mg/dl. The control group remained high, with an average of 246 mg/dl. At the same time, the average blood level of the good HDL cholesterol increased in the treatment group to 42 mg/dl. The control group remained high risk at 33 mg/dl.

BLOOD PRESSURE

GLA supplementation has proven beneficial for reducing high blood pressure. High blood pressure increases blood turbulence and may damage blood vessel walls, leading to the development of plaque in the arteries. Several laboratory studies on hypertensive rats have shown that dietary supplementation with GLA containing oils significantly lowered blood pressure.

Studies on humans demonstrate that GLA supplementation reduces stress-induced hypertension. In a 1996 study published in the *Journal of Human Hypertension*, patients received 1 g of GLA from black currant seed oil daily for four weeks. During subsequent stress tests, the rise in blood pressure of the treatment group was up to 40% less than in the control group. In an earlier study, investigators compared the effects of GLA and EPA on stress-induced hypertension. In the 28-day study, one treatment group received 1.3 g of GLA daily, while the other received 1.6 g of EPA daily. During subsequent stress tests, the GLA group demonstrated a lower rise in stress-related blood pressure than either the control or EPA groups.

> *Recommended Dosage:* Effective doses for lowering blood pressure are in the range of 250–1,000 mg of GLA per day. To obtain these levels consume one to four 1,000 mg borage capsules or three to ten 1,000 mg evening primrose oil capsules. The positive effects of GLA can be generally seen after one month of supplementation, although some people may experience the effects much faster. The full effects of GLA supplementation are seen over longer periods.

Heart-Friendly Flax

Flax is the richest plant source of the omega-3 ALA. Research has shown that ALA is extremely beneficial for the heart as well.

CORONARY ARTERY DISEASE

The National Heart, Lung, and Blood Institute Family Heart Study examined the relationship between ALA-rich omega-3 fatty acids and coronary artery disease (the build up of plaque in the blood vessels leading to the heart). The 4,584 participants filled out food frequency questionnaires and results of the study showed that a higher intake of ALA and LA had synergistic effects on the risk of developing coronary artery disease, with higher intakes of ALA and LA corresponding to lower risks.

A study looking at the relationship between the Mediterranean style diet (rich in olive oil, tomatoes and fish) and prevention of coronary heart disease clearly showed that increasing ALA in the diet reduced the incidence of sudden death significantly, by 70% after two years. Another study comparing the cholesterol levels in Crete, Greece and Zutphen, Netherlands, reported that the Cretans had higher concentrations of ALA and lower cholesterol levels than the Dutch. ALA in the Cretan diet comes from purslane, walnuts, and other wild green leafy plants.

Similarly, the population of Kohama Island, Japan, which has the longest life expectancy in the world and the lowest death rate due to coronary heart disease, has high concentrations of ALA in their blood. It is an interesting observation: two populations (the Japanese and the Greek) are documented to have the greatest life expectancies in the world and both have high intakes of ALA.

HEART ATTACK

One of the most significant landmark studies examining the relationship between dietary ALA and heart disease was that of the Nurse's Health Study. The dietary habits of more than 120,000 registered nurses were followed for more than 10 years. Nurses with the highest dietary intake of ALA experienced 30% fewer fatal heart attacks than those who consumed lower amounts of ALA. Regular consumption of flaxseed and/or flaxseed oil would provide similar results.

CHOLESTEROL

Not only is flax a valuable source of ALA, but flaxseed contains significant quantities of fiber. Fiber has been reported to help lower cholesterol and triglyceride levels. Flaxseed really is a super food!

Research with flaxseed and cholesterol began on animals and found that rats fed 20–40% flaxseed for 90 days showed significantly lower total cholesterol and triglyceride levels than rats fed no flaxseed. The researchers decided to add flax oil to the regime, and cholesterol levels fell dramatically. The combination of flaxseed and oil provided the most significant cholesterol lowering results. In a more recent study, when milled flaxseeds were added to bread and fed to rats for 19 days, their average blood cholesterol and bad LDL cholesterol dropped by 47% and 48.5%, respectively.

In human trials, the results are equally as impressive. A group of nine female volunteers was given a diet containing 50 g ground raw flaxseed daily for four weeks. Their total cholesterol was reduced by 9% and bad LDL cholesterol by 18%. In another study, 10 volunteers (five male, five female) were given 50 g of flaxseed daily in the form of muffins. After four weeks their cholesterol levels and the ratio of bad LDL to good HDL cholesterol had both fallen by 6%.

New research is also showing how the lignans in flaxseed decrease the bad LDL cholesterol, increase the good HDL cholesterol, decrease blood pressure, suppress the plaque development and inflammation, and enhance blood vessel tone. Increasing the flax and lignans naturally through diet or supplement form is an effective method to achieving health and preventing chronic disease, especially heart disease.

Recommended Dosage: To achieve optimal health and wellness, flax should be a part of your daily diet. For general health maintenance, 1.1 to 1.6 g of ALA daily is recommended. To obtain this level, take two to three 1,000 mg flax oil soft gels, or 1/2 to 1 teaspoon of oil. To receive the added benefits of protein, fiber and lignans that the milled seed brings also consume 1 to 2 tablespoons of flaxseeds daily. Higher doses of ALA and flaxseed may be required to lower cholesterol levels.

Recommended Products: Health From The Sun's EFA Heart Formula; Preferred Nutrition's FemmEssentials FemmOmega™; Herbal Select's Organic Flax Oil with Lignans; and Swanson's EFA OmegaTru™ High Lignan Flaxseed Oil.

Fishing for Heart Health

We have examined how obesity, cholesterol and transfatty acids can make a big impact on your heart and your risk of developing heart disease. While dietary advice is clear—reduce your body weight and cut down on the transfats in your diet—what else can be done? Over the past few decades an impressive number of studies have shown that fish is good for the heart. In 2000, the American Heart Association released dietary guidelines recommending that everyone consume at least two servings of fatty fish per week to protect against heart disease. In fact, omega-3 fatty acids from fish oil may be just what your heart is fishing for.

FATTY FISH: IT'S IN YOUR BLOOD

Research has shown that some populations have a lower incidence of heart disease than other populations, showing that heart disease can be prevented. During a visit to Greenland during WWII, Hugh Sinclair, one of the world's greatest nutritional researchers, noticed there was a surprising absence of heart disease among the Inuit population. This was in spite of the fact that their diet was extremely high in fat. He concluded that the type of fish fat in their diet must be helping to keep them healthy. Thirty years later, he set out to prove it.

Using himself as a guinea pig, Sinclair ate only seal and fish for 100 days. Afterwards, he cut himself and recorded the time it took for his blood to clot. He had induced the longest bleeding time ever recorded in Western civilization, excluding hemophiliacs. Although this was not a wise experiment, it did show that his body's blood-clotting function was altered. The result led him to conclude that consuming marine oils can dramatically change the properties of blood.

FATTY FISH: LOWERS BAD CHOLESTEROL AND TRIGLYCERIDES

"The Eskimo Diet Doctor"—as Sinclair became known—was not alone in his studies. In 1969 two Danish scientists, Bang and Dyerberg, were astonished by the low occurrences of heart disease in the Inuit population in Greenland. Their studies showed that heart disease among the Inuit was consistently much lower than the average of the rest of the Danish population who consumed a "conventional, industrialized" diet.

In spite of the approximately same intake of total fat, the Inuit had a high intake of seals, whales and fish, whereas Danes ate milk and meat products. One of the most significant dietary differences between Danes and Inuit was the type of dietary fatty acids they consumed. The Danes had a high intake of saturated fat and low intake of very long-chain omega-3 fatty acids, whereas the Inuit had on average 14 g of long-chain omega-3s (EPA and DHA) daily. From this the researchers concluded that a diet rich in fish oils had a profound effect on people with high blood cholesterol and high blood triglyceride levels.

BANANA CHOCOLATE CHIP MUFFINS

1 1/4 cups (325 mL) unbleached
  flour
1/4 cup (75 mL) LignaMax®,
  coarse
2/3 cup (150 mL) honey
1 1/2 tsp baking powder
1/4 tsp salt
1 large egg

1/4 cup (75 mL) milk or soymilk
1 cup (250 mL) mashed ripe
  bananas (about 2 large)
1/2 cup (125 mL) unsalted melted
  butter
3/4 cup semisweet chocolate
  chips or carob chips

Preheat oven to 350°F. Mix dry ingredients (flour through salt) in a large bowl. Mix bananas, egg, butter and milk in a medium bowl. Stir banana mixture into dry ingredients. Stir in chips.

Prepare muffin tin by buttering or lining with cup liners. Spoon batter into muffin cups, filling each about 3/4 cup full. Bake muffins until tops are pale golden and tester comes out clean, about 32 minutes. Cool on a rack. Makes a dozen muffins.

Recipe courtesy of the Bioriginal Food & Science Corporation

Their published observations on this population of people initiated widespread interest in omega-3 fatty acids.

The triglyceride lowering effects of fish oil have been well established. Clinical studies show a reduction in blood triglycerides by 25–30% when using approximately 4 g of EPA and DHA daily. The results are very effective even in comparison to some pharmaceutical agents. A dose-dependent relationship exists for fish oil and triglyceride lowering: the higher doses used, the greater the reduction in triglyceride levels.

In the case of reducing heart disease, the majority of data available on lowering triglyceride levels has been done on men. The effect of omega-3s in postmenopausal women has received little attention. However, in a clinical trial published in the *American Journal of Clinical Nutrition* in 2000, the researchers sought to determine the effects of fish oil on triglyceride and HDL cholesterol risk for heart disease in postmenopausal women, some of whom were receiving hormone replacement therapy and others were not. The results showed that supplementing with 2.4 g EPA and 1.6 g DHA daily was associated with a 26% lower triglyceride level and a 28% lower triglyceride to HDL cholesterol ratio. The researchers concluded that this approach could potentially reduce the risk of heart disease by 27% in postmenopausal women.

FISH OIL: YOU CAN LIVE LONGER

Later observational studies demonstrated that a moderate intake of fish (one to two meals per week) was associated with a 50% decrease in risk of developing coronary heart disease. Studies from coastal and inland villages in Japan suggested that a high intake of omega-3 fatty acids from fish was associated with low mortality of heart diseases. This is because fish oils contain the two heart healthy fatty acids, EPA and DHA. The typical North American diet is deficient in these fats, leading to a potentially harmful imbalance. Increasing your consumption of fish or supplementing with a high quality fish oil source will help to ensure you have the sufficient levels you need. It is important to note it is not just any kind of fish that will provide the EPA and DHA but only cold, deep water fatty fish, such as salmon and mackerel.

The research in the area of fish oils and heart health is so important that we will now discuss the effects of fish oil on different aspects of heart health, such as arrhythmia (heart palpitations), atherosclerosis, blood pressure, coronary heart disease, heart attack and stroke.

CORONARY HEART DISEASE

There is a strong relationship between the fatty acids EPA and DHA and reduced occurrence of coronary heart disease and atherosclerosis, a disease in which a plaque-like substance forms on the blood vessel walls. Atherosclerosis is a major cause of illness and death from heart disease. Numerous studies show that EPA and DHA can prevent the development of atherosclerosis. There are many mechanisms by which this has been proposed, including effects related to hormone production and decreased inflammation; decreased stickiness of blood platelets; reduced chemotactic affect (migration of cells associated with infection); and relaxation of the smooth muscles, which promotes an increase in blood flow and a decrease in blood pressure. EPA and DHA can also inhibit the proliferation of vascular smooth muscle cells, which helps reduce the buildup of plaque in the blood vessels.

Population and observational studies report that those who eat some fish weekly have a lower heart-related death rate. In a 30-year follow-up of the Chicago Western Electric Study, fish consumption was found to affect coronary heart disease mortality favorably, especially non-sudden death from heart attack. Men who consumed 35 g or more of fish daily compared to those who consumed none had a lower risk of death from coronary heart disease.

The majority of information available on coronary heart disease risk and fish consumption has been on men, until recently. A study conducted with women in the Nurses' Health Study, published in the *Journal of the American Medical Association* 2002, reported an inverse association between fish intake and death due to coronary heart disease—the more fish they ate, the lower the occurrence of coronary heart disease. When women ate fish one to three times per month, they had a 21% reduced risk for coronary-related death; once per week correlated with a 29% decrease risk; fish consumption two to four times per week showed a 31% reduction; and women who consumed fish more than five times per week had a 34% lower risk for deaths related to coronary heart disease than women who ate fish less than once per month.

BLOOD PRESSURE

The blood pressure lowering effects of dietary fish oil have been well evaluated by a multi-study analysis of 31 placebo-controlled trials comprising 1,356 patients. Fish oil's effect appears greater in patients with high blood pressure, exhibiting a dose-dependent effect. DHA seems to be more effective than EPA in lowering blood pressure.

HEART PALPITATIONS

Recent evidence links fish and fish oils to the prevention of ventricular arrhythmias (life-threatening abnormal electrical conductivity in the heart) and sudden heart attack. The severity of arrhythmia can range from mild to critical, where the heart may stop beating completely. There is strong clinical evidence suggesting the protective role of fish oil for this condition. Studies have identified the most anti-arrhythmic component of fish oil as DHA or its combination with EPA.

Dr. Marchioloi of Consorzio Mario Negri Sud in Italy was the main investigator of the most recent study set out to determine if fish oil concentrate containing 85% EPA/DHA could lower the risk of fatal arrhythmia (irregular heartbeat). His team looked at 11,323 patients who had suffered a heart attack within the previous three months. A randomly selected group was given 1 g of fish oil daily. Over a three and a half year period, 1,031 patients died but the data showed that patients receiving the fish oil supplements had a 41% lower risk of death from any cause after just three months. At the end of the study, 45% were less likely to die from a heart-related cause.

Dr. Alexander Leaf, Professor of Clinical Medicine at Harvard Medical School, who has also performed research on the anti-arrhythmic effects of fish oil, commented in an editorial accompanying this study that these results were very significant because there is no effective pharmaceutical drug therapy available for arrhythmias.

HEART ATTACK

Other recent research reports that men with high blood levels of omega-3s were strongly protected against sudden death from heart attacks. This study, published in the *New England Journal of Medicine* in 2002, was based on data from the Physicians' Health study. The degree of protection was 81% in men with the highest blood levels of omega-3s. The researchers concluded that omega-3s reduce the risk of sudden death from cardiac causes even among men without a history of heart disease.

Some of the most impressive research comes from clinical trials suggesting that the benefit of dietary fish is centered on a reduction in sudden cardiac death. Because these trial results were so significant, we feel they deserve an in-depth look.

The Diet and Reinfarction Trial (DART), reported in 1989, was the first randomized, clinical trial to evaluate the effects of omega-3s on survival. DART included 2,033 men who were recruited in 21 British hospitals an average of 41 days after having a heart attack. The patients were randomized in groups to receive or not receive advice on the following: lower fat intake, increase fatty fish intake to at least two fish meals per week (200–400 g of fatty fish per week, which provides an additional 500–800 mg of omega-3 fatty acids), and increase fiber intake. After two years, the group who was advised to increase their fatty fish intake had an impressive 29% reduction in deaths of any cause, mainly seen with a reduction in fatal heart attacks.

Ten years after that, the second randomized clinical trial, the world famous GISSI-Prevenzione trial, was conducted. The purpose of the GISSI study was to investigate the effects of omega-3 fatty acids and vitamin E on cardiovascular events after heart attack. Between October 1993 to September 1995, 11,324 patients participated in this trial. To qualify as a participant for the study, the patients had to have survived a recent heart attack (less than three months prior to being enrolled in the study). Patients were randomly assigned to four treatment groups:

Group 1 – Patients received 1 g of fish oil
(containing 85% EPA and DHA in a ratio of 1.2:1)

Group 2 – Patients received 300 mg of vitamin E
(synthetic alpha-tocopherol)

Group 3 – Patients received a combination of omega-3 and vitamin E

Group 4 – Control-group patients did not receive treatment

The results were very significant for dietary supplementation with omega-3s from fish oil. Treatment with omega-3s resulted in a 45% reduction in the risk of having a sudden fatal heart attack, a 30% decrease from heart-related death and a 20% reduction in overall death. Vitamin E was found to have no benefit and its effects on fatal heart events require further exploration. The investigators concluded that omega-3s from fish significantly reduced death, particularly sudden death, but not stroke. An anti-arrhythmic effect from fish was also supported by these findings.

The omega-3 supplementation in the GISSI trial corresponds to approximately 100 g of fish per day, an amount beyond what can normally be obtained with a balanced diet. Therefore, supplementing with a fish oil concentrate may be indicated. However, other population studies suggest a substantial benefit from fish at a level of one to two fish meals per week, but the benefit is definitely dose-dependent, and seems to plateau with higher fish intake. An important consideration with these trials is that no adverse effects were seen from these natural treatments.

Overall, clinical trials and population data support the use of fish oil for anti-arrhythmic effects, reduced risk of sudden death, and reduced triglyceride and high blood pressure levels in both men and women.

STROKE

Studies suggest that regular fish oil consumption can produce "thinner blood" allowing it to flow more easily through blood vessels. This helps reduce the risk of heart attacks and strokes from blood clotting for those with "sticky" blood. If you are prone to longer bleeding times or are on blood thinning medication such as Warfarin or Coumarin, consult your health care practitioner. You should not consume more than 3 g of EPA and DHA daily (more than 10 fish oil 18/12 capsules per day).

Recommended Dosage: The dosages required to prevent and treat heart disease vary based on the risk factor you are trying to treat. Overall, results with fish oils are dose-dependent results, showing the higher doses you take, the greater results you will see. However, for general health maintenance a dosage of 2 g of a high quality 18% EPA and 12% DHA fish oil are recommended.

Recommended Products: Herbal Select's Fish Oil Concentrate; and Health From The Sun's Super High Potency Fish Oil with Garlic.

What We Learned In This Chapter:

- Diet, weight, diabetes and heart disease are closely interrelated and positive changes in diet and weight can greatly influence diabetes and heart disease.
- GLA has been shown to lower blood pressure, normalize cholesterol levels, and reduce plaque formation in the arteries.
- Flaxseed and its oil reduce bad cholesterol and triglycerides, as well as sudden death from coronary events.
- Eating fatty fish and fish oil can thin the blood, lower bad cholesterol and triglycerides.

In the next two chapters we will discuss the importance of essential fatty acids in brain development and how a deficiency can affect our mental health.

Chapter 5

BOOST YOUR BRAIN, IMPROVE MENTAL HEALTH

Are you a fat head? The human brain is more than 60% fat. The majority of fat in the brain is the type that cannot be made by the body, but must be supplied by the diet in the form of omega-3 fatty acids: EPA, DHA, and, to a lesser extent, ALA.

During this past century there has been a marked increase in the lifetime risk for major depression and decreasing age of onset. Over the same time period, there have been marked changes in dietary intake of fatty acids—we consume substantially more saturated fatty acids and less polyunsaturated fatty acids. Countries with high rates of fish oil consumption have low rates of depressive disorders. Other conditions studied for links with omega-3 deficiency are bipolar disorder, schizophrenia, Alzheimer's disease, chronic fatigue syndrome and stress.

MIND YOUR OMEGA-3S

The brain requires more omega-3 fatty acids than any other system in the body. With sufficient quantities of EPA and DHA in the diet, the membranes of the brain perform at their peak level, which is essential for regulating mood, emotions, and staving off depression. The brain also contains high proportions of the omega-6 fat arachidonic acid from linoleic acid.

Low levels of EFAs can be found in people with numerous mental conditions, including learning disorders, attention deficit disorder and attention deficit hyperactivity disorder (see Chapter 6 for further information on these three problems), depression, bipolar disorder, memory impairment, anxiety, psychological stress, Alzheimer's disease, Parkinson's disease and schizophrenia. This is not to say that an EFA deficiency will cause you to develop these mental conditions, more so that there is a link between a fat imbalance in the brain and a development of these conditions.

Fish Fats Relieve Stress

We live in a hectic environment, one full of numerous responsibilities and stresses. Careers, family, illness, aging parents and finances are problems that can be overwhelming. Periodical bouts of stress can be helpful... it motivates us to do what needs to be done. However, prolonged periods of stress, when there is little or no relief, inhibits the body's ability to cope and recover.

Stress is a complex series of events in response to stressors, often referred to as the "fight-or-flight" response. It is the response that helps organisms deal with stressful situations. Physiologically speaking, a multitude of events occurs with stress, whether it's as minor as being late for school or as serious as surviving a car crash. One such event is a release of hormones, including epinephrine, norepinephrine, cortisol and others. These hormones are released in situations of both acute and chronic stress, to sharpen the senses, stimulate the heart, increase blood pressure, and prepare us for increased exertion. A certain level of stress is essential for survival, but too much can lead to such problems as hypertension, heart disease, fatigue, and digestive disturbances, as well as emotional impairment.

Research shows that essential fatty acids may be able to reduce several symptoms of stress and minimize the damage caused by high levels of stress hormones. Stress management is clearly important in reducing current and chronic stress and its effects on the body. In addition, research has suggested that essential fatty acids, such as the omega-3s, may be able to minimize the symptoms of stress, and reduce the damage caused by high levels of the stress hormones.

DHA LOWERS HOSTILITY

In one study Dr. Hamazaki of Toyama University in Japan studied normal students under stress. Hamazaki provided medical students with 1.5 to 1.8 g of DHA or a fake pill containing soybean oil for three months prior to university exams. At the beginning of the study and again at the end he measured the participants' levels of hostility by presenting them with potentially emotionally-charged cartoon illustrations of various human interactions that had empty bubbles for each person to write in.

There was a much higher rate of hostile and aggressive dialogue in the 19 medical students who received the fake pill during the high-stress period as compared to the 22 medical students receiving the fish oil supplements. The rating of the students' hostility jumped 58% in the control group but did not change at all in the omega-3 group.

Further studies are being done examining omega-3 fatty acids in reference to stress, and evidence of their benefits are continually being reinforced.

Depression

Research has shown that in the U.S. more than 17 million people experience depression and in Canada more than 1 million people experience depression each year. Depression can cause changes in eating and sleeping patterns, problems with memory and concentration, decreased energy, and feelings of hopelessness, worthlessness, and negative or pessimistic thinking. Women are affected by depression more so than men, experiencing it at roughly twice the rate of men. Eleven other countries over the world report the same ratio.

Research continues to explore how the illness affects women, but a variety of factors that are unique to women's lives are suspected to play a role in developing depression. Reproductive, hormonal, genetic or other biological factors, abuse, and certain psychological and personality characteristics may be factors in the development of depression, yet the specific causes of depression in women remain unclear, and many women exposed to these factors do not develop depression.

Depression is more than just sadness or "feeling blue." Depression is a biochemical change in the brain where serotonin ("the mood enhancer") levels drop affecting one's outlook and perceptions dramatically from what the reality might be. It affects everything you do and feel (see the "Check Yourself for Depression" quiz). In order for depression to be the diagnosis, these feelings must be prevalent for at least two consecutive weeks.

The biochemical change can be ignited by any number of factors, including family problems, death of a loved one, loss of employment, substance abuse, genetic inheritance, physical/sexual/emotional abuse, allergies, nutritional deficiencies, the effects of media and technology and even toxic pollutants in the environment. Treatments for depression can vary to include psychological, social, physical and spiritual remedies. Not only those with susceptible genes can be affected by depression, but anyone who has gone through a period of trauma, grief, or abuse.

Researchers are investigating many of the triggers for depression, and new evidence documents that the steady decline in omega-3 fatty acids in our diet may be a large factor. Various population studies link eating large amounts of fish to low rates of major depression.

"FEEL-GOOD" FISH

There are many mechanisms thought to be involved in the antidepressant effects of omega-3 fatty acids. Further research is required in this area, but some of the possibilities include that EPA is converted into different hormones which may affect mood by triggering specific brain receptors; ALA, EPA and DHA decrease the inflammatory response responsible for inflammation, pain and mood; and ALA, EPA and DHA are incorporated into the cell membrane, which may potentially increase the response of serotonin, the "feel-good" hormone. Science will continue to evaluate the mechanisms involved in these amazing effects, but

CHECK YOURSELF FOR DEPRESSION

Mark each symptom if it applies to you. Four or five checkmarks indicate the likelihood of depression.

☐ emotions provoked with little cause
   (crying, nervousness, anger or guilt)

☐ lethargy or hyperactivity

☐ apathy, lack of interest in regular pursuits

☐ change in sleeping patterns (too little or too much)

☐ difficulty in maintaining concentration

☐ low self-esteem

☐ diminished sex drive

☐ poor or excessive appetite, digestive distress

☐ recurring thoughts of death or suicide

Chart courtesy of Healthy Immunity

for now we will look at the research that examines the beneficial roles that omega-3s play with our mental health.

Dr. Hibbeln, a respected psychiatrist and researcher at the National Institutes of Health in Bethesda, Maryland, is a leading expert on omega-3 fatty acids and depression. *The Lancet* published his study comparing annual rates of depression worldwide with levels of fish consumption. His findings were significant and noted that among selected nations, Japan has a high consumption rate of fish and also has the lowest rate of depression at 0.12%. New Zealand has one of the lowest consumption rates of fish and also has the world's highest rate of depression at 6%—some 50 times higher than Japan. Dr. Hibbeln concluded that the differences from country to country could be predicted by how much fish the population ate.

HIGH FISH INTAKE, LOW SEVERITY OF SYMPTOMS

Analyzing blood samples of patients with major depression has also helped prove the direct relationship between omega-3 fatty acids, depression and hostility. In 50 patients hospitalized for major depression after attempting suicide, the ratio of omega-6 to omega-3 was strongly positively correlated with the severity of depression. In patients without major depression, having high levels of EPA was associated with less severe symptoms on six different rating scales. In other words, the lower the omega-3 contents of the diet the greater the severity of depression.

Published in the *American Journal of Psychiatry* 2002, a recent study involving 20 people with recurrent depression reported the effects of EPA on their symptoms. Patients received either a fish oil capsule or a fake pill in addition to the antidepressant medication they were already taking. After four weeks, six out of ten patients receiving EPA and only one out of ten receiving the fake pill had significantly reduced symptoms of depression. Patients' symptoms of depressed mood, insomnia and feelings of guilt and worthlessness had all significantly improved by week four with EPA treatment, and those on the placebo remained in their depressed state despite the antidepressant medication.

Bipolar Disorder

Bipolar disorder, or manic depression, is a neuropsychiatric illness with a high associated ailment and death rate. Patients with bipolar disorder suffer from mania, an extreme elevation of mood exhibited as hyperactivity, insomnia, impulsiveness, erratic or dangerous behaviors, feelings of having "superhuman" qualities, obsession and compulsion. The mania phase is followed by a depression as deep as the mania was high. The cycle is never-ending; although it may begin mildly, each cycle becomes more extreme in both phases.

A new study in 2003 by the Bipolar Disorders Research Clinic at the New York Presbyterian Hospital confirmed that suicide remains highly prevalent among patients with bipolar disorder. Despite mood-stabilizing drugs, such as lithium, the illness has high rates of recurrence. As well, people can be resistant to taking their prescription because they feel it suppresses their ability to think and interact.

New research has identified the same mechanism in omega-3 fatty acids as is in mood-stabilizing pharmaceutical drugs, and it has been hypothesized that omega-3 fatty acids may be a useful adjunct in the treatment of bipolar disorder. The first published scientifically rigorous clinical trial was conducted in 1999 and published in the *Archives of General Psychiatry*. Patients between 18 and 65 years of age with bipolar disorder were randomized to take either omega-3 fatty acids or a fake pill in addition to their ongoing usual treatments for four months.

The researchers found that omega-3 fatty acids used as adjunctive treatment in bipolar disorder resulted in significant symptom reduction and a better outcome when compared with the control group. Only 13% of patients receiving fish oil experienced the recurrence of mania or depression, compared to more than 50% in the control group. Dr. Andrew Stoll, director of Psychopharmacology Research Laboratory, McLean Hospital and Faculty at Harvard Medical School was the lead researcher in this trial and he concluded that "omega-3 fatty acids may represent a new class of membrane-active psychotropic compounds, and may herald the advent of a new class of rationally designed mood-stabilizing drugs."

The potential for using omega-3s as antidepressants is significant and new antidepressant drug treatment using omega-3s as an ingredient could be on the market within the next few years due to the overwhelming evidence. Dr. Stoll has reported that omega-3 oils might be compared to the antidepressant Prozac™.

Memory

Forgetfulness, aging, having a "senior moment"—the decline in memory generally plagues us as we age. Since research indicates that age is the best predictor of memory performance, many people believe that memory problems really are a consequence of aging. The fact that there are 90-year-olds who show little loss of cognitive function yet there are middle-aged and younger individuals who exhibit varying degrees of mental impairment indicates that factors other than age are involved. Therefore, research on potentially modifiable risk factors, such as diet, is of enormous relevance. A few studies have reported on the relation between diet and memory loss.

OMEGAS FOR ALZHEIMER'S

One particular study focused on different components of fat intake, including total fat, saturated fat, cholesterol and polyunsaturated fat. Saturated fat and cholesterol may increase the risk of dementia, because they negatively affect heart problems and heart disease has been associated with dementia (memory loss). These events have been related to Alzheimer's disease. On the other hand, omega-3 fatty acids may reduce the risk of dementia due to their anti-clotting properties and beneficial effects on lipid profile, respectively.

Data from the Rotterdam Study was used, which is a single-center prospective population-based study designed to investigate determinants of chronic disease and disability in older persons. The investigators examined the association between fat intake and dementia among 5,386 participants aged 55 years old and older. Dementia with a vascular component was most strongly related to total fat and saturated fat. Low fish consumption was related to an increased incidence of dementia, and in particular Alzheimer's disease. The investigators concluded that high saturated fat and cholesterol intake increases the risk of dementia, whereas fish consumption may decrease this risk and delay or prevent the development of Alzheimer's.

Chronic Fatigue Syndrome

Chronic fatigue syndrome is a multi-system disorder that presents with unexplained prolonged fatigue, pain, sleep disturbance, anxiety, depression and impaired concentration; it is also diagnosed two to four times more often in women than in men. The Centers for Disease Control and Prevention reports that chronic fatigue syndrome affects approximately 500,000–800,000 people in the U.S. Because so many of the body's systems are involved and the symptoms vary with individuals, chronic fatigue syndrome is extremely difficult to diagnose. Its origin is unknown, although a viral infection often acts as a precipitating factor and the term post-viral fatigue syndrome is used to describe one of the causal factors for CFS.

There is no standard treatment, but one of the most significant studies has shown that patients with post-viral fatigue syndrome had lowered blood levels of EFAs and elevated levels of saturated fatty acids compared to normal patients. This was first observed over 50 years ago in patients with a variety of acute illnesses. Sixty-three patients with post-viral fatigue syndrome were entered into a double-blind placebo-controlled randomized study and given high doses of GLA, EPA and DHA (4 g). After three months, 85% of patient's receiving the EFAs were reported to have improved, while only 17% in the control group had improved.

GIVE YOUR BRAIN THE FATS IT NEEDS

We are relatively deficient in these powerful brain building omega-3 fatty acids. Diets that emphasize packaged and processed foods are missing the good, essential fats. To ensure you are receiving sufficient quantities of omega-3 fatty acids, fatty, cold-water fish, such as salmon, mackerel, sardines and anchovies should fill your plate, as well as other valuable omega-3 sources derived from oil-bearing nuts and seeds, such as flaxseed and flax oil.

While consuming a fatty type of wild fish twice a week is important, it may not be enough to provide you with the essential fatty acids your body needs to protect your mental health. It would be very difficult to obtain high amounts of omega-3s just from eating fish. It would take anywhere from 6–32 cans of tuna per day to achieve the omega-3 dosages used in some of these clinical trials. Also, if you are pregnant, it is recommended that you limit your intake of canned tuna (see Chapter 6) to avoid ingesting mercury and other heavy metal and environmental contaminants.

> *Recommended Dosage:* To ensure you are receiving adequate levels of omega-3s, taking a high quality fish oil supplement is recommended. If you are using omega-3 fatty acids for general health, mood or cognitive enhancement, 1–2 g daily of total omega-3 fatty acids (EPA plus DHA) is adequate. If you are using omega-3s to treat depression, higher amounts may be required. Pregnant women who are wishing to supplement with omega-3s should work with their health care provider to determine a correct dosage.

> *Recommended Products:* Herbal Select's Fish Oil Concentrate; Health From The Sun's Ultra DHA.

Flaxseed and oil, walnut and perilla oil are plant-based sources of omega-3 fatty acids that contain high concentrations of ALA. Because so many factors can influence the rate of conversion for ALA into EPA and DHA, it can only be estimated to be at a rate of about 7–10%. It is therefore beneficial to supplement with a fish oil source to ensure optimal levels of EPA and DHA are obtained.

However, plant oils are great options for vegetarians requiring a plant-based omega-3 source, as well as for those individuals with an allergy or are unable to tolerate fish supplementation. ALA has many independent health benefits of its own including cardiovascular protection and immune system enhancement. Although ALA has not been studied by itself in the treatment and prevention of mental disorders, eating foods containing or supplementing with ALA is more beneficial than not receiving any omega-3 fatty acids at all.

> *Recommended Dosage:* If you are using omega-3s from flaxseed oil, walnut or perilla oil for mood enhancement, take three to four 1,000 mg softgels, or 2 teaspoons of cold-pressed flax oil or perilla oil. However, these dosages will depend on the individual and the severity of the depression. Higher doses may be required, and can be determined by trial and error.

What We Learned In This Chapter:

- In times of stress, ensure that you get enough fresh fish and other healthy fats to reduce stress and quell aggression and hostility.
- Memory and dementia are related to low levels of omega-3 fatty acids.
- Countries with higher fish consumption have lower rates of depression and bipolar disorder.

In the next chapter we will discuss how healthy fats and oils like those from fish can benefit expectant mothers, infants and children, and help prevent and treat learning and behavioral disabilities.

Chapter 6

ESSENTIAL FATS FOR MOTHER, INFANT AND CHILD

Essential fatty acids (EFAs) were considered to be of marginal importance in prenatal and infant nutrition until the 1960s when signs of deficiency became apparent in infants fed skim milk-based formula which is void of any fat. Research performed by Dr. Hansen established that certain fatty acids were essential for the development of healthy normal infants. He conducted a study where 428 infants were divided into several groups and fed cow's milk-based formulas with no fat or varying amounts of fats or essential fatty acids. Those infants consuming the lowest levels of omega-6 linoleic acid were found to have skin that was dry and thick. Dr. Hansen also found that the infants who were omega-3 deficient had abnormal vision.

It was at this time that the importance of EFAs was generally accepted for their role in infant nutrition. While essential fatty acids are required for good health by everyone, they are crucial during pregnancy and lactation, and the need during infancy and childhood remains high. This is because DHA, EPA, arachidonic acid and other EFAs are absolutely critical for nervous system, brain and retina development, as well as fetal growth.

EATING FOR TWO

"Eating for two" should be your mantra not only during pregnancy, but if you are actively trying to get pregnant, supplementation with omega-3s should begin before conception. The diet before pregnancy plays an important role in determining maternal EFA status. Because EFA deficiency is so commonplace, boost your EFA intake beforehand in anticipation of the extra nutritional requirements of pregnancy and lactation. Proper development of the mammary glands, placenta and uterus, and, most importantly, fetal development depend on sufficient levels of EFAs. The greatest amount of the polyunsaturated fatty acids are absorbed by the fetus during the last trimester of pregnancy. This makes premature babies especially vulnerable for essential fatty acid deficiencies (in particular omega-3 deficiency) as they may not have had enough time to absorb them.

Fetal needs of DHA and AA are extremely high during this time because 70% of brain cell development takes place while the fetus is in the womb. The fetal liver is not mature enough to be able to metabolize shorter chain fatty acids into the long-chain omega-3s and is unable to supply sufficient EFAs until 16 weeks after birth. Therefore, to obtain sufficient levels of EFAs the fetus depends on the transport of the fatty acids from the mother across the placenta. It is important for pregnant women to have adequate amounts of EFAs in their diet to cover their own requirements plus the requirements of the growing baby. If the pregnant woman is depleted of omega-3s before pregnancy, neither the mother nor developing baby will have adequate levels of omega-3s.

DHA may be most critical since women deficient in DHA may deliver pre-term, as well as low birth-weight babies, or develop behavioral or mood disorders, including postpartum depression.

Evening Primrose Oil and Pre-eclampsia

As we discussed at the beginning of the chapter, omega-6s are very important for infants to prevent against skin deficiencies that result in thick, dry skin. Evening primrose oil, containing the important omega-6 GLA, has also been hailed as an effective treatment against the development of pregnancy-induced high blood pressure, known as pre-eclampsia. Pre-eclampsia generally develops in the second half of pregnancy occurring in approximately one in ten women and is caused by damage to the placenta (the special organ which supplies the baby with oxygen and food from the blood).

Problems in circulation are developed which can lead to high blood pressure and swelling throughout the hands, legs and ankles. In some cases pre-eclampsia can become more dangerous, resulting in blood clots that could eventually lead to stroke. Research is ongoing into trying to determine the cause of pre-eclampsia; however, prevention remains the key. Different drugs and supplements, such as evening primrose oil, fish oil, dietary protein, calcium supplements, magnesium oxide and aspirin, have been suggested as possible preventive measures.

In a study published in 1992 in *Women's Health* a combination of evening primrose oil and fish oil was compared to magnesium oxide and to a fake pill in preventing pre-eclampsia of pregnancy. All were given as nutritional supplements for six months to a group of pregnant women. Some of these women had personal or family histories of hypertension (21%). Compared to the control group (29%), the group receiving the mixture of evening primrose oil and fish oil containing GLA, EPA and DHA had a significantly lower incidence of swelling (13%). At the end of the study there were only three cases of eclampsia, all in the control group, showing the preventive effect of evening primrose oil and fish oil.

It is thought that one cause of pre-eclampsia may be related to a deficiency of beneficial prostaglandins (responsible for decreasing inflammation and decreasing blood clots) that are formed from GLA in evening primrose oil. An early study published in 1985 in the *British Journal of Clinical Pharmacology* examined the effect of dietary supplementation with 3 g/day linoleic acid and 32 mg/day GLA on 10 pregnant and 10 non-pregnant women for a week. The evidence suggests that increasing linoleic acid concentrations and increasing the availability of gamma-linolenic acid is associated with a rise in beneficial prostaglandins which will protect against the development of pre-eclampsia.

While clinical research is ongoing, we feel supplementing with evening primrose oil is essential for pregnant women to prevent against the development of pre-eclampsia.

> *Recommended Dosage:* For prevention of pre-eclampsia and the production of beneficial prostaglandins, we recommend pregnant women consume 1,000 mg of evening primrose oil daily.

Omega-3s for Longer Gestation

Every year over 13 million babies are born prematurely across the world. It is important to identify modifiable causes of preterm delivery and fetal growth retardation, which are strong predictors of an infant's later health and survival. There is evidence that Inuit populations, such as those from the Faroe Islands, with a high fish intake have longer gestation periods, larger babies and reduced incidence of the potentially life-threatening condition known as pre-eclampsia (pregnancy-induced high blood pressure), compared to those populations eating less fish.

The first studies from Olsen, published in *The Lancet*, showed that mothers on the Faroe Islands gave birth to bigger babies than babies born in Denmark, partly due to longer gestation periods. This observation is supported by data from a study where supplementation of omega-3 fatty acid (2.7 g/day) from the 30th week of the pregnancy was associated with increased gestation (4 days) and higher birth weight (107 g heavier), compared to the control group receiving olive oil as a supplement.

More Fish, Higher Birth Weight

Fish oil has been shown in randomized trials and animal experiments to have the potential to delay spontaneous delivery and prevent preterm delivery, but the minimum amount of omega-3 fatty acids needed to obtain this effect remains to be determined. Researchers from Denmark set out to investigate these issues in a study of 8,729 women whose seafood intake in early pregnancy was assessed by a questionnaire. They tested whether a low intake of seafood in early pregnancy was a risk factor for preterm delivery and low birth weight and whether it was associated with a lower fetal growth. The group found that 1.9% of women who ate fish at least once a week had a premature birth, but this increased to 7.1% among women who never ate fish. The researchers concluded that low consumption of fish was a strong risk factor for preterm delivery and low birth weight.

However, pregnant women in North America should know that there is increasing evidence of mercury and heavy metal poisoning in our fish supply

TZATZIKI (CUCUMBER YOGURT) SAUCE

1 cup (250 mL) plain yogurt

1/2 cup (125 mL) grated cucumber

4 T sunflower, flaxseed or olive oil

2 T onion, finely minced

2 garlic cloves, minced

Combine ingredients. Chill for one hour. Serve with falafels, pita bread, chicken, spanakopita or fresh vegetables. Makes 1 1/2 cups (375 mL).

Recipe originally appeared in Healthy Immunity

and if they are consuming fish in their diet, they should either omit fish during pregnancy or reduce their intake to once every couple of weeks if they do not know the source of their fish. In Canada, the Health Protection Branch tests tuna (see their website http://www.hc-sc.gc.ca/hpfb-dgpsa/index_e.html) but there is no such testing in the United States.

Fish for Brawny Brains

A recent study published in the *American Journal of Clinical Nutrition* found that pregnant women who ate more fish gave their babies a better chance at mature brain development. The study also found that mothers with more DHA in their blood had babies with better sleep patterns in the first 48 hours following delivery compared to those whose mothers consumed less fish. It has been hypothesized that infant sleep patterns are thought to reflect the maturity of a child's nervous system, and have been associated with more rapid development in the first year

---

EXCELLENT GINGER SAUCE

1/2 cup (125 mL) finely chopped onion

2 T peeled and grated (or finely sliced) ginger root

3 garlic cloves, minced

2 T olive oil or hazelnut oil

1/2 cup (125 mL) organic and wheat-free tamari

1/2 cup (125 mL) water

2 tsp apple cider vinegar

1 T cornstarch

2 T high quality oil

Frizzle onion, ginger root and garlic in olive oil in a saucepan on low heat. Combine tamari, water, apple cider vinegar and cornstarch. Whisk until mixed well. Add mixture to saucepan and stir until sauce thickens, about three to five minutes. Remove from heat and stir in high quality oil. Goes great with broiled fish and veggies. Refrigerate in an airtight container. Makes 2 cups (500 mL). Ginger is excellent for nausea.

Recipe originally appeared in Healthy Immunity

of life. The omega-3 fatty acid DHA, along with the omega-6 arachidonic acid, are the key building blocks for healthy brains and eye development.

> *Recommended Dosage:* If you're pregnant, try eating fish at least once a week (see chart on page 72 for safe fish to consume), or take 1 g of a high quality fish oil supplement daily. If you are vegetarian you may prefer to take 1,000 mg flaxseed oil softgels, or 1/2 to 1 teaspoon of oil.

BABY BLUES

A sufficient supply of omega-3s is not only crucial for the baby during the gestation stage, but also for the mother. During pregnancy and lactation DHA levels are low because the body is giving the nutrients to the baby. After giving birth, the mother is often left depleted of omega-3 fatty acids and numerous health problems may result. For example, new, ongoing research finds women with low levels of DHA may be at an increased risk of developing a condition known as postpartum blues or postpartum depression.

Approximately 15–20% of women who give birth in the United States develop postpartum depression, according to the Director of the Mother and Child Foundation. Dr. Hibbeln of the National Institute on Alcohol Abuse and Alcoholism in Bethesda, Maryland has studied the effects of fish consumption and risk for postpartum depression. His conclusions were similar to those we discussed in Chapter 5: countries with higher fish consumption, such as Japan, Hong Kong, Sweden and Chile, had the lowest levels of postpartum depression, while countries with the lowest fish consumption, Brazil, South Africa, West Germany and Saudi Arabia, had the highest rates of postpartum depression.

OMEGA-3S ARE BABY FUEL

Lactating women have an increased need for EFAs since breastfed babies require a constant supply of DHA, GLA, and AA. While omega-3 fatty acids are critical for the development of a healthy fetus, they are equally important as the infant grows and matures. Human breast milk is 50% fat, which is the fuel for the tremendous growth rate of newborn infants. While breast milk has been known as the "perfect food" for an infant and is a source of EFAs, the proportion of DHA and other omega-3s in breast milk varies from population to population. Numerous studies have found that the content of DHA in mother's milk depends largely on the type and quantity of food consumed. Research has shown that the breast milk of women living in Canada and the United States is deficient in omega-3s in comparison to women in China and Japan. Certain dietary changes or supplementation with an omega-3 source may be necessary for breastfeeding women in North America to ensure their babies are receiving adequate quantities of DHA.

While breastfeeding women can provide their babies with omega-3 fatty acids, other women who choose not to breastfeed, or are unable to, must rely on infant formulas to provide their babies with the necessary nutrients. The European Society for Pediatric Gastroenterology and Nutrition in 1991, the British Nutrition Foundation in 1992 and the World Health Organization expert committees on Fats and Oils in Human Nutrition in 1993 have recommended that not only alpha-linolenic acid (ALA) be present, but that DHA and arachidonic acid should be added to formulas destined for preterm infants.

In 1994, the International Society for Fatty Acid and Lipid Research issued recommendations for infants that are in accordance with the other expert committee recommendations. Infant formulas fortified with omega-3 fatty acids are available in approximately sixty countries worldwide, including throughout Europe and Asia.

> ## ONE FISH, TWO FISH, BAD FISH, GOOD FISH
>
> Heavy metal content in longer living fish is a growing concern among health authorities. Pregnant women in particular must be careful to limit their intake to five ounces per week as dangerous elements such as mercury can pass to the fetus.
>
> | Fish to Avoid | Safer Fish to Eat |
> | --- | --- |
> | fresh tuna | grouper |
> | king mackerel | halibut |
> | shark | lobster |
> | swordfish | orange roughy |
> | snapper | salmon |
> | | trout |

In 2001, the U.S. Food and Drug Administration approved the addition of DHA in infant formulas. Unfortunately, in Canada and the U.S., very few omega-3 formulas exist despite overwhelming evidence of their nutritional value to an infant's health and well-being. Two formulas we know of are Enfamil Lipil by Mead Johnson and Similac Advance by Ross Products. As more infant formula companies begin to recognize the importance of omega-3 fatty acids, there is hope that more formulas fortified with omega-3s will be made commercially available.

While the long-term consequences of inadequate levels of omega-3s are not completely understood, research supports the observations that infants who are lacking in omega-3s have lower visual acuity and are at greater risk for developing attention deficit disorders (ADD and ADHD) and depression later on in life. Breastfed infants perform better on cognitive function tests later in life than those fed standard formula.

Visual acuity maturation in full-term infants fed either human milk or cow milk formula containing 12–18% LA and 0.5–1.0% ALA were studied, the results indicate that visual acuity was more mature in the 4-month-old exclusively breastfed infants receiving DHA in comparison to infants of the same age receiving formula devoid of DHA.

BEHAVIOR AND LEARNING DISORDERS: THE LINK TO EFAS

Childhood should be a special time filled with fun and excitement. While this may be true for many children, more and more are being diagnosed with behavior problems. Many children have a short attention span. The energy and wonder of youth can spur kids from one occupation to another in a blink, but when you notice that your child is unable to concentrate on a task, becomes bored with activities quickly and is always looking for something else to do, then a behavioral problem may be present.

Because they are unable to pay attention to instructions, these children perform poorly in an academic environment. Based on their symptoms, children can be classified as hyperactive, aggressive or a combination of both. A child who is both aggressive and hyperactive is neither willing nor able to comply with the expectations of structured environments. These conditions are classified as attention deficit disorder (ADD) or attention deficit hyperactivity disorder (ADHD). Both conditions are noticed in the first few years of life and become especially evident when the child starts school.

ADHD is being identified as an epidemic throughout the United States, affecting 3–6% of school-age children. ADD and ADHD were first believed to undergo remission during or prior to adolescence, but it is now established that, in many patients, the symptoms may be carried into adulthood.

The exact cause of ADD/ADHD is not known, though the medical and scientific communities are working hard to understand the cause. ADD/ADHD is multidimensional and many factors interact to cause the problem. Recent studies have suggested a link between abnormalities in cell communication and cognitive and behavioral disturbances associated with neuropsychiatric disorders including ADD/ADHD.

Other hypotheses suggest maternal smoking and alcohol use during pregnancy, an ischemic insult during pregnancy or a trauma to the head in early childhood as possible causes. Nutritional deficiency during the prenatal period and in early childhood may also be responsible for the development of ADD later in childhood. Studies have shown a deficiency of EFAs and trace minerals in patients with hyperactivity and ADD.

Because the exact cause is not understood, treatment is far from satisfactory. Psycho-stimulants are used in the majority of patients. The drugs, however, need to be used for long periods and are very prone to abuse. Many of these stimulant drugs have serious side-effects, including loss of appetite with resulting weight loss, insomnia, headache, and liver damage. As well, these drugs do not address the underlying causes of ADHD and are not free from side/toxic effects, including headaches, nervousness, anxiety, insomnia, nausea, diarrhea and liver damage.

DHA Suppresses Aggression

EFAs are an important part of a balanced diet and have been recognized for the normal growth and functioning of the brain. Dietary DHA has been recognized for its importance to learning by increasing acetylcholine levels in the hippocampus, an area of the brain involved in learning and memory. We also know that those suffering with ADD or ADHD are also affected by stress and have bouts of aggression. The following study shows that DHA has secondary benefits to improving the ability to learn by reducing aggression.

A group of Japanese researchers evaluated the effects of DHA on aggression in young adults. The study began at the end of summer vacation and ended in the middle of final exams, a time believed to be stressful. During this stressful period, the control group exhibited an increase in aggression toward others, while the group taking a DHA supplement (1.5 to 1.8 g/day) did not change significantly. The researcher's concluded "DHA intake prevented extra aggression from increasing at times of mental stress."

Possible Suspect: EFA Conversion Problem

L.J. Stevens and his group helped establish the link between fatty acid deficiency and behavioral and learning disorders. Some of his research, published in the *American Journal of Clinical Nutrition*, suggested that altered fatty acid metabolism was a key contributor to the nutritional deficiencies they discovered. The 53 study participants with ADHD had lower concentrations of EFAs in their blood cells compared to the 43 controls. In addition, 21 ADHD participants also had many symptoms of fatty acid deficiency with lower blood EFA concentrations.

The same researchers continued their studies on young boys with learning disorders. They found a greater number of behavior problems, temper tantrums, learning disorders, and sleep difficulties in the participants with lower total omega-3 concentrations. The reason for this EFA deficiency in this group of children is unknown. Some researchers believe that a fatty acid nutritional deficiency and/or a conversion problem may exist among children with learning disorders such as ADHD and dyslexia.

DYSLEXIA AND MOTOR SKILL PROBLEMS

ADHD is often associated with developmental dyslexia. Dyslexia can be defined as a significant gap between general intellectual ability and writing skills; inhibited reading and writing abilities via letter and word reversal; poor visual language memory; and difficulty distinguishing similarities and differences in words. Dyslexia is a common condition and may be becoming more prevalent, although the cause is unclear.

In the late 1980s, the British Cohort Study involved 17,000 children from birth to maturity, and became the largest study ever performed to assess predictors of dyslexia. This study found an association between EFA supplementation and statistically significant improvements in the same children, with respect to manual dexterity, ball skills, static and dynamic balance, and total impairment.

Dyslexic individuals have problems with visual and central processing. They have poor vision in low light, which is known as dark adaptation. Frequently associated with dyslexia is dyspraxia, a developmental coordination disorder that affects handwriting, balance and ball skills. DHA is an important component of retinal and brain membranes. In preliminary studies, dark adaptation was shown to be impaired in 10 dyslexic young adults when compared to the control group. Dark adaptation improved in five dyslexic patients after supplementation with a DHA-rich fish oil (480 mg DHA/day) for one month. Movement skills in 15 dyspraxic children improved after four months of EFA supplementation (combination of omega-3 and omega-6).

A recent study by Richardson and Puri, published in *Progress in Neuro Psychopharmacology & Biological Psychiatry* in 2002, studied the effects of EFAs on ADHD-related symptoms in children with specific learning disabilities (mainly dyslexia). Forty-one children aged 8–12 years with both specific learning difficulties and above average ADHD ratings were randomly allocated to the EFA supplementation group or the control group for 12 weeks. After 12 weeks of EFA supplementation, significantly lower cognitive and behavioral problems were noted compared to the placebo group. The researchers concluded that EFA supplementation appears to reduce ADHD-related symptoms in children with dyslexia.

Currently, British school children with learning difficulties are taking part in a major trial to see if EFAs from both plant and fish sources can help raise their learning and concentration levels. A total of 120 children aged 6–11 with dyslexia, dyspraxia, ADHD and autism are being studied. The researchers feel that the significant dietary changes that have taken place over the last 20 years (the reduction of good fats in the diet) are responsible for the increase in the number of children (as much as four to five times) being diagnosed with these conditions. The researchers expect to see a significant improvement in the children's learning abilities following EFA supplementation.

The studies described show that there is some value in providing DHA to children with specific learning disabilities. Further studies, including double-blind, placebo-controlled trials, are in progress to determine the value of EFA supplementation for learning disorders.

However, omega-3s aren't just for children; EFAs are required for as long as we are alive. As we mentioned in Chapter 5, research has connected omega-3 deficiencies to overall depression and other mental health conditions.

Recommended Dosages: See chart on page 72 for a list of safe fish to eat. If you are using omega-3 fatty acids for general health, 1–2 g daily of total omega-3 fatty acids (EPA plus DHA) is adequate. Pregnant women who are wishing to supplement with omega-3s should work with their healthcare provider to determine a correct dosage.

As far as recommendations on ADD/ADHD, the jury is still out to determine the necessary ratios of omega-6 to omega-3 and dosages. Clinical research has shown improvements with 500 mg DHA and 200 mg EPA, but the dose will depend upon the learning disability and age of the child. If you are vegetarian or would rather not take fish supplements, you may prefer to take a daily dose of 1,000 mg flaxseed oil softgels, or 1/2 to 1 teaspoon of oil.

Recommended Products: Herbal Select's Tuna Oil; and Health From the Sun's Attention EFA Formula.

PASTA PESTO

3 cups (750 mL) packed fresh basil leaves, washed, dried and thick stems removed

4-6 garlic cloves, peeled

1/2 cup (125 mL) pine nuts

1/2 cup (125 mL) freshly grated Parmesan or Romano cheese

1/2 cup (125 mL) high quality oil

Add basil leaves, garlic, pine nuts, cheese and half of the oil to the food processor and blend until ingredients are well mixed. While the processor is still running, pour in the remaining oil. Pesto will become a thick paste. Keep sealed in refrigerator and use within one day or basil will oxidize and turn black. Cook your favorite pasta, add seafood or fish, and serve it dressed with this delicious pesto. Makes 2 cups (500 mL).

Alternate variations: substitute half of the basil with either 2 ounces of drained sun-dried tomatoes; or 2 large red peppers that have been roasted in the oven at 250F for 25 minutes, then cooled, peeled and seeded.

Recipe originally appeared in Healthy Immunity

What We Learned In This Chapter:

- Prenatal nutrition, in particular the supply of essential fatty acids, is of utmost importance to the development of the fetus. To protect the fetus and the mother from EFA deficiency-related conditions, such as premature delivery and problems with growth, brain development and behavioral disorders, extra supplementation will be necessary.

- Other conditions related to pregnancy, such as postpartum depression, pre-eclampsia and the increased demands of lactation, can be alleviated with a consistent intake of omega-3 fatty acids.

- Omega-3 fatty acids, such as DHA from fish, have been proven useful in the treatment of such learning disorders as ADD, ADHD, dyslexia and dyspraxia.

One of the challenges of pregnancy is coping with the hormonal fluctuations. The next chapter explains how essential fatty acid deficiency can throw your hormones into chaos, resulting in PMS or exacerbating symptoms of menopause.

Chapter 7

HEALTHY FATS,
HEALTHY HORMONES

The two most significant times in a woman's life, menstruation and menopause, were once celebrated, but in today's society they are culturally demonized as inconvenient, troublesome and debilitating. For some women, though, it is more than a cultural burden.

The hormonal fluctuations that arise during these times can upset the body's balance. Hormones are tiny but their influence over the body is far-reaching. Even the slightest changes in diet, environment, stress and lifestyle can stimulate them to keep you centered and calm or thrust your body into turmoil with a slew of symptoms that can be severe. This chapter will demonstrate that premenstrual syndrome and menopause are not diseases but signs that your body needs something to restore its inner balance.

PREMENSTRUAL SYNDROME

Quite prevalent amongst North American women, premenstrual syndrome (PMS) affects around 50% of menstruating women, with some reports claiming up to 70%. Unfortunately, many believe that PMS is an expected event—a normal, regular occurrence.

PMS is a condition that usually presents itself up to 14 days before menses. However, women can experience the various symptoms at different times during the cycle and to varying degrees. Some may suffer from PMS to such an extreme that they only feel normal a few days out of the month. Signs and symptoms include:

- Female organ sensitivities: tender, painful and enlarged breasts; cramping in the uterus; changes in sex drive.

- Digestive problems: bloating; constipation or diarrhea; swing in appetite with increased cravings, usually for carbohydrates, salt, chocolate and sugar.
- Physical well-being: fatigue; migraines and headaches; backaches; skin problems; water retention with edema of fingers, face, ankles and feet; heart palpitations; dizziness with or without fainting; insomnia; and lowered immunity.
- Mental or emotional well-being: anxiety, irritability, nervousness, mood swings, and depression.

The Menstrual Cycle

There are three stages to the menstrual cycle: menstruation, the follicular stage and the luteal phase. The length of a woman's cycle varies among different women, as well as from month to month in the same individual. The following description is based on a 28-day cycle.

On Day 1, if conception has not occurred, the endometrial lining (capillary-rich tissue that would nurture a fertilized embryo) sheds. Low estrogen and progesterone levels initiate the extraction of the tissue which rips the capillaries away, causing bleeding. The low estrogen levels stimulate luteinizing hormone (LH) to promote the maturation of eggs, as well as encouraging follicle-stimulating

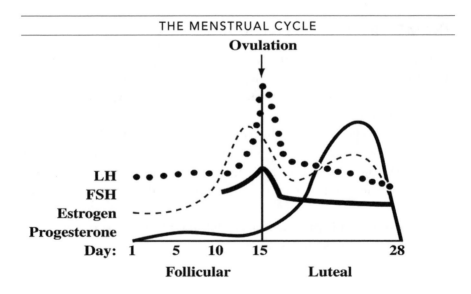

THE MENSTRUAL CYCLE

hormone (FSH) secretion, which, in turn, induces the follicles to secrete more estrogen.

The follicular stage lasts from about Day 6 to Day 14 of the cycle. The eggs are continuing to grow as FSH and LH bump up estrogen levels so as to allow the endometrium to develop. As the estrogen rises, a surge of LH occurs, causing ovulation. Between Day 12 and Day 14, an egg is usually released and carried along to settle in the womb.

The last two weeks of the cycle, Day 14 to Day 28, comprises the luteal phase. The follicle that released the egg secretes progesterone, the hormone that triggers the endometrium to prepare for a potential implantation. If the egg remains unfertilized, both estrogen and progesterone levels will drop again, and the cycle starts over.

THE CAUSES OF PMS

It wasn't that long ago that the American Psychiatric Association described severe PMS as a psychiatric illness, where a pattern of significant emotional and behavioral symptoms presented during the second half of the menstrual cycle, between the end of ovulation and the beginning of menses.

The main causes of PMS from a holistic point of view are poor diet, lack of exercise, liver and bowel congestion, and general toxicity. Once a long-term strategy is enacted to address those factors, sometimes along with short-term support from botanical, nutritional or homeopathic remedies, most women will find a dramatic improvement, if not elimination, of their symptoms.

The causes of PMS can result in many imbalances. The following have been identified in women with PMS:

- Dysglycemia (blood sugar imbalances)—poor blood sugar control, it can lead to further emotional and physical symptoms.

- Hormonal imbalances—estrogen excess; progesterone deficiency or excess; thyroid hormone imbalances; prolactin excess; high aldosterone levels (an adrenal hormone that, in excess, can cause muscle spasms).

- Nutritional deficiencies—magnesium, B-complex vitamins, especially vitamin B6, vitamin A and vitamin E. Vegetarian women do not have the same incidence of PMS as non-vegetarian women because they consume more fiber and less low-quality or harmful fats. Studies show that vegetarian women also have lower estrogen levels than women who eat meat. Research also shows that women who suffer from PMS have very low levels of essential fatty acids, specifically GLA.

- Prostaglandin imbalances—prostaglandins are hormone-like compounds made in every cell of the body that function as regulators of a variety of physiological responses, including inflammation, muscle contraction, blood vessel dilation, blood platelet stickiness (platelets are blood cells involved in blood clotting), and some reproductive functions. Symptoms can result with prostaglandin excesses or deficiencies. In PMS, there is often a decrease of the anti-inflammatory prostaglandins and an increase in inflammatory prostaglandins.

- Psychological difficulties—serotonin, the "feel good" hormone, is a brain chemical crucial in regulating mood, especially depression. Some research has shown that an increase in estrogen is associated with a decrease in serotonin. Leading researcher Dr. Guy Abraham has identified four distinct types of PMS, each with specific symptoms, hormonal patterns, and metabolic mechanisms. See the chart Four Types of PMS. You may find that your symptoms fit almost perfectly into one of the PMS types described or your symptoms may fall into several types.

NATURAL, EFFECTIVE MEDICINE FOR PMS

Conventional treatment is starting to look beyond over-the-counter remedies and pharmaceuticals, as more and more good research demonstrates that vitamin, mineral and herbal supplements are effective in relieving PMS symptoms.

GLA: EASES CRAMPS AND BREAST PAIN

GLA deficiency is one major cause of PMS. A healthy body creates GLA by converting dietary linoleic acid found in many healthy oils, such as organic hemp oil, sunflower oil, safflower oil as well as borage and evening primrose oil. The body metabolizes GLA into prostaglandins, hormone-like compounds made in every cell of the body that function as regulators of a variety of physiological responses including inflammation, muscle contraction, blood vessel dilation and blood clotting.

Before menstruation, arachidonic acid (the omega-6 that produces inflammation) is released and a cascade of prostaglandins is initiated in the uterus. The inflammatory response initiated by these prostaglandins results in vasoconstriction and contractions, causing the pain, cramps, nausea, vomiting, bloating and headaches that can coincide with PMS.

Painful menstruation and breast pain are known to be affected by low levels of anti-inflammatory prostaglandins. Symptoms of PMS have been specifically attributed to these deficiencies and the supplementation of beneficial prostaglandins can soothe PMS. The prostaglandins that worsen the pain in the

FOUR TYPES OF PMS – TYPES 1 AND 2

PMS-A (ANXIETY)

SYMPTOMS	MECHANISMS	PREVALENCE
• Anxiety • Irritability • Mood swings • Nervous tension	• Estrogen excess • Progesterone deficiency	• 68–80% of PMS sufferers

The estrogen excess in PMS-A is due to decreased breakdown of estrogen by the liver. The result is that not enough progesterone is produced to balance the excess estrogen.

PMS-H (HYPERHYDRATION)

SYMPTOMS	MECHANISM	PREVALENCE
• Weight gain • Abdominal bloating • Breast tenderness and congestion • Fluid retention, with swelling face, fingers, hands, or ankles	• Increase in adrenal aldosterone production • Estrogen excess • Deficient dopamine (a central nervous system compound)	• 60–66% of PMS sufferers

Increased levels of aldosterone (adrenal hormone) due to stress, estrogen excess, and dopamine deficiency cause sodium and water retention.

breasts and other tissues are found in excess in women suffering from PMS, in whom the conversion to GLA is often impaired.

Both the deficiency of anti-inflammatory prostaglandins and an imbalance of healthy fats (too many bad and not enough good) may result in increased sensitivity

FOUR TYPES OF PMS – TYPES 3 AND 4

PMS-C (CRAVINGS)

SYMPTOMS	MECHANISMS	PREVALENCE
• Increased appetite • Craving for sugar, carbohydrates, salt • Fatigue, dizziness, fainting • Heart palpitations • Headaches	• Increased carbohydrate tolerance • Low levels of prostaglandin PGE1	• 24–35% of PMS sufferers

Deficiency of PGE1 in the pancreas and central nervous system leads to increased insulin secretion and lowered blood glucose levels.

PMS-D (DEPRESSION)

SYMPTOMS	MECHANISMS	PREVALENCE
• Depression and insomnia • Crying • Forgetfulness and confusion	• Low estrogen • High progesterone • Elevated adrenal androgens • Possible heavy metal toxicity (lead)	• 23–37% of PMS sufferers

The increase in estrogen results from a stress-induced increase in adrenal androgens or progesterone. It has been found that PMS-D patients often have higher heavy metal levels and lower magnesium levels as determined by hair mineral analysis. The heavy metal lead binds estrogen to receptor sites and has no effect on progesterone.

Charts here and on previous page courtesy of No More HRT: Menopause Treat the Cause

to hormones. Some symptoms of PMS, especially breast pain, may be due to high levels of saturated fatty acids found in the red meat, milk and processed foods we eat, and because we don't have enough GLA. Women with breast cysts and pain have abnormal fatty acid profiles, with increased proportions of saturated fatty acids and reduced proportions of essential fatty acids. Supplementation with essential fatty acids will shift the abnormal levels towards a more healthy level.

A trial done at the breast clinic at the University of Hong Kong evaluated evening primrose oil for the treatment of cyclical breast pain. Among the 66 women who were referred to the clinic for disturbing breast pain, 97% responded to treatment with GLA after six months. The authors conclude that evening primrose oil may be recommended as a first-line treatment for women experiencing cyclical mastalgia (breast pain).

GLA deficiency may also be responsible in menstrual depression, since research has shown that GLA can help stimulate serotonin (see Chapter 5 for more information).

> *Recommended Dosage:* Dosage varies for each woman, but the general recommendation for PMS is two to four 1,000 mg capsules of borage oil or four to eight 1,000 mg capsules of evening primrose oil, every day.
>
> *Recommended Products:* Swanson's EFA OmegaTru™ Evening Primrose Oil; Health From The Sun's Evening Primrose Oil; and Preferred Nutrition's FemmEssentials FemmOmega™.

FISH OIL FOR PAINFUL MENSTRUATION

Painful menstruation is often found in women with low levels of omega-3 fatty acids. The *European Journal of Clinical Nutrition* published a Danish study in 1995 where the researchers found that among 181 healthy Danish women, low intake of animal and fish products was correlated with menstrual pain, with an average dietary omega-3 to omega-6 ratio of women with menstrual pain being 0.24. A higher intake of fish omega-3 fatty acids correlated with milder menstrual symptoms, and results were highly significant.

Another study, published in the *American Journal of Obstetrics and Gynecology*, found that supplementation with omega-3 fatty acids in the form of fish oil was effective in relieving symptoms of painful menstruation in adolescents. The double blind study examined 42 adolescents on either a fake pill or fish oil for two months. After two months of treatment the girls treated with fish oil experienced a significant reduction in symptoms compared to those in the control group. The authors concluded that dietary supplementation with fish oil was beneficial for painful menstruation.

FLAXSEED-BASED ALA: RELIEVES BLOATING, PAIN AND TENSION

Flax oil is an excellent source of ALA, another fatty acid that is associated with menstrual symptoms. ALA has numerous health benefits, including the ability to improve blood flow and relieve such symptoms as cramping, nervous tension, bloating and breast pain. ALA is an important precursor of other omega-3 fatty acids, namely EPA and DHA (found in fish and fish oil). Omega-3s in the diet positively correlate with milder menstrual symptoms. The intake of ALA is critical and must be balanced with GLA at the same time to reduce breast pain, cramping and bloating.

Flaxseed contains lignans, which help to balance the body's estrogen. Flaxseed can block the binding of xenoestrogens, foreign environmental estrogens that come from chemicals (e.g., plastics and pesticides). The liver sends xenoestrogens into the intestines to be removed via the feces. Flaxseed promotes elimination, moving waste through the bowels regularly to prevent a build-up of xenoestrogens. Menstruating women who consume about 10 g of milled flaxseed daily showed significant positive hormonal changes. The changes seen are similar to those in women who consume soy isoflavones. Lignans help reduce hot flashes, cycle changes and ovarian dysfunction.

Cyclical mastalgia, a syndrome of breast pain, swelling and lumpiness that recurs every menstrual cycle, responds well to lignans. Dr. Paul Goss, associate professor at the University of Toronto, and Director of the Breast Cancer Prevention Program at the Princess Margaret Hospital and the University Health Network, and his team of researchers examined the role of flaxseed in cyclical mastalgia. Cyclical mastalgia has been associated with breast cancer risk.

The researchers found that dietary supplementation with 25 g of flaxseed daily (also eaten in muffins) was effective in relieving symptoms of cyclical mastalgia without significant side-effects. The researchers believe that the benefits may have been the result of the anti-estrogenic effects of the lignans found in flaxseed.

> *Recommended Dosage:* If you are interested in supplementing with a high ALA source, recommendations are around 3–4 g of flaxseed oil capsules, or 1 to 2 teaspoons of flaxseed oil per day. Combining borage or evening primrose oil and flax oil will be more effective for treating

PMS symptoms as it will help to balance the body's omega-3 and omega-6 ratio.

FISH OIL AND VITAMIN B12: COMBAT FATIGUE

Fish oil made from cold water fatty fish is a beneficial source of the omega-3 fatty acids EPA and DHA. A study published in *Nutrition Research* 2000 involving 78 Danish women showed those who supplemented their diet with omega-3 fatty acids in fish oils along with vitamin B12 found relief from menstrual pain, fatigue and headache. Researchers reported that omega-3s and vitamin B12 may serve as an "alternative treatment to NSAID medication."

OTHER NUTRIENTS FOR PMS

Vitamins and Minerals

A study of 500 women published in the *American Journal of Obstetrics and Gynecology* reported that 1,200 mg of calcium carbonate reduce the physical and psychological symptoms of PMS by nearly 50%. Women taking 200 mg of magnesium a day noted reduced fluid retention, breast tenderness and bloating by 40%. Vitamin E is thought to help reduce PMS symptoms through regulating the production of prostaglandins that help reduce cramps and breast tenderness. Dosage varies but most doctors recommend 400 IU/day.

Bioflavonoids exhibit strong antioxidant effects and inhibit an enormous number of enzymes. These activities result in diminished formation of various pro-inflammatory mediators, including prostaglandins and leukotrienes. With the suppression of these inflammatory compounds, this may alleviate many of the symptoms associated with PMS.

Herbal Remedies

Find the remedy that seems to suit your symptoms and begin supplementation 10 days prior to when your symptoms usually begin. If your symptoms usually occur during menstruation as well, continue taking the remedy until the symptoms would typically stop. If your symptoms end with the onset of menses, you may stop until the next cycle. If your symptoms last for most of the month, take the remedy throughout the month. Be sure to make the necessary lifestyle and dietary changes to reduce or eliminate the need for other remedies.

- Alfalfa (*Medicago sativa*) acts as an estrogen balancing herb.

  Recommended Dosage: 500–1,000 mg powdered extract (4:1) daily.

- Black cohosh (*Cimicifuga racemosa*) can be effective for excess estrogen and inhibit inflammatory prostaglandin production. Traditionally, it has also been used to treat symptoms such as restlessness and nervous excitement. It is also beneficial for breast tenderness and headaches associated with menstruation.

  Recommended Dosage: 250–500 mg solid extract (4:1) twice daily; 40 mg solid extract standardized to contain 2.5% triterpene glycosides once or twice daily.

- Black hawthorn (*Viburnum prunifolium*) is an excellent tonic for the female organs and gastrointestinal system. It helps calm the nervousness or anxiousness that may occur.

  Recommended Dosage: 2–8 mL bark tincture (1:5) daily.

- Blue cohosh (*Caulophyllum thalictroides*) has been used traditionally in the treatment of PMS where there are emotional symptoms, and ovarian or breast pain. It is very effective for cramps.

  Recommended Dosage: 20–30 drops root tincture three to four times daily.

- Chaste tree (*Vitex agnus-castus*) is the primary botanical remedy used in Europe to treat PMS symptoms. It works by helping the body balance progesterone levels relative to estrogen levels. Chaste tree berries may help alleviate irritability, anger, headaches, breast tenderness, and reduce stress.

  Recommended Dosage: 175–250 mg solid extract standardized to contain 0.5% agnusides twice daily.

- Cramp bark extract (*Viburnum opulus*) is remarkably effective for relaxing the uterine muscles. These actions may help prevent or reduce abdominal cramping and discomfort.

  Recommended Dosage: 2–8 mL root tincture daily.

- Ginkgo (*Ginkgo biloba*) has been shown to be effective for congestive effects of PMS, particularly breast tenderness.

Recommended Dosage: 120–140 mg solid extract (4:1) one to two times daily; 80 mg solid extract standardized to contain 24% ginkgo flavone glycosides two to three times daily.

- EstroSense™ is a formula used by many with PMS. It helps relieve painful menstruation, scant or flooding periods, ovarian cysts, breast pain and estrogen dominance by balancing the estrogen to progesterone ratio.

Recommended Dosage: 2–4 capsules daily with meals.

STUDY PRAISES EFA-HERBAL COMBINATION

Research conducted at the University of Saskatchewan and published in the September 2001 *Journal of Obstetrics and Gynaecology of Canada* showed that a herbal formulation combining borage oil, flax oil, vitamin E, bioflavonoids, cramp bark extract and chaste berry fruit extract taken three times daily every day of the month was clinically effective for women with PMS. The three-month study showed a 67% reduction in 15 of the most common PMS symptoms at the end of the trial. The symptoms studied included:

- Premenstrual cramps
- Nausea, diarrhea or any stomach or bowel problem
- Depression, crying easily, feeling down or hopeless
- Anxiety, tension, feeling on the edge
- Anger/irritability
- Feeling hopeless or worthless or guilty
- Wish to be alone
- Difficulty concentrating
- Food cravings
- Fatigue/less energy
- Bloating/swelling
- Breast tenderness
- Headache
- Less sleep
- Hot flushes

Recommended Dosage: It is recommended to take three 1,000 mg softgels of the herbal formula daily.

Recommended Product: Herbal Select's Alphea™.

MENOPAUSE ... THE NEXT STEP

Menopause is defined as the total cessation of the menses for 12 months. The fertility hormones become less active and the ovaries cease the release of eggs, marking the end of a woman's ability to conceive. Some women experience a range of symptoms that may present as being very minor or severe, and which may appear years before menstruation stops. Other menopausal women will have no symptoms other than the cessation of their period. Symptoms may include:

- ❑ Accelerated aging (wrinkles may appear overnight)
- ❑ Anxiety or panic attacks
- ❑ Bone pain (often associated with osteoporosis/osteopenia)
- ❑ Digestive problems (bloating, indigestion, gas)
- ❑ Heart palpitations
- ❑ Heightened sensations in the skin, especially of the lower limbs (restless leg syndrome)
- ❑ Hot feet, worse in bed
- ❑ Hot flushes and/or night sweats
- ❑ Inability to breathe deeply
- ❑ Increase in facial hair, especially on the chin and upper lip
- ❑ Insomnia, or interrupted sleep
- ❑ Itching around the vaginal area, with or without discharge
- ❑ Joint and muscle aches and pains
- ❑ Lack of energy
- ❑ Lower sex drive, painful intercourse
- ❑ Lightheadedness, dizzy spells, vertigo
- ❑ Memory problems, clouded thinking
- ❑ Migraine headaches
- ❑ Mood changes, depression, irritability, or anger
- ❑ New sensitivities or allergies to food or environment
- ❑ Rise in blood pressure or cholesterol

❑ Urinary incontinence (worse with coughing or laughing)

❑ Vaginal or urinary tract infections

❑ Weight gain, usually around or on the abdomen, hips, and breasts

The number of menopausal women with:
- no discernible symptoms at menopause = 10–15%
- mild to severe symptoms = 70–80%
- severe symptoms; may require hospitalization = 10–15%

Menopause Is Not a Disease

While the symptoms of menopause for some woman can be uncomfortable and difficult to cope with, try to remember that it is not a disease. One-third of our life is spent in this transitional phase. Think of menopause as a time that heightens our wisdom and power.

Some women have a difficult time accepting the loss of youth; for them, aging is interconnected with unbearable loss. Much of this resistance and unhappiness over the reality of aging is due to their acceptance of unreal, impossible superficial standards of appearance perpetuated by a bombardment of glamourous images in the media. For a more detailed look at menopause, consult Lorna's latest book, *No More HRT: Menopause Treat the Cause*.

CONVENTIONAL HORMONE REPLACEMENT THERAPY

Estrogen has continually been among the top 10 selling drugs in North America, even though it was never adequately tested when launched in 1960s. The perception in North America is to view menopause as a disease of the endocrine system that needs to be treated with drugs, and that every woman will require estrogen for optimal health during and after the transition. There is something fundamentally disturbing about turning a natural event such as menopause into a disease that demands decades of drug treatment.

Most menopausal and postmenopausal women at this time have been raised in an era in which it was generally considered wrong to question medical authority. There is vast wealth of health information that is available to help you. The better equipped you are to make the choices that feel right to you, the better you will feel about this phase of your life.

THE ESTROGEN ILLUSION REVEALED

Until recently, estrogen therapy's destructive side-effects were mostly ignored or downplayed ... but no more. In the U.S. a statement released by the National Heart, Lung, and Blood Institute (NHLBI) of the National Institutes of Health (NIH) on July 9, 2002 declared that an 8-year estrogen study was abandoned after five years due to the dangerous effects of estrogen; researchers concluded that the risks were far greater than the benefits and that it would be unethical to continue. On December 12, 2002 it was announced that a U.S. government body, the National Institute of Environmental Health Sciences, put estrogen replacement therapy on its list of cancer-causing agents.

HRT has been prescribed to alleviate a variety of symptoms, such as hot flashes, night sweats, insomnia, but the two most commonly promoted reasons to take HRT are for the prevention and treatment of osteoporosis and protection from heart disease. No longer will doctors be prescribing HRT to reduce our risk of heart disease after the study's release. A reduction in fractures was noted in the above mentioned study but the risk of serious side effects will deter any woman from taking HRT for osteoporosis. See Chapter 10 for more information on osteoporosis.

The North American diet is typically deficient in EFAs, which are as essential to your diet as vitamins and minerals. This EFA deficiency results in a negative menopausal experience. Supplementing your diet with EFAs may be beneficial for menopause.

GLA: Relief from Bloating, Depression, Flushing, Pain

The enzyme that converts linoleic acid into GLA is impaired in many people but it appears to be particularly low in those experiencing advancing age and in women. Supplementation with GLA has been found to relieve symptoms of perimenopause (the years leading up to menopause) and menopause, including night-time flushes, breast pain, inflammation, fluid retention, depression and irritability.

> *Recommended Products:* Herbal Select's Alphea 50+™; Preferred Nutrition's FemmEssentials FemmOmega™; Health From The Sun's The Woman's Oil; and Swanson's EFA OmegaTru™ Borage Oil.

Flaxseed-based ALA: Stop Hot Flashes with Lignans!

Lignans are naturally-occurring substances found in plants that can balance estrogen in the body. Lignans are effective at preventing breast cancer and inhibiting cancer-causing forms of estrogen. Recently, one study published in *Nutrition and Cancer* reported that 28 postmenopausal women who added ground flaxseed to their diets showed significant improvement in estrogen balancing. Lignans work in cases of estrogen dominance, characterized by uterine fibroids and fibrocystic breast disease. Over the past five decades, more than a thousand studies have examined the role of flaxseed and lignans in maintaining health and in protecting against or modifying disease. The National Center for Complementary and Alternative Medicine is currently funding research on the effectiveness of flaxseed, and its lignans, for treating menopausal symptoms.

Lignans can potentially reduce menopausal symptoms, including hot flashes, sweating, and vaginal dryness and have even been proposed as an alternative to hormone-replacement therapy in post-menopausal women.

A new study, published in September 2002, was the first to examine the effects of natural therapies such as flaxseed supplementation in comparison with hormone therapy. Researchers at Laval University in Quebec, Canada, assigned 25 postmenopausal women with high cholesterol to a four-month cholesterol lowering diet followed by two months on either flaxseed supplements or hormones. After a two-month break, the groups switched treatments. The flaxseed was provided in bread and in ground flaxseed that was added to other food. The study found that flaxseed supplementation and hormone therapy were equally effective in treating hot flashes.

Other effects of lignans have been shown to reduce inflammation, have antioxidant properties and enhance the immune response.

Flaxseed and oil are also a source of the essential fat ALA. Flaxseed contains approximately 40% ALA, while flax oil contains between 50–60% ALA. The anti-inflammatory prostaglandins derived from ALA reduce the inflammatory and vasomotor properties associated with hot flashes.

Flaxseed: Lowers Cholesterol in Menopausal Women

Women are more susceptible to developing coronary heart disease upon the onset of menopause. Flaxseed is known to be effective in lowering cholesterol and serum lipoprotein levels, which are powerful predictors of heart attacks. Thirty-eight women with high cholesterol were assigned to two treatment groups and supplemented their diet with either flaxseed or sunflower seed for six weeks. The subjects were provided with 38 g of either treatment in the form of breads and muffins. Significant reductions were seen in bad cholesterol levels and lipoprotein levels with the flaxseed treatment, but not with the sunflower seed treatment, confirming the benefits of flax for post-menopausal women in reducing cholesterol.

A recent study involving researchers from the University of Oklahoma Health Sciences Center assigned postmenopausal women who were not using HRT to take 40 g of flaxseed or a wheat-based control diet for three months. Both groups were also given 1,000 mg/day of calcium and 400 IU/day of vitamin D. Total cholesterol levels, including LDL, HDL and triglyceride levels, fell by 6% in the flaxseed group compared to no change in the control group. This is an extremely positive study for postmenopausal women at risk for heart disease to help lower levels of total and bad cholesterol.

Not only do flaxseed lignans provide benefits for the prevention of heart disease but the essential fat ALA found in flaxseed and flaxseed oil is also well known for its heart health benefits, including lowering cholesterol and decreasing atherosclerosis (hardening of the arteries), thereby lowering the risk of heart disease.

> *Recommended Dosage:* For general health and to ease symptoms take 1–2 tablespoons of milled flaxseed daily.

> *Recommended Products:* Health From The Sun's Super FiProFLAX; Herbal Select's Organic Milled Flax Seed; and Swanson's EFA OmegaTru™ Milled Flaxseed.

Multi-EFA Therapy Prevents Heart Attack

A recent study published in the *American Journal of Nutrition* in 2003 suggests that a combination of EPA/DHA and GLA may be most effective in prevention of heart disease in postmenopausal women. The study examined the effect of EPA/DHA or GLA alone and in combination on lipid and fatty acid levels in healthy women. A mixture of 4 g EPA/DHA and 2 g GLA favorably altered blood lipid levels and fatty acid profiles in these women. This group was estimated to have a 43% reduction in the 10-year risk of heart attack.

Earlier studies have shown that both postmenopausal women on HRT and those not taking HRT who supplemented with 2.4 g EPA plus 1.6 g DHA daily over a 28-day time period exhibited beneficial improvements in the ratio of good to bad cholesterol, reducing the risk of coronary heart disease by 27%.

Awareness of the risks associated with hormone replacement therapy is growing, and as we understand hormonal fluctuations better, women will need somewhere to turn, to help ease their transition into the next exciting phase of their life. We now have a myriad of natural options for relief of PMS and menopause symptoms. Begin with eating the right fats and getting support from the herbs that will put the balance back in your hormone levels.

What We Learned In This Chapter:

- GLA is useful for PMS because of its anti-inflammatory action on cramps, painful menstruation and breast pain. It also benefits those menopausal women who have night sweats, bloating and hot flushes.

- Flaxseed, in particular the lignans in milled flaxseed, are recommended for improving blood flow and reducing breast pain and bloating during PMS. They are also shown to help against hot flushes, sweating, vaginal dryness. Lignans work in cases of estrogen dominance, such as uterine fibroids and fibrocystic breast disease.

- EFAs in combination with other nutrients or herbs can enhance their potency in relieving symptoms. For example, MenoSense™ is a combination of black cohosh, vitex chasteberry, dong quai, gamma-oryzanol and hesperidin. This combination reduces hot flushes, night sweats, sleep disturbances, irritability, nervousness,vaginal atrophy and dryness, leg cramps, menstrual abnormalities and triglycerides and cholesterol.

In the next chapter we will explain the relationship between diet and cancer and how essential fatty acids can prevent or slow the progression of breast cancer.

Chapter 8

THE DIET AND
BREAST CANCER LINK

Cancer rates are on the rise and few of us have been untouched by cancer. No other disease strikes as much fear in our hearts as cancer. We all know a friend or loved one who has been ravaged by this disease. Breast cancer is one cancer that affects far too many people. Breast cancer is the leading cause of death in women ages 35 to 54 and the risk of developing it are rising. In 1960 one in 20 women had breast cancer. Today 1 in 8 women will develop breast cancer and of those who have breast cancer, 1 in 4 will die. The ages of women affected by breast cancer are becoming younger and younger. Genetics plays a role in less than 10% of breast cancer cases so heredity does not play a big role.

With these facts in mind we should be asking what is causing the other 90% of breast cancer cases. Environmental factors are believed to be involved in 80% of all cancers and diet is a concern in at least 35% of all cancers. We are not destined to get cancer. We can reduce our risk and adopt a strategy for prevention, but first we have to know what influences our personal risk. We suggest you take the following Breast Cancer Risk Assessment to evaluate your own personal risk.

CAUSES OF BREAST CANCER:
THE ONES YOU MAY NOT KNOW ABOUT

We have been trained to believe that the only way to prevent breast cancer is through regular mammograms. This is a diagnostic method, to diagnose breast cancer once you have it—not a prevention method. Early diagnosis is key to acquiring fast and appropriate treatment, but it does not prevent breast cancer.

What are the most common but unpublicized risks for breast cancer? Estrogen replacement therapy in high doses with prolonged use; oral contraceptive use in young women with prolonged use; pre-menopausal mammography with early and repeated exposure; non-hormonal prescription drugs, such as some anti-hypertensive medications; silicone gel breast implants, especially those wrapped in polyurethane foam; diets high in bad fat contaminated with undisclosed cancer-causing and estrogenic chemicals; extended cell phone usage; exposure in the workplace or home to household chemicals or pollution from chemical plants and waste sites; alcohol and tobacco use with early or excessive use; lack of exercise; and the use of dark hair dyes from a young age or over a prolonged period.

You Are What You Eat: The Diet/Cancer Relationship

One area that has received a lot of attention in the media and research world is the link between diet and cancer, especially fat in our diet. If you have ever heard the old saying "you are what you eat," many researchers feel this theory is applicable for those who develop cancer.

The incidence of cancer has increased as humankind has advanced both industrially and technologically. Cancers of the lung, breast, prostate and colon have all become more frequent in countries where such risk factors as cigarette smoking, exposure to dangerous chemicals in the environment and poor nutrition are now more common; however, unhealthy dietary habits that include too many bad fats from processed, convenience foods, as well as red meat and not enough good fats from healthy oils such as olive, flax, hemp, and coconut are well within our power to control.

Bad Fats Increase Cancer Risk

As we have discussed earlier in this book, bad fats have a role in causing heart disease, obesity and diabetes, but often these conditions don't motivate us to make the necessary dietary changes. Perhaps it is because we've accepted that the fates of our relatives are to be our own. It is the same with cancer. Cancer is a powerful enemy, but it is not the inevitable victor. You make choices every day that will determine how well you can prevent or fight cancer. Bad fats in the diet promote cancer by stimulating abnormal cell division. These fats also produce toxic free radicals, and if the damage caused by free radicals overwhelms your body's natural defenses, the damage can contribute to aging and cancer.

Scientists agree that bad fats in the diet have a significant effect on cancer development. The harmful effects of excess calorie consumption and bad fat

BREAST CANCER RISK ASSESSMENT

☐ Have not had children and are under 25 1

☐ Have not had children and are 25 to 35 2

☐ Have had no children and don't intend to 3

☐ Did not breastfeed 2

☐ Took birth control pills during teens or early 20s. A few months use may increase risk of breast cancer by 30%. Ten years use may double it. 3

☐ Have taken or are taking HRT (Premarin, Provera, Prempro) ..3

☐ Have had regular mammograms before menopause 2

☐ Don't exercise three times per week 2

☐ Have had depression where tricyclic anti-depressants were prescribed (studies showed increase in mammory tumors in rats) 2

☐ Have breast implants (cause breast trauma) 1

☐ Had chest x-rays as a teenager or during 20s 2

☐ Are exposed to EMFs due to excessive computer usage, hair dryer usage or live close to power lines 1

☐ Dye your hair with dark-coloured dyes (a source of xenoestrogens) 2

☐ Wear dry-cleaned clothing (a source of xenoestrogens) 1

☐ Use bleached sanitary products, eg tampons, pads (a source of xenoestrogens) 2

☐ Eat pesticide- and herbicide-laden foods 3

☐ Use nail polish remover containing tolulene or phthalate ..1

☐ Periods started before the age of 12 2

☐ Late onset menopause starting after the age of 50 2

☐ Eat a diet high in animal fat, dairy and meat (a source of
xenoestrogens) 3

☐ Smoke, with early or excessive use 3

☐ Alcohol, with early or excessive use 3

☐ Don't eat cruciferous vegetables (these vegetables
detoxify carcinogenic estrogens) 3

☐ Take cholesterol-lowering drugs which depletes the
body of Q10 (Q10 is used to treat breast cancer) 3

☐ Using anti-hypertensives for lowering high blood pressure
which deplete Q10 3

☐ Using tranquilizers (studies show an increase in breast
tumors) 2

☐ Using ulcer medications which disrupts estrogen
metabolism which decreases good estrogen 2

☐ You are overweight or obese (fat stores estrogens) 3

☐ Use or have used Flagyl for yeast infections (studies show
an increase in mammory tumors) 2

☐ Family history in a first degree relative (mother, sister or
daughter—less than 10% of breast cancer is hereditary).........1

Total Score: ‗‗‗‗

0-18   lower risk

19-35   moderate to high risk

35-65   high risk

Courtesy of No More HRT: Menopause Treat the Cause

content in the diet on breast cancer were first demonstrated in animal studies in 1945. A review of 100 animal studies has indicated that higher calorie intake and higher fat intake increases breast cancer risk in rats and mice. The relationship between bad fat and excess calorie intake on human breast cancer risk has also been demonstrated. Studies have shown that populations with the highest consumptions of bad fat, refined sugars, red meat and milk also have the highest rates of cancer.

The link between fat and cancer has been studied most in breast, prostate and colon cancers, with much evidence showing a link between poor diet and cancer development. Dietary recommendations developed by the American Institute for Cancer Research (AICR) focus on increasing the fruits, vegetables and fiber in the diet and replacing the bad fat in the diet with healthy fats.

These nutrients have a well-established role in the prevention of cancers. In their 1997 report *Food, Nutrition and the Prevention of Cancer*, the AICR provides a comprehensive review of data surrounding intake of fats and cancer risk. They state that diets high in total fats, particularly saturated fat, may increase the risk of breast cancer. A study of more than 61,000 Swedish women found a relationship between breast cancer risk and fat type. The risk of breast cancer was lower among women who ate diets high in olive oil, avocados and nuts. However, diets high in refined oils, such as canola oil and refined sunflower oil (found in grocery store salad dressings, mayonnaise, etc.), were associated with increased risk of breast cancer.

The diet and cancer relationship clearly focuses on the importance of reducing total bad fat and replacing bad fat with good fat. The relationship with fat and cancer has another important component and that is fat is also calorically dense at 9 calories/g in comparison to protein and carbohydrates at 4 calories/g. People who eat a high fat diet are often overweight due to excess calorie consumption; they tend to eat less fruit and vegetables, an absence of which contributes to the increase risk of breast cancer.

More recent research has shown the cancerous component of diet is also due to specific foods, such as red meat, especially well-done meat. Animal studies have demonstrated that meats cooked at high temperatures result in heterocyclic amines which are cancer causing. In a case-control study, researchers sent out a questionnaire to 41,836 women with breast cancer. They obtained information about their intake of meat and on meat preparation. The researchers found a relationship between well-done meat consumption and breast cancer.

Women who consumed hamburger, steak and bacon well done had a 4.62 times higher risk of developing breast cancer than women who consumed meats rare or medium done. The researchers concluded that consumption of well-done meats and thus exposure to cancer-causing amines formed during high-temperature cooking may play a role in the development of breast cancer.

As well a high meat or high fat diet is generally low in vegetable and fruit content, and therefore low in such protective factors as antioxidants and fiber. The links between diet and cancer may have as much to do with what is not in the diet as what is.

NATURAL SOLUTIONS: OMEGA-6 AND OMEGA-3

GLA: Restrain Breast Pain

Good fats can provide protection against the development of breast cancer. Research has shown that evening primrose oil and borage oil, both omega-6s, can help reduce pain and tenderness of benign breast disease (non-cancerous but is a risk factor for the later development of breast cancer) and breast pain (another risk factor for breast cancer).

Both evening primrose and borage oils contain GLA, which is responsible for these beneficial effects. In fact, researchers have found that women with breast pain may have unusually low concentrations of GLA. GLA produces anti-inflammatory prostaglandins that help decrease inflammation as well as decrease breast

What is a Free Radical?

Molecules are joined together with electrons. If the electons are in pairs, the molecule is said to be stable. When there is an extra electron, instability arises and the electron will make itself a pair by stealing an electron from another molecule. The "robbed" molecule reacts by stealing an electron from another molecule and the process repeats itself.

In moderation the process is good for the body because free radical reaction produces energy; however, when there is too much free radical activity, it can cause serious damage to the body. Antioxidants are a good way to combat free radical damage.

pain. Low levels of GLA in breast and other body tissues are usually associated with high levels of bad fats in the body, such as those from saturated fats found in red meat and dairy products. This is because of the high bad fat North American diet that encourages excess fat storage in body tissues. Therefore, when patients consume good fats, such as evening primrose and borage oil, the concentration of GLA in breast tissue increases and the concentration of saturated fats in the breast decreases, improving overall breast health.

GLA: The New Anti-Cancer Agent

Regardless of the cause of cancer (diet, genetics, environment and so on), some form of therapy or treatment is required to kill cancer cells and stop the spread of cancer, ideally without any adverse effect on normal cells. Scientific research in recent years has shown that GLA from borage and evening primrose oil may be useful in the treatment of breast cancer. GLA has been found to kill cancer cells without harming normal cells, making it a good possibility as an alternative or addition to treatments for such cancers as breast, gastric, brain and pancreatic. Research with GLA has come a long way, evolving from cell studies done in a laboratory to a very promising treatment of cancer in humans.

GLA: A Potent Partner for Tamoxifen

A recent British study published in 2000 observed women who had locally advanced and metastic breast cancer (when cancer cells have spread out from the primary tumor). They found that women with breast cancer who were taking Tamoxifen (common breast cancer treatment drug) and received GLA from borage demonstrated faster clinical response than those on Tamoxifen alone. Patients received about 3 g of GLA (approximately twelve 1,000 mg borage softgels).

Tamoxifen by itself is associated with significantly improved survival rates in postmenopausal breast cancer patients whose breast cancer is estrogen-receptor positive. The researchers concluded that GLA was a useful adjunct to primary Tamoxifen treatment with no serious side effects: "... our Phase II study suggests high dose oral GLA to be a valuable new agent in the treatment of hormone-sensitive breast cancer." There is increased awareness of the potential anti-cancer benefits of GLA in the United Kingdom, and the Cancer Research Campaign (CRC) has designed borage pins to show their support for the use of borage in cancer treatment. The Director of the CRC states, "This humble herb holds great potential as the CRC strives to find new treatments for cancers."

In other research, the fatty acid composition was examined among a group of 197 pre- and post-menopausal breast cancer patients and their matched controls in the New York University Women's Health Study. Increases in total saturated fatty acids were associated with an increased risk of breast cancer, whereas, overall, total polyunsaturated fatty acids were suggestive of a small protective effect against breast cancer in postmenopausal women.

Other studies also show that EFA supplementation may improve the effectiveness of cancer chemotherapy. The activity of another pharmaceutical used in patients with breast cancer was found to be enhanced when combined with GLA or other fatty acids. A study published in the *European Journal of Cancer* in 2001 found that the effectiveness of Paclitaxel on breast cancer cells was enhanced by GLA. GLA alone was also observed to stop the spreading of cancer cells. While GLA was most effective at enhancing the activity of the anti-cancer drug Paclitaxel, ALA, EPA and DHA also showed benefit.

A more recent study published in 2002 in *Breast Cancer Research and Treatment* examined the effect of GLA and other unsaturated fatty acids on the effectiveness of the drug Vinorelbine in breast cancer cells. GLA was most effective in enhancing the anti-cancer effect of the drug, followed by DHA, EPA and ALA. The authors conclude that some unsaturated fatty acids can increase a tumor cell's sensitivity to drug therapy and that GLA is the most promising unsaturated fatty acid in the treatment of human tumors.

GLA: Not Just for Breast Cancer

Not only does GLA help with breast cancer treatment, but research has shown great potential for GLA in the treatment of brain tumors. An injection of 1 mg per day of GLA resulted in tumor mass reduction, and two years later, 12 out of 14 patients were still alive while typical survival time is less than one year.

Pancreatic cancer has responded well to GLA injections, in which subjects were initially given 5.7 g/day. Later the dosage was reduced to 3 g/day which resulted in an increase in immune cells and a decrease in inflammatory immune cells, corresponding to an increased survival rate from four to eight months.

As well, a high dietary consumption of GLA is thought to prevent the occurrence of gastric cancer. In a 1993 Spanish study on borage and cancer occurrence, a three-fold reduction of gastric cancer was observed for regular consumers of borage oil.

Overall, GLA from evening primrose and borage oil shows great potential as a non-toxic treatment for certain kinds of cancer, and research on humans will continue in this area to confirm the efficacy of GLA treatment.

> *Recommended Dosage:* For prevention we recommend two to four 1,000 mg capsules of evening primrose oil or one to two 1,000 mg capsules of borage oil daily. For treatment purposes much higher doses may be required, but this should be done under the supervision of your healthcare practitioner.

The Omega-6 Controversy

While linoleic acid is an important omega-6 with beneficial effects as a precursor to anti-inflammatory prostaglandins (responsible for decreasing inflammation, blood vessel constriction and blood clotting), too much LA from refined oils is not advised. Some recently published articles have raised concerns about whether or not refined omega-6 oils are safe for women who are either at risk for breast cancer or who are breast cancer patients.

Some of the commonly consumed refined omega-6 oils include corn oil, canola oil, safflower oil and sunflower oil. These oils all contain differing amounts of LA. However when the AICR examined the role of polyunsaturated fatty acids, including LA, they found no relationship to breast cancer other than the contribution these fats make to total fat intake.

A 1998 review of the data on this relationship did not find a significantly increased risk of cancer with high versus low intakes of LA. The review was conducted by Peter Zock and Martijn Katan of Wageningen Agricultural University. They reported that none of the studies conducted within populations indicated a significantly increased risk of cancer with high vs. low intakes of LA or polyunsaturated fats. The researchers concluded that, "it seemed unlikely that a high intake of linoleic acid substantially raises the risks of breast, colorectal, or prostate cancer in humans."

It is interesting to note that the studies which linked LA to breast cancer did not consider the total amount of fat in the diet. In animal studies where LA was linked to cancer, the link was the strongest when the diet was high in total fat. Research to date has been inconclusive; however, we feel that everyone should be replacing their refined cooking oils with healthier alternatives, such as coconut, hemp, flaxseed and other unrefined organic oils, and supplementing with healthy omega-6 oils from borage and evening primrose oil. See page 20 for information on how to cook with fats and oils.

Flaxseed: Super Food for a Reason

If you are searching for the perfect food to help with your overall health as well as to protect against diseases like breast cancer, look no further because researchers say the weapon of choice is flaxseed. Flaxseed is gaining popularity in the marketplace as a dietary supplement that can have a big impact on your health. This ancient grain is fast becoming the newest super food. In the last five years, studies have shown adding flaxseed to your diet can prevent and slow the progression of breast cancer. Why? Flaxseed is bursting with important cancer-fighting agents known as lignans. Other components, such as fiber (which helps to decrease estrogen levels) and the essential fat ALA, have also been linked to lowering breast cancer risk.

Lignans Balance Estrogen Levels

New research shows that one of the best things you can do to prevent the onset of breast cancer is to make sure you get your share of lignans. Flaxseed is nature's most abundant source of lignans with a concentration of 75 to 800 times that of other plant foods. Lignans are naturally-occurring substances found in plants that can balance estrogen in the body. Some lignans are also formed by bacteria in the gut. Studies have indicated that a semi-vegetarian diet rich in fruits and vegetables and lignans, compared to a standard North American diet that is high in bad fat, red meat, milk and refined sugar, will give a positive effect on the body's ability to burn fat, enhance immune function, and balance estrogen. Lignans help by reducing the bad estrogens in the diet, balancing overall estrogen levels, thus reducing the risk of breast cancer.

Evidence is increasing to support the view that lignans are principally responsible for the anti-cancer properties of vegetarian diets. Lignans are eventually excreted in the urine. A high urinary lignan excretion corresponds with a high dietary intake of lignan-rich foods, while a low urinary excretion of lignans indicates a low dietary intake of the lignan-rich foods found in fruits, vegetables and other plant foods like flaxseed. In breast cancer patients and individuals at high risk of breast and colon cancer, the urinary excretion of lignans is significantly lower than in individuals who consume vegetarian diets. High lignan diets are found in populations living in areas with low rates of several diseases, including heart disease and cancer. It has been found that Asian populations that consume large amounts of lignans have a lower frequency of breast and prostate tumors than North American populations that consume lower quantities of lignan-rich foods.

Lignans Reduce Estrogen Exposure

Flaxseed lignans exerts physiological effects, such as increasing menstrual cycle length, which has also been associated with lower breast-cancer risk. A study conducted by the Department of Obstetrics-Gynecology at the University of Rochester confirmed this relationship. The researchers evaluated the effect of the ingestion of flaxseed powder (concentrated source of lignans), which has been known to produce high concentrations of urinary lignans.

Urinary lignan excretion when consuming the flaxseed powder was similar to that previously noted for women consuming a macrobiotic diet containing unpolished rice, legumes, vegetables, fermented foods, nuts, seeds and fruit. Ovulation and the days following until menstruation were longer in those consuming flaxseed powder. Longer cycles correspond with less exposure to the body's estrogen production. This is significant as high levels of estrogen promote breast and ovarian cancer.

Lignans Protect You Against Breast Cancer

The potent anti-cancer effects of lignans, especially in hormone-sensitive cancers like breast and prostate cancer, are becoming widely acknowledged and accepted by the scientific community. An impressive number of studies have shown that flaxseed lignans are very potent anti-cancer agents because of their ability to block the action of estrogen, and eliminate excess cancer-causing hormones produced in our bodies. We believe flaxseed and its high lignan content is essential for the treatment of cancers of the breast and prostate.

In a 2002 study, researchers from the Department of Nutritional Sciences at the University of Toronto examined in a well-controlled study the effect of flaxseed or soy supplementation on urinary excretion of estrogen. Postmenopausal women were randomized into three groups. Two groups supplemented their diet with either a muffin containing 25 g of flaxseed or soy, and the third group received a muffin with no supplementation. Urine samples were collected, and after 16 weeks results showed that flaxseed, not soy or the control, significantly increased urinary estrogen excretion. The researchers confirmed that flaxseed supplementation has a more anti-estrogenic effect on estrogen metabolism than soy and therefore may be more cancer protective. We believe that flaxseed rather than soy would be better for women with positive estrogen-receptor breast cancer.

Flaxseed Slows Breast Cancer Cell Growth Rate

For women who already have breast cancer, flaxseed can slow its progression. Researchers at the University of Toronto, Princess Margaret Hospital and Toronto Hospital studied a group of 39 women with newly diagnosed breast cancer tumors. The women received a muffin each day that contained 25 g of ground flaxseed, or a muffin that contained no flaxseed. The researchers found that women who received the flaxseed muffins experienced slower tumor growth.

This research is significant because it suggests that consumption of ground flaxseed in the diet may reduce the risk of developing breast cancer as well as slowing the progression of the disease. This research confirms population data that suggests people who consume flaxseed have lower breast cancer risks. Previous animal studies also showed that flaxseed helps prevent and slow down hormone-dependent tumor growth.

In a related study, Dr. Goss and his team of researchers also examined the role of flaxseed in cyclical mastalgia (a syndrome of breast pain, swelling, and lumpiness) that recurs in each premenstrual cycle. This syndrome has been associated with an increased breast cancer risk. The researchers found that dietary supplementation with 25 g of flaxseed daily (also eaten in muffins) was effective in relieving symptoms of cyclical mastalgia, without significant side effects. The researchers believe that the benefits are the result of the anti-estrogenic effects of the lignans found in flaxseed.

Researchers feel that one of the reasons lignans may be so beneficial for fighting breast cancer is because the lignan structure is very similar to anti-cancer compounds such as Tamoxifen, which have anti-estrogenic properties. Lignans are able to block excess estrogen. Some lignans have also been found to improve immune function; in addition, they have antiviral, antibacterial and anti-fungal properties.

Recommended Dosage: For prevention we recommend 1 to 2 tablespoons of milled flaxseed daily. For treatment purposes much higher doses may be required, but this should be done under the supervision of your healthcare practitioner.

Recommended Products: Health From The Sun's FiProFLAX; Herbal Select's Organic Milled Flaxseeds; Swanson's EFA OmegaTru™ LignaMax® Concentrate.

ALA-Rich Flaxseed Oil: One More Weapon in the Breast Cancer Arsenal

Flax oil is nature's richest source of the omega-3 essential fat, alpha-linolenic acid (ALA), which has been shown to be cancer protective. Numerous studies have examined the role ALA plays in breast cancer prevention. For example, one study published in 2000 in the *European Journal of Cancer* showed that alpha-linolenic acid has a protective effect in breast cancer. This case-control study used fatty acid levels in adipose breast tissue as a marker of intake of fatty acids. The subjects studied were 123 women with invasive non-metastatic breast cancer along with 59 women with benign breast disease that served as controls. The lowest breast tissue levels of ALA were associated with the highest risk of breast cancer. This research shows a protective effect of ALA in the risk of breast cancer. We encourage women to consume flaxseed oil to ensure they are receiving plenty of ALA.

Another similar recent study conducted in Tours, central France, published in *International Journal of Cancer 2002*, examined the fatty acid composition in breast fat tissue from 241 patients with invasive, nonmetastatic breast cancer and from 88 patients with benign breast disease. Fatty acid composition in breast adipose tissue was used as a marker of past intake of fatty acids. The researchers found that the highest levels of omega-3 fatty acids in the breast tissue corresponded with the lowest breast cancer risk. In conclusion, their data based on fatty acid levels in breast adipose tissue suggested a protective effect of omega-3 fatty acids on breast cancer risk and supported the hypothesis that the balance between omega-3 and omega-6 fatty acids plays a role in breast cancer.

Research has also shown the benefit of alpha-linolenic acid in helping to stop the spread and growth of existing breast cancer cells.

Recommended Dosage: For prevention we recommend a daily dose of one 1,000 mg capsule of flaxseed oil, or 1/2 to 1 teaspoon of flaxseed oil.

Fish Oil: Up Your Intake, Increased Protection

We have discussed throughout the book the amazing health benefits of omega-3s from fish oil, especially in relation to cardiovascular health and depression. These omega-3s are also beneficial for breast cancer. The protective effect of omega-3 fatty acids was first observed in Greenland Inuit women who seemed to have a strikingly low rate of breast cancer. These women have a diet that is probably the highest in total fat but they are eating good fat from fish oil. This is why adding omega-3s to your diet even with a high fat diet will be beneficial.

High doses of fish oil have been shown to change the fat composition in women's breast tissue by lowering the amount of bad fat and increasing the good fat, thereby lowering the risk of breast cancer. A study published in the *Journal of the National Cancer Institute* shows breast tissue changes three months after

Fresh Bean & Apple Salad with Dijon Flaxseed Dressing

Dressing Preparation:
3 T red wine vinegar
2 tsp Dijon mustard
3 T honey
4 shallots, finely minced
2 T milled flaxseed
1/2 cup (125 mL) flaxseed oil, or a combination of flaxseed and olive oil
Combine all the dressing ingredients and shake well to blend. Taste and adjust with salt, pepper, Dijon and honey to your preference.

Salad Preparation:
2 lb yellow or green beans, blanched and drained
2 tart apples (such as Granny Smith),
    diced and tossed with lemon juice to keep white
1 medium red onion, minced
1 lb baby greens
1/2 cup (125 mL) fresh basil, torn
Toss beans and apples in dressing. Fill a large platter with baby greens. Top with the marinated bean mixture and sprinkle with sliced basil. Serve immediately.

Recipe courtesy of Bioriginal Food & Science Corporation

dietary changes to include more fish oil and a higher consumption of soy, green leafy vegetables, Brussels sprouts, cauliflower, and carrots. Taking 3 g/day of fish oil resulted in a four-fold increase in the ratio of omega-3 to omega-6s (such as the linoleic acid found in refined oils like canola oil and sunflower oil and margarines) in the blood and a 1.4 fold rise in the ratio in breast tissue.

The high omega-3 blood ratios are consistent with levels found in Japanese women, whose breast cancer rate is much lower than North Americans. However, when Japanese women move to the U.S. and adopt the traditional North American diet, their breast cancer rate equals that of U.S. women and their fat ratios become that of North American women.

Fish Oil: Good Benefits for Other Cancers

Not only are omega-3s beneficial for breast cancer, but other cancers, including colon, pancreatic, lung and skin, can find benefit from an omega-3 rich diet. It is well known that the nutritional status in cancer patients is poor and research has shown that the omega-3 content of the blood in these patients is also low.

In a recent study researchers measured the omega-3 fatty acid in 71 newly diagnosed, untreated cancer patients of three tumor types—esophageal, lung cancer and pancreatic cancer—and in 45 healthy subjects. The researchers found that the omega-3 fatty acid levels were reduced in pancreatic cancer and lung cancer, but were not altered in esophageal cancer. Therefore, patients with lung and pancreatic cancer would benefit from an omega-3 supplement to improve the fatty acid content of their blood.

In a study including 24 European countries, fish and fish oil consumption were shown to protect against the later promotional stages of colorectal cancer. Experiments with animals have shown that omega-3s decreased colon cancer at both the initiation and promotion stages.

Skin cancer is the most common type of cancer in North America. A number of research studies, including a recent one published in 2002, have shown that omega-3 fatty acids from fish have a protective effect on the skin from ultraviolet light exposure. Omega-3s offer this protective effect because of the prostaglandins they produce that are anti-inflammatory, acting to reduce the UV-induced release of inflammatory components from a variety of skin cell types. For more information on how to keep your skin healthy and glowing, see Chapter 9.

A recent study published in November 2002 showed the results of animal studies that have demonstrated consumption of omega-3 fatty acids from fish oil can slow the growth of cancer, increase the efficacy of chemotherapy and reduce the side effects of the chemotherapy or of the cancer. There are numerous mechanisms by which fish oil could contribute to these beneficial effects, including suppressing the proliferation (rapid growth) of cancer cells; allowing cancer cells to die; and reducing cancer-induced cachexia (extreme loss of weight and muscle mass). The researchers concluded that it seems reasonable that after appropriate cancer therapy, consumption of omega-3 fatty acids might slow or stop the growth and spread of cancer cells, increase longevity of cancer patients and improve their quality of life. It is easy to see how important the omega-3 fatty acids are for your health. Research will continue in this area to strengthen the recommendations for omega-3s for all types of cancer.

Along with other nutrients, fatty acid supplementation improves the immune response of patients with cancer. A study published in *Surgery* in 2002 found that preoperative supplementation with omega-3 fatty acids and arginine improves the immune response and outcome of patients undergoing surgery for gastrointestinal cancer. Patients receiving supplementation for five days before surgery had a significantly better immune response and decreased infection rate compared to the groups not receiving supplementation.

Patients with advanced cancer may exhibit an altered supply of essential nutrients and may have an imbalance or deficiency of omega-3 fatty acids, as suggested by reported beneficial effects of fish oil supplementation.

A recent study in advanced cancer patients before and after 14 days of supplementation with fish or a fake pill of olive oil found that changes in body weight related directly to increases in the level of EPA. Advanced cancer patients may have alterations in fatty acid metabolism due to nutritional status or the effects of chemotherapy.

Omega-3 fatty acids may lower the risk of hormone-responsive cancers. A study published in 2002 in *Cancer Epidemiology and Biomarkers* found that increased consumption of fatty fish lowered the risk of endometrial cancer. The study, involving 709 cases of endometrial cancer and 2,888 controls, found that women who consumed the highest consumption of fatty fish exhibited the lowest risk of endometrial cancer.

Recommended Dosage: For prevention we recommend 1–2 g of mixed fish 18/12 daily. For treatment purposes much higher doses may be required, but this should be done under the supervision of your healthcare practitioner.

Conjugated Linoleic Acid: The Power of One

As we discussed in Chapter 2, conjugated linoleic acid, or CLA, refers to a group of fatty acids that we must supplement or consume from foods with high CLA concentrations. Because our current food sources have an insufficient levels of CLA, we are typically CLA deficient.

In addition to its fat loss properties* and its protective role in preventing type 2 diabetes, heart disease and immune function, CLA may inhibit the growth of certain kinds of cancers such as breast, prostate and colon cancer. CLA was first isolated from ground beef in 1983 and examined as a potent anti-cancer compound. Unlike most other anticancer substances, CLA appears to act on all three stages of cancer—initiation, promotion and metastasis (the spread of cancer cells).

The interest in the research community has been tremendous, and since its discovery hundreds of studies have explored the health benefits of CLA. CLA has been shown to have anticancer effects against breast, colon, and prostate cancer cell lines. Numerous animal studies have examined and confirmed the anti-cancer affects of CLA. In one Finnish study the CLA content from food was examined in breast cancer patients. Dietary CLA was lower in breast cancer patients and the researchers confirmed that a diet composed of CLA rich foods may offer protection against breast cancer in postmenopausal women. Research is preliminary and ongoing however we feel this is a promising area for cancer prevention and treatment.

Recommended Dosage: For prevention we recommend 3 g of CLA daily. For treatment purposes much higher doses may be required, but this should be done under the supervision of your healthcare practitioner.

Knowing that poor diet plays a role in breast cancer, this is the first area to improve on. Insist on organic fruits and vegetables, dairy products and wild or free-range meats to reduce your exposure to environmental estrogens. Eat less animal products and more fruit and vegetables, especially those from the cruciferous

* *See footnote on page 30*

family: broccoli, cauliflower, kale and Brussels sprouts as they contain breast cancer inhibitors. Reduce your intake of sugar as it suppresses the immune system and supplement with essential fatty acid sources.

What We Learned In This Chapter:

- Evening primrose and borage oil contain powerful omega-6 fatty acids that can reduce breast pain (a risk associated with breast cancer) and kill cancer cells while leaving healthy cells alone. The GLA found in these herbs is considered a positive adjunctive therapy for hormone-sensitive breast cancer that can enhance pharmaceutical drug therapy, for example, Tamoxifen.

- Cancer-fighting flaxseed not only protects you from cancer, but may be able to slow the rate of tumor growth.

- Occurrences of breast and other cancers coincide with low levels of omega-3 in the blood or tissues.

In the next chapter we will explain how to protect your skin—your shield against harmful bacteria and other invaders—and alleviate irritating and painful skin conditions.

Chapter 9

BEAUTIFUL SKIN STARTS
FROM WITHIN

Did you know that your skin is the largest organ in your body? Your skin is much more than an outer surface for the world to see. It protects you from bacteria, dirt and the ultraviolet rays of the sun, and contains nerve endings that let you know if something is hot or cold, soft or hard, sharp or dull. Your skin also plays an important role in regulating your body's fluids and temperatures. The smooth, hairy outer layer is called the epidermis, and beneath it lies a thick, strong and elastic layer of tissue known as the dermis. The dermis is richly supplied with blood vessels, sweat and oil glands, and nerve endings.

Healthy skin mirrors a healthy body. Most of us will spend an exorbitant amount of money on creams, lotions and potions "formulated" to give us smoother, younger-looking skin. Spend $10 or $200 if you prefer, but know this: all the product in the world won't help if your body is ill or malnourished. Healthy looking skin comes from within. That is why eating a well-balanced diet full of fruits, vegetables and high quality protein, and, of course, drinking plenty of water for hydration, is so important.

HEALTHY FATS FOR HEALTHY SKIN

Essential fatty acids (EFA) are especially necessary for moisturizing skin, preventing aging, decreasing wrinkles, treating acne and protecting the skin from sunburn. Research from the 1930s to the 1950s established that an omega-6 deficiency leads to inflammatory skin conditions like eczema and psoriasis in both animals and humans.

More recently, it has been established that it is a deficiency of gamma-linolenic acid (GLA) that can be attributed to inflammatory skin conditions. Mounting research studies suggest that the natural and non-toxic GLA found in borage and evening primrose oil has dramatic healing results when taken orally and/or applied topically to treat dry skin, sunburn, cradle cap and other more serious skin disorders. In fact, the basic science and clinical evidence for the effectiveness of GLA in maintaining healthy skin and treating skin problems is so promising that GLA should be the natural skin product of choice, replacing dangerous drugs and greasy, irritating ointments.

GLA for Skin Health

As a contributor to the healthy function of cellular membranes, the GLA found in borage oil and evening primrose oil helps to maintain the stability and fluidity of the natural water loss barrier in our skin to prevent toxic substances from entering or irritating the skin. Optimal structure and performance of the skin is necessary in order for it to function properly. When the barrier function of the skin is defective, skin disorders and damage can result.

Common skin disorders include dry skin, eczema, sunburn, acne and psoriasis. Dry skin is the most common skin condition and is characterized by rough, scaly skin and itching, particularly in the winter or in climates with low humidity. Dry skin is especially common in the elderly. By the age of 80 years, the epidermis may lose as much as 50% of its thickness, which accelerates water loss, leading to skin dryness. Dry skin also exacerbates many other conditions, including eczema and psoriasis.

ECZEMA

Atopic (allergic) dermatitis, or eczema, is a chronic inflammatory disease that affects up to 25% of the population and is characterized by dry, itchy and inflamed skin. The incidence of eczema has doubled in the last decade. Most people have dry skin to some degree, especially during winter and in climates of low humidity; however, those who suffer from eczema can experience itching so intense that they lose sleep at night, causing irritability and daytime fatigue. The itching, increased skin sensitivity and inflamed skin can induce severe skin trauma in which secondary infections can occur as a result of the scratching.

Conventional Treatment for Eczema

Conventional treatment for eczema includes antihistamines, oral steroids, topical steroids and antibiotics to help control the symptoms of itching and inflammation.

These drugs often have long-term side-effects and are not recommended for continuous periods. A more natural, effective solution is needed to help provide eczema sufferers with the relief they so desperately need.

GLA: Keep Skin Moist

A dietary deficiency of the omega-6 linoleic acid (LA) results in a scaly skin disorder and excessive epidermal water loss. Because of the inability of normal skin epidermis to convert LA into GLA (human skin lacks the D6D enzyme, which metabolizes EFAs; for more information see chapter 1), we become relatively deficient in healthy skin GLA.

Clinical research has found that people who suffer from eczema have low blood levels of GLA and increased levels of allergy-promoting inflammatory factors which may result in inflammation and itching. Therefore, supplementing with GLA is vital for keeping healthy skin cells moist and strong by improving the barrier function of the skin, reducing water loss through the skin and acting as a powerful anti-inflammatory agent to reduce itching and inflammation.

Borage Oil: An Elixir for Eczema

Clinical trials have demonstrated that patients with eczema showed dramatic improvements with GLA supplementation. Andreassi and colleagues at the University of Italy set out to determine the effects of GLA from borage oil on the treatment of eczema in a study published in the 1997 *Journal of International Medical Research*.

Sixty patients with eczema (30 men and 30 women) participated in the 12-week trial. Of these, 30 patients were treated with 274 mg of GLA twice daily (one to two 1,000 mg borage soft gels twice daily), while the remaining 30 received a fake pill. Their symptoms were assessed by a dermatologist and by the subjects themselves every four weeks. Gradual and significant reductions in itching, inflammation, blisters and oozing were noted in patients who received GLA in comparison with the control group. Some noted as much as a 90% improvement in symptoms following borage oil supplementation.

Patients receiving GLA were able to reduce their dosage of antihistamine and steroid therapies by 73%, antibiotics by 80% and the use of topical steroids by 50%. The investigators concluded that GLA supplementation in the form of borage oil is effective in the treatment of eczema, with noticeable benefits between six and twelve weeks. Borage oil does not produce the side-effects common to antihistamines.

Borage Oil: Improves Efficacy

In another study, the effectiveness, safety and usefulness of borage oil on eczema was studied. Twenty-eight Japanese eczema patients were treated with borage oil 180 mg/day for 4, 8, 12 and 16 weeks. The borage oil supplement reduced the symptoms of eczema with an increased effectiveness being noted with a longer period of treatment. Following 8 and 12 weeks of treatment, respectively, the researchers noted a reduction of 52.7% and 63.2% in symptoms, with a more significant degree of improvement being reported in the patients with the more pronounced symptoms (itchiness, flaky skin and red rash).

No significant side effects of the borage oil treatment were reported. The researchers concluded that their results indicated that borage oil appeared to be

Effects of GLA Therapy on Symptoms of Eczema

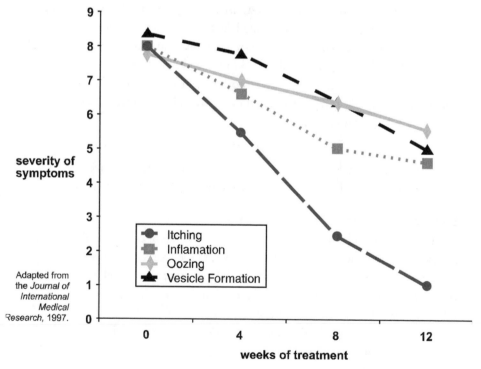

Adapted from the *Journal of International Medical Research*, 1997.

Diagram courtesy of Bioriginal Food & Science Corporation

an effective and safe supplement, which could provide further control of eczema in combination with traditional medical treatments.

Borage Oil: Protects Mature Skin

Published in *Archives of Gerontology and Geriatrics* in 2002, researchers examined the effect of borage oil supplementation in 29 healthy elderly people with respect to skin barrier function, skin water content and fatty acid metabolism. Subjects received a daily dose of 360 or 720 mg of GLA (two to three 1,000 mg borage oil soft gels) for two months. Barrier function of skin improved an average of 10.8%; water loss through the skin was reduced significantly; and the water content of the stratum corneum (outer most layer of the epidermis) increased slightly. Thirty-four percent of subjects suffered from itch before supplementation, while no subjects experienced it after. The percent of subjects who evaluated their skin as more dry decreased from 42% to 14% during the study. Increases of GLA and DGLA (the immediate derivative of GLA) from the borage oil were observed in cell membranes, with corresponding decreases of saturated, monounsaturated and omega-9 fatty acids.

The increase in the skin's water retention observed after borage oil supplementation may also counteract age-related decline of the skin barrier function and trauma due to scratching. As the study shows, borage oil counteracted itch in all subjects and itch is frequently observed in normal elderly people—even those without skin disease. Therefore, it is hypothesized that if supplementation with borage oil eliminates itch, scratching trauma would be eradicated, thus protecting the skin barrier function.

Recommended Dosage: Take one to two 1,000 mg of borage oil daily.

Recommended Products: Swanson's EFA OmegaTru™ Borage Oil; Health From The Sun's Borage Oil; and Herbal Select's Borage Oil.

Evening Primrose Oil for Eczema

Evening primrose oil, another natural source of GLA, is also beneficial to eczema patients. In a double-blind trial, patients with eczema received either evening primrose oil or a fake pill for 12 weeks. In the evening primrose oil group a statistically significant improvement was observed in the overall severity and grade of inflammation, and in the percentage of the body surface affected by eczema, as well as in dryness and itch. Patients in the evening primrose oil group showed a significantly greater reduction in inflammation than those receiving the placebo.

In a 2002 study published in *Skin Pharmacology and Applied Skin Physiology*, the researchers determined the effectiveness of evening primrose oil in selected eczema patients with dry and itchy skin lesions without apparent patchy redness of the skin, and oozing and dry, thickened, scaly skin. The study also examined whether the treatment effect of evening primrose oil is related to two specific immune system indicators in eczema.

Fourteen patients (five males and nine females) with eczema and a control group of six volunteers (four males and two females) without skin disease or respiratory atopy (itch) were enrolled in this study. Each variable, including the extent of skin lesions, pruritus (severe itching reaction often resulting in blisters) and the recurrence of skin lesions, were given scores ranging from 1 to 3. Both groups received dietary supplementation with evening primrose oil (40 mg of GLA or 500 mg evening primrose oil) administered in two capsules twice a day until the combined scores of pruritus, and the extent and recurrence of lesions remained below 1 for two weeks. Blood levels were taken before and after treatment in order to measure the two immune system indicators.

The data showed that after evening primrose oil supplementation, 42.8% of the eczema group was completely clear of itching and skin lesions and only 28.6% complained of mild pruritus without skin lesions. The authors concluded that their data provides strong evidence that EPO could be highly effective in the treatment of eczema characterized by dry scaly skin and pruritus. Furthermore, they suggest that EPO may play a role in the balance of one of the two immune system indicators tested.

> *Recommended Dosage:* When supplementing with evening primrose oil, we recommend three 1,000 mg soft gels daily for adults. Babies and toddlers up to age 2 use 500–1000 mg of evening primrose oil which can be added to formula or the capsule can be pricked with a pin and the contents rubbed on the infant's belly (may discolor clothing).

> *Recommended Products:* Preferred Nutrition's FemmEssentials FemmOmega™; Herbal Select's Evening Primrose Oil; Swanson's EFA OmegaTru™ Evening Primrose Oil.

Omega-3s Fight Skin Conditions

Flax oil is very beneficial for many health conditions, especially where a deficiency of omega-3 fatty acids is a contributing factors as in heart disease, arthritis, obesity and other conditions. Consumption of certain foods like flaxseed and flax oil as well as fish and fish oil are known to decrease the inflammatory components in the skin and, therefore, are invaluable in the treatment of such inflammatory skin disorders as eczema. Not only do flax oil and fish oil help treat dry skin, eczema and psoriasis, they are also beneficial for dandruff and sun-sensitive skin. There are hair product companies that formulate hairsprays and shampoos with flax oil to help increase shine and decrease a dry, itchy scalp.

> *Recommended Dosage:* To help treat your eczema and dry skin, try supplementing with 1 to 3 tablespoons of flaxseed oil daily or use five to eight 1,000 mg flaxseed oil capsules daily. When supplementing with fish oil, use 500 mg softgels three times daily.

PSORIASIS

According to the National Psoriasis Foundation, 7 million North Americans suffer from psoriasis. It is characterized by raised patches of red with white flakes or scales that appear on the torso, elbows, knees, legs, back, arms, and scalp. When it is in the scalp, it can promote hair loss. In some, the nails may become dull, pitted or ridged and may separate from the nail bed. Psoriasis fluctuates between periods of inflammation and remission and is categorized as mild, moderate, or severe. If the skin becomes too badly damaged, there can be fluid loss, bacterial infection, and temperature dysregulation. Approximately 400 people die every year from psoriasis and another 400 are on disability pension. There are psychological ramifications as well, as people may feel shame, embarrassment, social rejection, and anger due to a lack of understanding on the part of their peers. This psychological aspect can significantly affect relationships.

Psoriasis can also be associated with an autoimmune form of arthritis called psoriatic arthritis. There is pain, morning stiffness, swelling, reduced range of motion, pitting of the nails, tiredness, and redness in the eye. In severe cases it can lead to deformity of the joints and spine. Difficult to diagnose in people with subtle symptoms, it is believed that 10–30% of those with psoriasis will also develop psoriatic arthritis. It usually appears between 30 and 50 years old.

Borage Oil: Sic it on Psoriasis

Most people find some relief with cortisone drugs to reduce inflammation, moisturizers and bath solutions; however, relief is only temporary. Psoriasis sufferers will be heartened to know that some publications and unpublished studies suggest that GLA may be effective in treating psoriasis.

For example, Dr. Darren Poncelet, a chiropractor and Alternative Medicine Practitioner in Newmarket, Ontario, began using borage oil to treat patients with eczema and psoriasis as early as 1994. Since then, he has seen borage oil clear up almost all of the cases of eczema he has treated. He has also had some success with psoriasis patients, of which about 60% have found relief from their itchy, scaly symptoms. He has commented that some patients call it a miracle.

Dr. Poncelet has a nine-year-old patient with such an extreme case of psoriasis that she seldom went outside. When she did, she had to wear a toque, gloves and turtleneck to camouflage the weeping, bleeding wounds that covered her body. Her skin was raw and itchy and she shed two to three tablespoons of scaly flakes in bed each night. Poncelet prescribed borage oil softgel capsules. A year after she started treatment, his patient had noticed a "dramatic improvement." Her bleeding and weeping wounds had healed and the itching was cleared up. She is now able to enjoy the outdoors without having to worry about covering up; a year earlier that was only a dream. Says Poncelet, "It's a huge emotional boost when they can wear shorts in the summer. She was elated the first time she went out."

> *Recommended Dosage:* When supplementing with GLA to treat psoriasis symptoms, use two to four 1,000 mg borage softgels or four to six 1,000 mg evening primrose oil capsules.

Fish For Flaky Skin

Omega-3 fatty acids found in both flaxseed oil and fish oil are potent anti-inflammatory agents that work to promote remission of psoriasis symptoms. A recent study published in 2002 in the *Journal of the American College of Nutrition* confirmed that many trials of fish oil in such chronic inflammatory diseases as psoriasis and psoriatic arthritis reveal significant benefit, including decreased disease activity and a lowered use of anti-inflammatory drugs.

> *Recommended Dosage:* When supplementing with omega-3s, use 1 tablespoon of flaxseed oil daily and three 1,000 mg of fish oil capsules daily.

CRADLE CAP

As we discussed in Chapter 6, EFAs are critical for the healthy development of your infant. Up to 25% of infants may be affected with eczema later on in life. One factor suspected in the rise of allergies and eczema is a decrease in the number of breastfed infants. Breast milk contains a blend of beneficial EFAs, especially GLA. Infants who are not breastfed may be missing out on this vital nutrient. In one study, the fatty acid composition of breast milk from 23 mothers of infants with eczema was compared to that of a control group with 18 mothers whose infants did not have eczema. The breast milk from mothers of children with eczema was higher in linoleic acid, but lower in GLA, DGLA and arachidonic acid compared to that of the control group. The researchers recommended doing further studies on GLA supplementation for breastfeeding mothers.

Infantile seborrhoeic dermatitis, or cradle cap, is described as dry crusts occurring on the scalp, face, armpits, chest, and groin area, and it can be successfully treated with topical applications of borage oil. Research appearing in the *British Journal of Dermatology* in 1993 examined 48 infants with cradle cap who were treated twice daily with topical borage oil. The skin cleared up within 10 to 12 days, but lesions resurfaced within a week after treatment was discontinued. Treatment needs to be continued for at least 6 months. There were no relapses once treatment was stopped when the infants were 6 to 7 months of age.

This study demonstrated that borage oil is effectively absorbed through the skin and serves as a source of available GLA to reduce inflammation. Immature functioning of the D6D enzyme (see Chapter 1 for causes of immature D6D enzyme) may be responsible for cradle cap in infants and can be corrected with topical or internal borage oil treatment.

In another study, when infants between one and seven months were treated with topical borage oil (0.5 ml oil per day) for cradle cap, they became completely free of all skin symptoms within three to four weeks. Conclusions were based on measuring the amount of water lost through the skin before and after treatment. The rate of water loss was restored to normal after the treatment. Improvements were even seen in areas where borage oil was not applied, proving its ability to penetrate and heal the skin as a whole.

FATS CAN REMOVE THE SPOTS

Not only are teenagers challenged with peer pressure, hormonal changes, and life-altering decisions about college and careers, but approximately 85% of adolescents

(20 million American teens) must also overcome acne. With heightened perceptions of their appearance and wanting to fit in, severe acne can be emotionally and physically scarring. In 30% of teenagers with acne, the acne will persist into adulthood. Acne vulgaris appears predominantly among teenagers and, women between the ages of 20 and 40 cope with acne conglobata.

Acne is a condition that has affected most of us at some time in our life. It is caused by an increase in the production of androgens (male hormones) stimulating the oil glands beneath the skin to enlarge and increase production of sebum (oil). Although they are male hormones, they exist in smaller quantities in women as well. The hair follicles, or pores in your skin, contain sebaceous glands (oil glands). These glands make sebum, the oil that lubricates your hair and skin. Most of the time the gland makes the proper amount of sebum, but sometimes the pores get clogged with excess sebum, causing the redness and eruptions seen as acne. Sebum moves along hair follicles to surface on the skin, and as it does, cells on the follicles are shed.

To prevent acne and maintain healthy skin, proper nutrition and circulation are vital. Healthy skin depends upon a consistent dietary intake of certain vitamins and minerals, as well as the right kinds of fatty acids. Deficiencies in essential fatty acids can cause an overproduction of sebum, resulting in acne. Research has shown that when the Inuit changed to standard North American diets, they developed acne. Far less acne is seen in those eating traditional diets versus the standard North American diet, which is high in bad fat and refined carbohydrates like white rice, pasta and sugar. Eating too many of the wrong fats has also been shown to cause excess sebum production.

GLA and Acne: Help is On The Way!

Over 150 acne drugs exist: topical creams (such as Retin-A), antibacterial creams, antibiotics such as tetracycline, anti-inflammatory medications (corticosteroids), low dose birth control pills and Accutane. Some of these treatments come with serious side-effects. Treating acne may be much simpler than taking hit-or-miss over-the-counter remedies, or harmful prescription drugs. In addition to eczema, psoriasis and cradle cap, natural treatments in the form of borage oil and evening primrose oil exist for acne as well.

Researchers explain that GLA from borage and EPO has the ability to inhibit androgens, male hormones that are present in men and women, and are thought to cause acne, common baldness, and seborrhea (skin lesions). GLA can reduce the symptoms related to acne, such as dryness, itching, oozing, inflammation and blister formation. Topically-applied GLA (from borage, evening primrose oil) in particular is showing great potential as a natural skin solution for androgen-related skin ailments. This statement takes into account symptom alleviation, as well as reduction in the use of prescription medications, including topical and oral steroids, antihistamines and antibiotics.

> *Recommended Dosage:* For treating acne try supplementing with two 1,000 mg of borage oil or four 1,000 mg of evening primrose oil daily.

GOOD BYE TO SUNBURN

You would be hard-pressed to find someone who has not had a sunburn at some time in their life, but some people (especially those with blonde or red hair) are particularly susceptible to the sun's ultraviolet rays (UVA and UVB). UVB rays are the shorter of the skin damaging rays, penetrate deeply and quickly burn the mid-layers of your skin. The damaged skin sends signals to the bottom layer of the epidermis, which responds by forming "melanin" to protect the active skin. It is the melanin which results in "tanning," and as the melanin remains higher in the skin, you set up some natural defense against the sun but only after damage has been done. A peeling burn occurs when active skin "commits suicide" and prematurely dies, creating extra top layers of skin which then peel.

UVA rays are longer, do not penetrate as deeply, but still cause damage. Often because sunblocks focus on absorbing UVB rays, you increase your exposure to UVA rays when you stay in the sun longer than you would without sunblock protection. The magnitude and total consequences of exposure to UVA rays is not fully understood, but it is generally agreed that UVA rays increase the aging and wrinkling of the skin and perhaps more.

Sunburn symptoms will typically appear a few hours after overexposure— usually redness, swelling, tenderness and blisters. Following this appearance is a scaling of the outermost layer of skin. The symptoms usually peak within three days and their intensity will gradually diminish. The new skin, however, will remain very sensitive to sunlight for several weeks. The UVA and UVB rays induce a myriad of changes to the skin, including damage to the water loss barrier of the skin that results in loss of skin smoothness.

Although the skin always needs EFAs, they are particularly important in times of distress and damage, such as sunburn. Experiments on cultured skin cells show that ultraviolet light causes significant release of fatty acids from cell membranes. The cell uses these fatty acids for the production of local hormones that regulate redness of the skin, swelling and pain. Typically, skin has a lot of arachidonic acid which, when released, exacerbates the severity of sunburn.

When GLA is given in the form of a supplement of either borage or evening primrose oil, it can quell the inflammatory effects of arachidonic acid. As a result, there is a reduction in the redness, swelling and pain that is created by the ultraviolet injury. Experiments on animals have proved GLA from borage oil has the ability to restore the damaged water loss barrier, bringing back previously lost skin softness. In a Scandinavian arthritis study, 20 patients who received GLA from borage oil were also noticed as having significantly reduced UV damage to their skin.

GLA is normally taken orally and its concentration slowly accumulates in the skin. The process can be significantly accelerated if GLA is given topically as well as orally since GLA can be absorbed by the skin quite quickly.

Recommended Dosages: In case of sunburn, take up to eight 1,000 mg capsules of borage oil a day in two doses until symptoms subside. For even more soothing results, borage oil can be applied topically to the skin two to three times daily. As a daily preventative against the sun's damaging rays, take one to two 1,000 mg capsules of borage oil or two to four 1,000 mg capsules of evening primrose oil.

SLOW THE AGING PROCESS

Not surprisingly, GLA is also a skin beautifier for aging, dry and wrinkled skin. Through a variety of dietary and environmental factors and as the effectiveness of the D6D enzyme (see Chapter 1) decreases with aging, it becomes more difficult for the body to produce GLA on its own. Without sufficient GLA, cellular membranes cannot lock in moisture and the skin takes on a dry and rough appearance. As we age or because of the various dietary and environmental metabolic roadblocks, we are at risk of losing GLA's moisturizing and anti-inflammatory benefits which produce a silky complexion and can soothe dry, scaly skin that may lead to wrinkles.

GLA is commonly used as an ingredient in skin care moisturizers and cosmetics to improve dryness, retain moisture of the skin, and help prevent the appearance of wrinkles. Ann Louise Gittleman, one of the premier nutritionists in the United States, and author of *Eat Fat, Lose Weight* and *The Fat Flush Plan*, recommends a GLA source from either borage or evening primrose oil to all her clients to help them maintain healthy, glowing skin and prevent aging and wrinkles.

> *Recommended Dosage:* one to two 1,000 mg of borage oil daily or two to four 1,000 mg of evening primrose oil daily.
>
> Recommended Products: Health From The Sun's The Woman's Oil; Preferred Nutrition's FemmEssentials FemmOmega™; Herbal Select's Essential 3-6-9; and Swanson's EFA OmegaTru™ EFA Complete.

What We Learned In This Chapter:

- The GLA found in borage oil is an effective adjunctive or alternative to antihistamine and corticosteroid therapy.

- Regular supplementation of borage and evening primrose oils can keep your skin supple, protect you from sun damage and prevent aging and wrinkling.

- There are fewer occurrences of acne in cultures that eat a more traditional diet that is high in good fats, low in bad fats.

Having covered how to protect our outer selves, the next chapter will discuss how to protect our inner workings—the bones and joints.

Chapter 10

OPTIMAL OIL FOR THE
BONES AND JOINTS

The Centre for Disease Control in Atlanta, Georgia released the results of a new study showing that 70 million (or one in three) Americans suffer from arthritis. More than four million Canadians live with this disease that can lead to disability, deformity and even death. The greatest misconception about arthritis is that it occurs only in the elderly. In fact, some forms of arthritis can strike at those as young as two years of age and many types will hit people in the prime of their life.

Of the conditions that affect women, arthritis is the most prevalent. Another misconception about arthritis is that it only attacks the bones and joints. While that may be true of osteoarthritis (the most common arthritis) and rheumatoid arthritis (an autoimmune disease), other types of arthritis (such as lupus) can infiltrate the skin, lungs and kidneys. Severe forms of arthritis may lead to lost work time, reduced productivity, and reduce the pleasure people get from everyday life.

OSTEOARTHRITIS

The most common form of arthritis, also known as "wear and tear" arthritis, osteoarthritis is a degenerative disease that can come with age or overuse. It usually affects the weight-bearing joints (hips, knees and lower spine), though other joints (fingers, thumbs, shoulders) may be afflicted.

"Osteo" refers to bone and the point at which two bones meet is called a joint. Osteoarthritis sets in when the inside of a joint is weakened or wears down, which it does with time. Cells and fluid from dilated blood vessels accumulate in the joints, causing pain and inflammation. The wear and tear causes the cartilage to become thinner, and it can progress, to the point where the cartilage may ultimately disappear. The bone underneath the worn out cartilage becomes thick and hard and can develop into spurs. The synovial membrane (soft tissue surrounding the joint) may be inflamed and produce excessive synovial fluid that contributes to the swelling of the joints.

Osteoarthritis affects 60–65% of people over age 65, and with the aging baby boomers, this population is expected to grow 30–50% over the next 20 years. Osteoarthritis is really the case of too much stress on a normal joint or normal stress on a damaged joint. People whose jobs require them to put strain on the joints, athletes or people with excess weight are at higher risk of developing osteoarthritis. Obese people are twice as likely as people with normal weight to suffer from osteoarthritis. There is a range of pain involved from mild to severe and disabling.

RHEUMATOID ARTHRITIS (RA)

The second most prevalent type of arthritis, rheumatoid arthritis, is an autoimmune disease. The body's immune system forms antibodies that attack the synovial membranes and the fluid that lubricates the joints. Rheumatoid arthritis can progress gradually but in 25% of sufferers it will hit hard and fast. Rheumatoid arthritis shares similar symptoms with osteoarthritis—swollen joints and stiffness or pain that is more apparent in the morning. However, that is where the similarity ends. Rheumatoid arthritis can strike at any age, even in children, and other symptoms are associated with it, such as depression, anemia, weight loss, fever, fatigue and night sweats.

JUVENILE RHEUMATOID ARTHRITIS

Juvenile rheumatoid arthritis (JRA) is the most frequent major connective tissue disease in children. The disease afflicts between 27,400 and 54,800 children under age 16 in the United States—some patients are as young as 6 months old. JRA is often a mild condition, causing few problems, but in severe cases it can produce serious complications.

There are several forms: the most common is polyarthritis, which affects multiple joints (five or more). There are a few telltale signs that will indicate if your child has JRA. Children may not directly communicate their symptoms. You as a parent must use careful observation and questioning to detect symptoms of the disease. The child may be increasingly irritable, may assume a posture of guarding the joints, and may refuse to walk. Fatigue and low-grade fever are common at the onset of the disease. Anorexia, weight loss, failure to grow, and psychological regression to a more infantile pattern of behavior are seen in many children. If you suspect that your child may be affected, consult your family doctor immediately.

Causes of Arthritis

Osteoarthritis is present in 70% of the elderly; however, it is not completely inevitable or unavoidable. Other factors come into play and if they are addressed, osteoarthritis may never arise. Guard against repetitive use or damage to joints due to occupation, injury or athletics. Poor nutrition, dehydration and environmental or food allergies can aggravate osteoarthritis progression. Excess weight puts even more strain on the joints. Rheumatoid arthritis is suspected to have a number of potential causes that include heredity and obesity, but may also be a result of bacterial or viral infection, an overactive immune system, vaccines, nutritional deficiencies and stress-induced hormonal disruption.

Conventional Treatment Options: Arthritis Drug Dangers

Present conventional treatments aim to reduce or alleviate the pain and inflammation of the affected joints and improve mobility. These treatments include analgesics, salicylates, non-steroidal anti-inflammatory drugs (NSAIDs), corticosteroids and reconstructive surgery. The most widely prescribed are NSAIDs, ranging from ASA (Aspirin, Entrophen, Novasen) to ibuprofen (Motrin). These drugs are associated with a large number of side-effects, such as gastric ulcers (salicylates, NSAIDs), renal failure (NSAIDs) and immunosuppression (corticosteroids).

A new family of NSAIDs called COX-2 inhibitors (Celebrex and Vioxx)

A Brief List of Types of Arthritis

- Ankylosing spondylitis
- Gout
- Infective arthritis
- Juvenile chronic arthritis
- Osteoarthritis
- Polymyalgia rheumatica
- Pseudo gout
- Psoriatic arthritis
- Reiter's disease
- Reynaud's phenomenon
- Sjogren's syndrome
- Systemic lupus erythematosus

List courtesy of Healthy Immunity

work by attacking inflammation (they block the COX-2 enzyme that produces bad prostaglandins). The COX-2 inhibitors were initially believed to be much safer than standard NSAIDS, yet long-term use and research are showing some serious concerns. Health Canada issued a warning advisory in 2002 for Celebrex, stating that hundreds of serious adverse reactions have been reported with nearly 70 cases of stomach bleeding and 10 deaths since its release in 1999. If this was a natural product, sales would be halted immediately.

In 1989, the *Journal of Gastroenterology* reported that NSAIDs used by people with rheumatoid arthritis result in approximately 20,000 hospitalizations and 2,600 deaths each year. As well, some evidence exists indicating that NSAIDs may actually cause cartilage to be further damaged or destroyed, thus causing further progression of the disease. The prescription and over-the-counter medication offers some symptomatic relief providing a bandage effect, but it does not get to the root of the problem.

Natural Treatment Options: Juice for the Joints

OSTEOARTHRITIS

Although much less research has been done in the area of essential fatty acids and osteoarthritis, as compared to rheumatoid arthritis, there are indications that EFAs are useful in this form of arthritis as well. Osteoarthritis is characterized by inflammation of the joints and cartilage damage, with pain often being the most

---

SIGNS OF RHEUMATOID ARTHRITIS

Check each box as it applies to you.
Four out of seven symptoms indicate RA.

- ☐   Morning stiffness lasting more than an hour
- ☐   Presents itself symmetrically (both wrists, both knees, etc.)
- ☐   X-ray can detect decalcification or erosions in the joints
- ☐   Rheumatoid factor levels in the blood are abnormal
- ☐   Arthritis appears in any of the hand joints
- ☐   Nodules are present beneath the skin on bony prominences
- ☐   Three areas are inflamed at the same time
       (not just bony overgrowth)

distressing symptom. Studies show that omega-3s decrease the inflammation and degradation, and help to prevent cartilage damage, that occurs in the joints, and this can slow the progression of degenerative joint diseases, such as osteoarthritis.

Early research also demonstrates that essential fatty acids affect levels of pain mediators and suggests that EFA supplementation may be potentially useful in decreasing the pain associated with arthritis, such as osteoarthritis. Thus, through slowing destruction and damage to cartilage and joints, through decreasing inflammation and preventing inflammatory-induced destructive processes from occurring, and possibly affecting levels of pain mediators, EFA supplementation can help chronic inflammatory degenerative diseases of joints, such as osteoarthritis.

Marya Zilberberg reports that GLA is not only safe, but it is also an effective natural therapy. In her review of close to 40 clinical papers on GLA, Zilberberg noted that GLA consistently reduces inflammation and joint stiffness without any of the serious side-effects associated with pharmaceutical drugs. "We saw about a 60–65% reduction in morning stiffness for these patients," said Zilberg. "In other words if you have two hours of morning stiffness, there is a 1.5 hour reduction compared to a 6.7 minute reduction with a fake pill. It is an extremely striking difference."

This is good news for arthritis patients who often see morning stiffness as the most debilitating effect of their disease. "If you were to ask an arthritis patient about morning stiffness you would find that it is an extremely important indicator of how their disease is doing," said Zilberberg. These results demonstrate the importance of long-term supplementation with large doses of GLA from borage or evening primrose oil for osteoarthritis and rheumatoid arthritis.

Dr. Ronald Lawrence, an assistant clinical professor at the UCLA School of Medicine in Los Angeles, is currently working to find a safe treatment for degenerative arthritis. He has begun to use GLA on some of his arthritis patients. "My patients say that they move freer and easier and seem to be more relaxed, sort of lubricated if you will. It's nice to hear because stiffness is a big problem with all types of arthritis but particularly rheumatoid arthritis."

RHEUMATOID ARTHRITIS

The omega-3 fatty acids found in flax and fish (EPA and DHA), as well as the omega-6 fatty acid GLA found in evening primrose oil and borage oil are useful in the management of rheumatoid arthritis by reducing pain and inflammation. Arachidonic acid (found primarily in red meat) produces inflammatory compounds.

Supplementing with GLA-rich evening primrose oil or borage oil helps to reduce the inflammatory components from arachidonic acid. GLA helps to suppress the inflammatory immune cells and the synovial cell proliferation in inflamed synovial tissue which will help decrease inflammation and pain. In clinical trials GLA has been shown to replace pharmaceutical drugs as an NSAID substitute and, in fact, might function as a disease-modifying anti-rheumatic drug.

GLA Reduces the Use of NSAIDs

Recent research suggests that GLA reduces the immune factors that promote inflammation and joint tissue injuries. It is important to decrease these dangerous immune factors in order to reduce cartilage damage (the event that leads to bone erosion and crippling), and joint swelling in patients suffering from rheumatoid arthritis.

Supplementing with GLA not only results in a decrease in the clinical symptoms of RA but taking GLA can reduce the effects of NSAIDs by repairing damage to the stomach lining. Studies show that GLA protects the stomach lining against gastric acid that could cause stomach ulcers due to repeated or overuse of NSAIDs.

For example, as early as 1988, researchers confirmed that daily supplementation with 540 mg of GLA from evening primrose oil could help patients reduce their usage of NSAIDs and therefore protect their stomach lining, as shown in the following table, Reduction of NSAIDs with GLA Treatment. At the beginning of the study 100% of patients were on their full NSAID dosage; after three months of supplementing with evening primrose oil, 70% of patients were still taking NSAIDs, and after six months only 30% of patients were still taking NSAID at full dosage. This is a remarkable 70% reduction in patients using NSAIDs.

GLA Reduces Symptoms

In 1993, researchers at the University of Pennsylvania conducted a randomized, double-blind, placebo-controlled, 24-week trial with 37 rheumatoid arthritis patients. Patients in the treatment group received 1.4 g of GLA from borage oil daily, and assessed their symptoms on a daily basis. Treatment with borage oil reduced the number of tender joints by 36%, the tender joint score by 45%, the number of swollen joints by 28%, and the swollen joint score by 41%, whereas the placebo group did not show significant improvement in any measure. The researchers concluded that "Borage oil in the doses used in this study is a well-tolerated and effective treatment for rheumatoid arthritis."

Three years later, researchers at the University of Massachusetts further explored the use of borage oil with a much longer study using twice as much borage oil in the treatment. In this study, 56 patients participated in a year-long trial. Their results indicated that 2.8 g of GLA (dosage of oil) were more effective than the 1.4 g used in previous research. Patients experienced significant improvements in their symptoms within the first six months, and continued to improve during the remaining six months. After 12 months of treatment, the number of tender joints reduced by 50%, tender joint score reduced by 54%, the number of swollen joints reduced by 42%, and swollen joint score reduced by 42%. Furthermore, morning stiffness decreased by 67% and overall pain assessment diminished by 27%.

GLA for Juvenile Rheumatoid Arthritis

Data from a recent study conducted at the Shriners Hospital for Children in Springfield, Massachusetts, found that borage oil can benefit children with Juvenile Rheumatoid Arthritis (JRA). Preliminary data from the study was presented by lead researcher Dr. Deborah Rothman, MD, PhD, during the Annual Meeting of the American College of Rheumatology in Boston. In her research, Dr. Rothman found that the effects of borage oil were strongest for patients with polyarthritis.

Reduction of NSAIDS with GLA Treatment

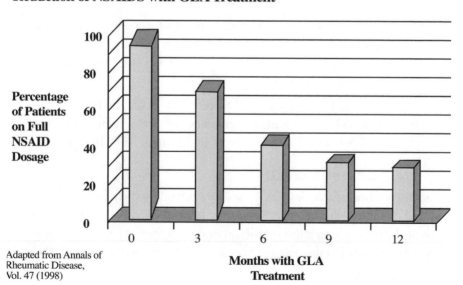

Adapted from Annals of Rheumatic Disease, Vol. 47 (1998)

Diagram courtesy of Bioriginal Food & Science Corporation

Use of borage oil in JRA may allow some patients to reduce their dosage of standard medications such as NSAIDs or corticosteroids. Approximately 15% of patients on long-term NSAID treatment develop ulcers of the stomach, which can lead to severe bleeding and death. Children with rheumatic disease receiving long-term corticosteroids are also at high risk of developing osteoporosis and infections.

> *Recommended Dosage:* Positive effects on rheumatoid arthritis can be seen with dosages in the range of 1.4 to 2.8 g of GLA per day (the equivalent of six to eleven 1,000 mg borage capsules). These high doses were used in the clinical trials with no safety concerns. However, dosages can vary from person to person.

> Start with two 1,000mg capsules of borage or four 1,000 mg capsules of evening primrose oil with your meal. Increase the number of capsules up to ten per day to achieve relief of symptoms. Some will need as little as 2,000 mg per day for relief and others will require higher doses. If diarrhea occurs, reduce dose.

> *Recommended Children's Dosage:* 1,000–2,000 mg of evening primrose oil or 500–2,000 mg of borage daily for children between the ages of 2 and 7; 8 to 12 year olds take 1,000–4,000 mg of evening primrose oil or 500–1,000 mg of borage oil; and those over 12 can take the adult dose as mentioned above.

> Reduction of symptoms may be observed after one month of supplementation. The full effects of GLA supplementation are seen over longer periods. Studies have shown that borage oil and evening primrose oil are safe and non-toxic, even in large amounts.

> *Recommended Products:* Herbal Select's Borage Oil; Preferred Nutrition's FemmEssentials FemmOmega™; Health From The Sun's Joint EFA Formula; and Swanson's EFA OmegaTru™ Borage Oil.

FISHING FOR JOINT HEALTH

The first scientific paper describing the use of fish oil for rheumatoid arthritis was published in the 18th century. Since then laboratory and clinical studies have revealed the beneficial effects of fish oil in various forms of arthritis. The benefits were attributed to the omega-3 fatty acids EPA and DHA. EPA and DHA are incorporated into the cellular membranes and compete with arachidonic acid for the enzymes responsible for the production of anti-inflammatory prostaglandins.

EPA and DHA reduce the formation of bad prostaglandins and regulate immune factor production, which controls how long, how fast and how much the immune system acts or reacts. EPA produces the anti-inflammatory prostaglandins (good guys). Fish oils improve joint mobility and reduce the severity of pain and inflammation without any short- or long-term side-effects.

Abnormalities of fatty acid composition in synovial fluid in the joints have been demonstrated in rheumatoid arthritis patients. In a 1999 study, 39 arthritic patients were included. Synovial cell fluid samples were obtained from nine of the patients and decreased levels of EPA and total omega-3 fatty acids were observed in blood and in joint fluid of patients with rheumatoid arthritis. The researchers concluded that the fatty acid pattern found in rheumatoid arthritis (decreased levels of omega-3s) may explain the beneficial effect of fish oil.

A 1998 review of the research confirmed the beneficial effects of fish oil in arthritis. Fish oil, like GLA, reduces symptoms of arthritis, such as pain, number of affected joints and morning stiffness, in a dose dependent manner. Clinical benefits were seen after twelve weeks, with a dosage of 3 g of EPA and DHA per day. Due to the relatively high doses required to obtain clinical improvements, a concentrated fish oil supplement would be recommended.

Just like GLA, it also appears that fish oil will help arthritis sufferers reduce the amount of NSAIDs needed, and some may even be able to discontinue usage completely. The first 12-month study of fish oil in RA patients examined NSAID requirements in 37 of 64 patients who were given fish oil at a dose of 1.7 g per day of EPA and 1.1 g per day of DHA in a randomized double blind study. After six weeks of therapy patients were advised to reduce their NSAID dose slowly. At 12 months all fish oil treated patients were crossed over to a fake pill and assessed again three months later. At the three-month mark a 41% reduction in NSAID usage was achieved. Overall, patient's taking fish oil had a dramatic reduction in their symptoms.

A clinical study conducted in 2000 and published in the *Journal of Rheumatology* evaluated the efficacy of fish oil concentrate in the treatment of RA. A placebo-controlled, double-blind, randomized 15-week study to determine the effect of supplementation on 50 subjects with RA was performed. Fish oil containing 60% total omega-3 fatty acids was supplemented at a rate of 40 mg/kg body weight.

After analyzing nine clinical variables, including tender joint count, swollen joint count, duration of early morning stiffness, and pain assessment, a significant difference between the group being treated with the omega-3s and the control group was noticed. The researchers concluded that fish oil supplementation at a dose of 40 mg/kg body weight results in cellular incorporation of omega-3 fatty acids and improvements in clinical status in patients with rheumatoid arthritis.

Some research has studied the usage of EPA and GLA together and their impact on reducing pro-inflammatory substances. A study at Wake Forest University School of Medicine found that patients supplementing with a combination EPA and GLA reduced production of pro-inflammatory substances. A research review in *Lipids*, conducted at the University of Southampton, England, noted that taking EPA supplements decreased production of pro-inflammatory immune factors that cause swelling, pain, redness and heat in the joints.

> *Recommended Dosage:* A healthy balance between omega-3s and omega-6s is important to reduce the production of inflammatory immune factors. See dosage for omega-6 on page 134. A combination of EPA and DHA up to 3 g is recommended to reduce pain and inflammation. This would be the equivalent of ten 1,000 mg capsules of a natural fish 18/12 supplement or six 1,000 mg capsules of a concentrated 30/20 fish oil supplement.

> *Recommended Products:* Health From The Sun's Ultra 30/20 Fish Oil; and Herbal Select's Fish Oil Concentrate.

OSTEOPOROSIS: BUILDING STRONG BONES

It is estimated that a 50 year-old woman has a 50% chance of suffering an osteoporosis-related fracture during the remainder of her life.

Osteoporosis is often known as a silent disease that can strike at any time. We have heard numerous stories of how women have bent over to pick something up or were vacuuming and have felt a pain and later discovered they fractured a rib. Osteoporosis is the most prevalent metabolic disease of bone leading to bone thinning and frequent fractures; it progresses painlessly and without symptoms until bones become so frail that a sudden strain, sprain or fall causes a bone fracture.

Osteoporosis affects one in four women and one in eight men over the age of 50 and is reaching epidemic proportions in the United States. Postmenopausal women are especially at risk since women in general have less bone tissue and lose bone more rapidly than men because of hormonal changes during menopause.

Data published in 1998 revealed that about 10 million individuals in the U.S. already have osteoporosis and 18 million more have low bone mass, which increases their risk of developing osteoporosis. Currently, one in four Canadian women and about 400,000 men are affected by osteoporosis annually; as a result, more than 25,000 hip fractures, with costs of $400 million annually, occur in Canada every year.

The incidence of osteoporosis is expected to increase dramatically world-wide as the proportion of older individuals is continually increasing. There is growing concern about this disease and the great health care costs that arise. Increased bone fragility and the risk of fractures, especially hip fracture, contribute significantly to mortality in older individual—only 50% of hip fracture patients leave the hospital. Osteoporosis is also linked to vascular and renal disease and can lead to height loss, limited mobility and diminished independence. For this reason, prevention of osteoporosis is of the utmost importance.

Early detection of osteoporosis is important and there are many risk factors that can be considered. Risk factors commonly associated with osteoporosis include genetics, medical disorders, drug use, lifestyle, menopause, disturbances in hormonal regulation and nutritional factors. The prevalence of malnutrition, particularly inadequate nutritional intake, increases with advancing age. Menopause, and the reduction of estrogen, have been blamed for osteoporosis in women.

However, just because estrogen levels fall, doesn't mean that giving estrogen is the answer. Read the following pages for more on estrogen and bone loss. Early menopause or surgically-induced menopause

OSTEOPOROSIS RISK FACTOR

- Family history
- High-stress lifestyle or Type A personality
- Northern European or Asian descent
- Low stomach acid
- Smoking
- High caffeine and sugar intake
- High-protein diet
- Thyroid disease
- Corticosteroid therapy (prednisone)
- Thin, small build
- Early menopause
- Sedentary lifestyle
- No pregnancies

is felt by some to increase risk because of the longer period of estrogen and progesterone deficiency these events cause in a woman's life. In one study, women who had both ovaries removed had two to three times the risk of hip fracture of other postmenopausal women. Women who have hysterectomies but do not have their ovaries removed are also at increased risk because the blood and nerve supply to the ovaries can be altered during such surgery. The ovaries thus become less efficient, resulting in decreased hormone production earlier than in women experiencing natural menopause.

Age is also a factor, as the older you get the more likely your chances are of developing osteoporosis. Family history, tobacco use, and certain medications such as Prednisone may contribute to weak bones as well. Diet is an important consideration. Ensuring your diet is sufficient in calcium, vitamin D, and phosphorous will help increase bone mass, and exercising regularly will help keep your bones strong. By being aware of the possible risk factors, you may be able to slow the disease if you already have it or prevent it if you are likely to develop it.

So What Happens to Your Bones?

Bone is a living, growing tissue composed of collagen, which provides a soft framework, and calcium phosphate, which adds strength and hardens the framework. Bone constantly undergoes a state of renewal, with osteoclasts resorbing (removing) old bone and osteoblasts laying down new layers of bone matrix in the remodeling (formation) process.

Bone formation continues at a faster rate than resorption until peak bone mass (maximum bone density and strength) is attained, usually between the ages of 16 to 25 years of age. Subsequently, bone resorption slowly begins to exceed bone formation. When an increase in bone resorption relative to formation occurs, there is a net loss of bone density, ultimately resulting in osteoporosis. Accelerated bone resorption is the principal physiological derangement responsible for both postmenopausal and age-related bone loss.

ESTROGEN AND BONE LOSS

In her book, *No More HRT: Menopause Treat the Cause*, Lorna discusses estrogen and bone loss:

Hormones play a very important role in bone health. However, the current almost exclusive focus on estrogens as a critical factor in bone health is seriously misplaced. Many more hormones are involved, and the estrogens alone do not necessarily have the beneficial effects many people think they do. Hormones, including parathyroid hormone, calcitonin secreted by the thyroid, androgens, progesterone and thyroid hormone, all contribute to bone health. Let's take a closer look at estrogen.

Estrogen stimulates the formation of calcitonin, thus increasing calcium uptake by the bones and inhibiting the action of osteoclasts, the cells that break down bone. For this reason, supplemental estrogen on its own or supplemental calcium is often touted as a preventive measure and treatment for osteoporosis. Many studies indicate that estrogen therapy decreases bone resorption and seemingly stabilizes bone mass, and may even be involved with a minimal increase in bone density. The promotion of estrogen's benefits for osteoporosis started with the whole "Premarin push," and the theme was well established by the 1970s and 1980s. The actual benefits of estrogen for osteoporosis were greatly exaggerated in the advertising hype.

A more recent eight-year study that involved more than 9,500 American women confirmed other studies that mentioned that the only benefit estrogen has on possibly preventing bone loss is in the first few years around the time of menopause. This study also showed that by seven years after menopause the decline in bone mineral density (BMD) was the same in women who were taking estrogen and women who were not. It is interesting to note that women treated with estrogen who showed less BMD loss during the earlier years of menopause had a higher BMD in the years before menopause, putting to question the so-called positive effects of estrogen on bone loss during the first few years of menopause.

In our opinion, this view of estrogen understates the harm it can do. Think about it... osteoclasts seek out and destroy old, damaged bone. Estrogen slows down the action of osteoclasts. If osteoclasts are not breaking down old bone, then the osteoblasts, which would normally fill the space with new healthy bone, become unable to build new bone because there is no space in which to put it. It seems logical that the result would be greater amounts of older damaged and brittle bone. More is not always better, especially when it comes to more old, brittle bone.

Studies show that women who have been on estrogen for a long time and suddenly stop have increased rates of bone loss. Given that estrogen inhibits the breakdown of old bone, rapid breakdown will occur once estrogen is stopped because now the osteoclasts, put on hold by the hormone, can finally do their work. In the meantime, so much old, damaged bone has accumulated that when it starts to be resorbed, the bone-building cells, probably already at a disadvantage due to the other causes that contribute to poor bone health, cannot fill the spaces fast enough.

Clearly, supplemental estrogen merely temporarily masks the symptoms of osteoporosis while doing nothing to address its causes and putting women's health at risk. When there are safe, natural, effective remedies and treatments available to support women through menopause, such as essential fats, treatments that not only prevent bone breakdown but stimulate new bone growth, why is synthetic estrogen replacement so popular?

FATS FOR BONE HEALTH

Recent animal and human research suggests that both GLA from borage and evening primrose oil and EPA in fish oil enhance calcium absorption and increase calcium deposition in bone. The anti-inflammatory prostaglandins produced from GLA have numerous beneficial effects on health, including increasing bone strength and bone formation and decreasing the rate of cardiovascular events. A deficiency of good fats leads to severe osteoporosis associated with loss of bone calcium. Deficits of EFAs may be the common factor which accounts for the close association between osteoporosis, vascular disease, and other diseases, such as hypertension and renal disease.

As we have discussed earlier in the book, the first step in the conversion of dietary linoleic acid and ALA to their by-products is a slow rate-limiting step. Numerous factors, including aging, diabetes, smoking and steroid use, are associated with a decrease in the enzyme that results in impairing this metabolism of essential fats. These same influences are risk factors in developing osteoporosis. Therefore, supplementing with a direct source of GLA, EPA and DHA causes the continuing production of beneficial prostaglandins.

Prostaglandins are important local regulators of cell activity in bone and are necessary for bone formation. Good prostaglandins have been shown to stimulate bone growth by causing inhibition of the osteoclast and stimulation of the osteoblast. Dietary supplementation with GLA and EPA increases the levels of beneficial prostaglandins that stimulate the formation and reduce the resorption of bone.

EFAs have been shown to affect bone formation in other ways as well. Supplementation with EFAs enhances calcium absorption, reduces urinary calcium excretion, increases bone calcium, increases bone protein synthesis and bone strength. Deficiency of EFAs impairs the actions of vitamin D on calcium absorption. In addition, EFA sources, such as borage, fish and flax oil, have numerous other health benefits, as we have discussed throughout this book.

A 1998 study was set up to test the interactions between calcium and GLA and EPA in humans. Sixty-five elderly women (mean age of 79.5) with a diet low in calcium were randomly assigned to take 6 g of a mixture containing both evening primrose oil and fish oil (GLA and EPA) or a fake pill. Each group also received 600 mg/day of calcium carbonate for a total of 18 months. The fatty acid supplementation increased calcium absorption and bone density and prevented bone density loss, while the group that took calcium without any essential fats actually resulted in bone density loss, as shown in the following table, GLA & EPA Supplementation.

This study confirmed what researchers had already thought: EFAs are critical for the absorption of certain vitamins and minerals. The researchers concluded that evening primrose oil and fish oil have beneficial effects on the bone and they are safe to take for prolonged periods of time.

GLA & EPA Supplementation Increases Bone Density Over 18 Months

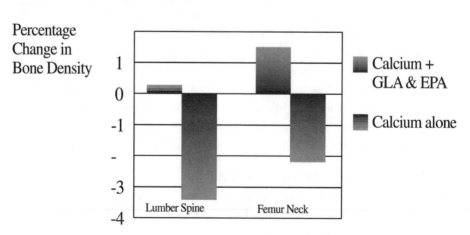

(M.C. Kruger, et al. *Aging Clin. Exp. Res,* Vol 10, No. 5, pp. 385-94 1998)

Diagram courtesy of Bioriginal Food & Science Corporation

FLAXSEED FOR BONE HEALTH

Not only do good fats help with bone maintenance, but flaxseed has proven beneficial for reducing the risk of osteoporosis. If you recall in Chapter 8 where we discussed lignans, they are active in treating numerous health conditions, including building stronger bones. Daily dietary intake of flaxseed lignans protects against bone loss, may increase bone density, and reduces the risk of osteoporosis. Increasing the lignans naturally through diet or supplement form is an effective method to achieve health and prevent chronic disease, including heart disease and osteoporosis.

OTHER NUTRIENTS FOR BONE HEALTH

Calcium and phosphate are major components of bone and represent more than 80% of bone mineral content. Both are essential for formation and maintenance of strong, healthy bones. Calcium is the fifth most abundant element in the body, with the majority being in bone. Low calcium intake is associated with reduced bone mass and increased risk fractures and osteoporosis. Adequate intakes of calcium ensure maximum bone mass and protect against increased bone resorption, as evidenced by reduced levels of serum osteocalcin, a parameter of bone turnover.

Calcium insufficiency due to low calcium intake and reduced absorption contributes to the accelerated rate of age-related bone loss in the elderly. Failure of older individuals to increase their calcium intake to offset age-related increases in calcium requirement contributes substantially to the development of increased bone resorption. In men and women over 65 years of age, calcium intakes are insufficient to prevent calcium-related erosion of bone mass and calcium supplementation is recommended.

Adult bone building requires that approximately 600 mg of calcium per day be absorbed. According to national health surveys conducted in the United States, calcium intake in adult women is 40–50% lower than in men, with 75–80% of women consuming less than 800 mg of calcium per day; one-quarter of American women consume less than 300 mg daily.

Calcium Sources: More than the Cow

If we believe what the Canadian Dairy Association informs us in their aggressive advertising campaigns, we would think that cow's milk is the only source of dietary calcium. But do cows drink milk in order to provide the calcium in milk? No, they eat grass! In fact, humans are the only species on the planet that continue to drink milk after weaning. Yet vegetable sources of calcium are more readily absorbed and easily utilized by the body than dairy sources, and occur in

CALCIUM CONTENT OF COMMON FOODS

FOOD	CALCIUM CONTENT (IN MG)
PLANT FOODS	
100 g hijiki (sea vegetable)	1 400
100 g wakame (sea vegetable)	1 300
100 g kelp (sea vegetable)	1 100
250 g sesame seeds	900
250 g almonds	660
250 g filberts	450
250 g turnip greens	450
250 g chickpeas	450
250 g tofu	400
250 g quinoa	340
250 g bok choy	330
250 g black beans	315
250 g kale	315
25 mL blackstrap molasses	300
7 corn tortillas	300
250 g broccoli	160
ANIMAL FOODS	
250 g goat's milk	330
250 g cow's milk	300
65 g Parmesan cheese	300
125 g plain yogurt	300
125 g ricotta cheese	300
30 g Cheddar cheese	300
250 g ice cream	240

Chart courtesy of No More HRT: Menopause Treat the Cause

abundance, as shown in the table Calcium Content of Common Foods. Furthermore, three out of four North American adults have some degree of lactose intolerance (sensitivity to milk sugars), while others are sensitive to casein, the protein in milk. Pasteurizing milk kills the enzymes that assist in the breakdown of these products, often causing digestive difficulties that result in poor assimilation of the calcium and other nutrients in milk.

Calcium Supplements

If, given your health history, current diet, and digestive strength, you determine that you need supplemental calcium (your health care practitioner can help establish whether supplementation is necessary), know that throwing calcium at your bones and expecting it to stick won't work. Your health, the type of calcium consumed, and the overall balance of minerals and vitamins taken in are critical factors in optimal absorption and assimilation.

Many people have difficulty digesting and assimilating the form of calcium most commonly recommended by medical doctors, calcium carbonate. Research has shown that about 45% of calcium in the citrate form is absorbed. Only 4% of calcium in the carbonate form is absorbed in people with low stomach hydrochloric acid (HCL) levels. It has been demonstrated that calcium citrate is more readily absorbed than carbonate in normal subjects. One study demonstrated that subjects absorbed more calcium from 500 mg of calcium citrate than from 2,000 mg of calcium carbonate.

Calcium and Other Minerals

To build bone, calcium works in concert with other minerals, such as phosphorous, magnesium, manganese, boron, strontium, silica, zinc and copper. All minerals in the body are in delicate balance with one another, and if a deficiency in calcium exists, other minerals will also be compromised. Vitamins that join in to complete the orchestration of bone building are folic acid, vitamin B6, vitamin D and vitamin K.

Magnesium is essential for the activity of many enzyme systems. Although dietary intake of magnesium is marginal in the whole population, deficiencies of magnesium are characteristic in the elderly population and in people with osteoporosis. Deficiencies of magnesium are accompanied by a variety of structural and functional disturbances. Magnesium influences mineral metabolism indirectly in hard and soft tissues and directly on the process of bone formation, resorption and mineralization. The large fraction of magnesium in bone is an integral part of bone crystal.

Vitamin D is manufactured in the body as a result of exposure to sunlight or is available from vitamin-enriched milk products. Normal levels of vitamin D are essential for optimum calcium absorption. Vitamin D deficiency is associated with reduced calcium absorption and an increased risk of fractures. Deficiency of vitamin D is being recognized more often, especially in geriatric populations. The body's ability to manufacture vitamin D decreases with age and worsens in the winter. Low dose vitamin D supplementation wards off vitamin D deficiency and ensures adequate absorption of calcium. The major metabolite, 1,25 dihydroxy-vitamin D3, stimulates active transport of calcium in the small intestine and colon and thereby enhances calcium absorption. Supplementation with magnesium, calcium, and vitamin D maximizes calcium uptake.

Zinc is also essential in bone metabolism as a cofactor for specific enzymes and directly stimulates bone formation and mineralization. Zinc is necessary for bone protein synthesis, optimal bone development and bone density sustenance. Additionally zinc enhances the bone formation and mineralization effects of EFAs. Preferred Nutrition's FemmEssentials contains all the nutrients mentioned above for healthy bone formation.

Recommended Products: Preferred Nutrition's FemmEssentials FemmOmega™ and OsteoBalance.

What We Learned In This Chapter:

- GLA found in evening primrose oil and borage oil are beneficial in reducing the inflammation and swelling of arthritis.

- Fish oil, like GLA, reduces symptoms of arthritis, such as pain, number of affected joints and morning stiffness.

- Osteoarthritis is not an inevitable part of aging. Diet and lifestyle changes can prevent the condition from arising.

- Other nutrients can be beneficial in preventing or treating osteoporosis, such as flaxseed, calcium, magnesium and more.

The next and last chapter addressing specific health conditions will focus on men's health issues and how essential fatty acids can help.

Chapter 11

PROSTATE PROTECTION

As you have read throughout this book, essential fatty acids are beneficial for many women's conditions, including PMS, menopause, breast cancer, osteoporosis and rheumatoid arthritis. Now we wish to address the powerful benefits of EFAs for specific men's conditions. Our female readers will find this chapter interesting as well because you will find the nutrition advice that your partner may need to treat benign prostate hypertrophy (BPH), prostate cancer and infertility.

BENIGN PROSTATE HYPERTROPHY (BPH)

Small in size but grand in problems, the prostate is a chestnut-sized gland located just below the bladder and wrapped around the urethra. The prostate gland is the gland that produces semen, the fluid that carries sperm, and is essential for reproduction. The urethra is the pathway for seminal fluid and urine, and when the gland swells, it can inhibit the normal urinary flow and the ejaculation of semen. The majority of the urinary problems men experience are due to inflammation (prostatitis) and enlargement of the prostate gland (benign prostatic hyperplasia) or, more seriously, prostate cancer.

Benign prostatic hyperplasia (BPH) is a condition arising from the enlargement of the prostate gland due to excessive growth of the glandular tissues. The enlarged prostate causes compression, elongation, displacement and distortion of the prostatic urethra, leading to the obstruction of urine flow. The incidence of enlarged prostate increases with age. Studies have revealed that when a man reaches approximately 40 years of age, the prostate gland has already started to enlarge but not to the point of interfering with urine flow. This disorder progresses slowly and therefore the reversal of symptoms may take several months of treatment.

Approximately 50% of men aged 60 years and 90% of those aged 85 years have BPH. Men with a family history of BPH are more likely to develop the condition, as are athletes or cyclists, who may sustain repetitive injury to the gland.

Recognizing BPH

Symptoms of enlarged prostate vary in severity and include frequent urination, nocturia (excess urination at night), urinary urgency or hesitancy, painful and difficult urination and incomplete urination. There may be pain or discomfort during ejaculation. Inflammation and infection may develop from not emptying the bladder effectively. Chronic constipation and low back pain are also symptoms.

Another sign is prostatitis, an infection of the prostate characterized by fever, pain while urinating, and a discharge from the penis.

Prostate Functioning

Normal growth and functioning of the prostate is influenced by male sex hormones (androgens), especially testosterone from the testes and the adrenal glands. Free testosterone is taken up by the prostate cells, where it is converted to dihydrotestosterone (or DHT, which we will refer to it as bad testosterone) by the enzyme 5 alpha (a)-reductase. Bad testosterone is physiologically more active than testosterone and is mainly responsible for prostatic growth and enlargement in BPH. Bad testosterone concentrations are four to five times higher than testosterone in an enlarged prostate gland.

The binding of DHT to androgen receptors in prostate cells is necessary for the cellular activity of testosterone. DHT appears to be very active in the prostate because it has a much higher attraction for androgen receptors than testosterone does. A minor fraction of testosterone is metabolized to 17 ß-estradiol by aromatase and also contributes to the growth of prostatic tissue. Recently, these growth factors have been reported to contribute to the enlargement of the prostate gland. They may stimulate the growth of the prostate gland by direct action or by a prostaglandin (see Chapter 1) pathway.

Prostatic fluid from patients suffering from BPH and chronic prostatitis has been shown to have higher amounts of inflammatory prostaglandins than prostatic fluid from people with a normal prostate.

Natural Treatment for BPH

Plants have been used for centuries in the treatment of urinary problems, including BPH and prostitis. Many of these plants have been subjected to laboratory and clinical evaluations. The results of these evaluations have confirmed the safety of these plants for prolonged use.

In Germany and Austria, plant-based products are the first line of treatment for BPH and make up more than 90% of total prescriptions for BPH. Based on scientific evaluations, the Commission E Special Expert Committee of the Federal Health Agency of Germany, the German equivalent to the U.S. FDA, has recently approved pumpkin seed and saw palmetto berries for the treatment of BPH. Those plants may act by inhibiting the 5 a-reductase enzyme that is responsible for the conversion of testosterone to bad testosterone.

Recent scientific studies have revealed that GLA from borage and evening primrose oil is a potent inhibitor of this enzyme and can be used for the treatment of BPH. Borage and evening primrose oil also decrease the production of inflammatory prostaglandins and increase the concentration of anti-inflammatory prostaglandins.

PUMPKIN SEED

Pumpkin seed oil contains mainly linoleic acid (LA), the monounsaturate oleic acid (OA) and palmitic acid, which is a saturate. Traces of ALA are also present, as well as sterols consisting mainly of spinasterol, delta-7-stigmastenol, stigmasterol, squalene, ß and gamma tocopherols and pigments, including carotenoids and chloroplasts.

The sterols and fatty acids appear to be responsible for its anti-prostatic effect. The oil fraction of pumpkin seed has been shown to inhibit 5 a-reductase. The mixture of sterols has been shown to inhibit the binding of DHT to androgen receptors. Sterols have anti-inflammatory actions that may contribute to the beneficial effects of pumpkin seed oil in inflammatory prostatic conditions (chronic prostatitis).

> *Recommended Dosage:* Take two to four 1,000 mg softgels for prevention. For treatment higher doses may be required.
>
> *Recommended Products:* Herbal Select's Pumpkin Oil softgels.

SAW PALMETTO

Saw palmetto extract contains fatty acids (lauric, myristic, oleic acid, linoleic acid, and alpha linolenic acid), phytosterols (ß-sitosterol and its glucoseides, stigmasterol and campesterol) and fatty alcohols (doosanol, hexacosanol, octacosanol and triacontanol). The fatty acids, notably lauric and myristic acids, present in saw palmetto extract are mainly responsible for the 5 a-reductase inhibition. ß-sitosterol, which is present in the highest quantities, may be acting by competing with estrogens, thereby reducing the overall estrogenic effect. Recently, a double-blind clinical trial has demonstrated beneficial actions of ß-sitosterol against BPH.

These natural plant extracts and essential fats have been proven to be efficacious to treat BPH. They are relatively free of side-effects especially in comparison to side-effects seen with pharmaceutical drugs and would be highly recommended for any man with BPH, or for any man over 40 in the prevention of BPH.

PROSTATE CANCER

Prostate cancer is the most commonly diagnosed cancer in men in the U.S., aside from skin cancers. It is the second leading cause of cancer deaths in American men. The chances of developing prostate cancer increase with age, and more than 75% of prostate cancers are diagnosed in men over age 65. The cause of prostate cancer can be attributed to many factors, including a poor diet (high in bad fats, red meat and low in fruits and vegetables), lifestyle and hormone metabolism.

As we discussed in Chapter 8, the scientific community has been investigating the effects of diet on cancer for some time. Published in a 1997 report by the American Institute for Cancer Research (AICR), scientists believe that 60-70% of all cancer cases could be prevented through sensible diet (rich in fruits, vegetables, fiber and low in bad fat and red meat), maintaining a healthy body weight, keeping physically active and not smoking.

Ongoing research suggests that eating a plant-based, low healthy fat diet will reduce the risk of prostate cancer. People who are described as eating a "high bad fat" diet are generally consuming higher amounts of fatty meats, which may be linked to an increased prostate cancer risk. However, it is important to remember that all components of the diet work together to influence cancer risk. That is why it is so important to have a diet rich in fruits, vegetables, fiber and low in refined sugars, red meat and bad fats.

Researchers from Laval University in Quebec, Canada studied the association between bad fat intake and prostate cancer survival. Nutritionists interviewed 384 men with prostate cancer on their diet history. The researchers found that men who had a higher saturated fat diet (found in red meat and dairy products) had a three times greater risk of dying from prostate cancer than did the group with the lower saturated fat intake. It was thought that a recommendation of saturated fat below 10% of energy should reduce the risk of dying from prostate cancer. Another study, published in the *Journal of the National Cancer Institute* in 1999, concluded that total fat in the diet is associated with the increased risk of prostate cancer.

Flaxseed Fights Prostate Cancer

New study results released in November 2002 confirm that flaxseed shows promise in the fight against prostate cancer. The study was carried out in mice. Researchers from Duke University Medical Center in the U.S. found that a diet high in flaxseed reduced the size, aggressiveness and severity in tumors in mice with prostate cancer. Human studies will be carried out to determine the effects of flaxseed on prostate cancer, and we feel this is a promising area of research.

The flaxseed benefits seen in this trial could be due to the fiber content of flaxseed, omega-3 fatty acid content or the lignans that are well known for cancer treatment and prevention. Lignans have been found to inhibit testosterone metabolism, and since testosterone is important in the progression of prostate cancer, lignans may inhibit the growth and development of the disease. This was the second study these researchers performed on flaxseed and its affects on prostate cancer. In the first study, published in July 2002 *Urology*, they showed that 25 men with prostate cancer consuming a low fat diet supplemented with flaxseed had slower prostate tumor growth. The men saw a decrease in their testosterone levels and a lower prostate specific antigen (PSA) marker, which is a marker for cancer.

> *Recommended Dosage:* For prevention, take 1 to 2 tablespoons of milled flaxseed daily. Treatment of the condition may require higher dosages, please consult your healthcare practitioner.

Recommended Products: Swanson's EFA OmegaTru™ Milled Flaxseed; Health From The Sun's FiProFLAX; and Herbal Select's Milled Flaxseed.

Fishing for Prostate Health

In a study published in the *British Journal of Cancer,* researchers examined the consumption of fish oils and the risk of prostate cancer. Experimental studies in animals suggest that the risk of prostate cancer is reduced with EPA and DHA. The authors examined the relationship between prostate risk and EPA and DHA in 317 prostate cancer cases and 480 controls. There was a 40% reduced prostate cancer risk with high blood levels of EPA and DHA. The researchers concluded that a reduced risk of prostate cancer was associated with fish oils.

A 2001 Swedish study that focused on fish consumption found that men who ate moderate to large amounts of fish had only one-third to one-half the risk of prostate cancer as compared to those who did not eat fish. As well, combinations of all the fatty acids may be just what the doctor ordered for treatment of prostate cancer. In a 1985 study published in *Clinical Biochemistry,* researchers showed that GLA, ALA, arachidonic acid and EPA killed prostate cancer cells in tissue culture, but did not affect the normal cells with which they were cultured. The normal cells continued to grow normally. When essential fatty acids were not present, the prostate cancer cells overgrew the normal cells.

Recommended Dosage: For prevention take 2 g of natural fish 18/12 softgels daily. To treat this condition higher dosages may be required, please consult your healthcare practitioner.

Conjugated Linoleic Acid (CLA) Anti-Cancer Effects

CLA is also preventive against the development of prostate cancer cells (see Chapter 2 for more on CLA). New research published in 2002 in *Cancer Letters* examined the cis-9, trans-11 and the trans-10, cis-12 CLA isomers in their action against human colon and prostate cancer. The cis-9, trans-11 isomer was effective in protecting prostate cancer cells from growing and the trans-10, cis-12 isomer was effective for colon cancer. The researchers concluded that CLA may prove effective as chemopreventive supplements for individuals at risk of, or diagnosed with, colorectal or prostate cancer. This is a promising area of research.

MALE INFERTILITY

The fact that many couples are not able to have children has become a very significant problem. Over 4.5 million men and women, approximately 1 out of 5 couples are unable to conceive during their first attempt at pregnancy. About 40% of male infertility problems are related to male reproductive problems. In men, infertility is caused in general because of a lack of sperm in the semen, deformed or structurally abnormal sperm, sperm that lack the ability to reach and fertilize a female egg, and genetic disorders. Fertility is often a reflection of overall health.

EFAs are responsible for the production of healthy sperm cells. The DHA omega-3 fatty acid found in fatty fish and fish oils is observed in extremely high levels in healthy sperm. Infertile men often have low levels of DHA. Sperm is produced in the sertoli cells of the testicles, one of five sites in the human body with an extremely high content of the omega-3 fatty acid DHA.

Most of the DHA is located in the sperm tail, and it has been speculated that this fatty acid provides elasticity to the tail structures necessary for normal flow. One researcher found low DHA values in the sperm of 145 infertile men correlated well with reduced sperm motility. Another researcher who published his study in *Molecular Human Reproduction* in 1998 reported identical results when comparing sperms from infertile men with normal controls.

Researchers at the Department of Endocrinology, University Hospital in Gent, Belgium, have shown in numerous studies that DHA is a major component of human sperm, that there is a significant positive correlation between DHA content in sperm cells and parameters related to fertilization, and that subfertile men have significantly less DHA in their sperm cells. The same researchers decided to study whether or not other dietary omega-3 fatty acids, such as ALA, found in highest concentrations in flaxseed and oil, had an effect on the concentration of DHA in sperm cells and whether sperm cells can be enriched in DHA by supplementation of ALA (ALA is converted to DHA, see Chapter 1).

The study consisted of 15 subfertile men whose food intake was evaluated by a food frequency questionnaire. DHA content in the sperm was not associated with dietary EPA or DHA; however, was positively associated with food intake of ALA. Interestingly, the DHA from fish oil was not able to cross the blood-testes barrier to make its way into sperm cells. The researchers suggested that sperm cell DHA is derived mainly from ALA that must pass the blood-testes barrier, which will then be converted into DHA in the sperm cell. Supplementation with ALA can correct the deficiency of DHA in sperm cells of subfertile men.

> *Recommended Dosage:* Supplement with 2–4 g natural fish 18/12 daily or take a daily dose of one to two 1,000 mg flaxseed softgels, or 1/2 to 1 teaspoon of flaxseed oil.

What We Learned In This Chapter:

- Borage and evening primrose oil are potent inhibitors of the enzyme that promotes prostate enlargement.

- Men who eat moderate to large amounts of fish can lower their risk of prostate cancer by up to 50% compared to those who do not eat fish.

- Flaxseed is being studied for its ability to reduce the size, aggressiveness and severity of tumors in the prostate.

- Supplementation with ALA can correct the deficiency of DHA in sperm cells of subfertile men.

Having absorbed the information provided in this book up to this point, you may have questions about facts that you have seen presented in other articles or news programs. The next chapter will help shed some light on those facts, fallacies and misconceptions about essential fatty acids.

Chapter 12

FACTS, FALLACIES
AND MISCONCEPTIONS

Throughout this book we have given you the facts about essential fatty acids (EFAs) and how their nutritional power can prevent and influence disease, resulting in a healthier you. However, just as with any drug, herb or other dietary supplement, there will be myths and misconceptions surrounding their usage and efficacy. These misconceptions arise for a variety of reasons, including difficulty in interpreting the science, media influence, marketing power, and competitive sales strategies. In our experience with EFAs, we have seen a few facts become misconstrued, and our job in this chapter will be to give you a clear, accurate understanding of some of the more common issues that have made its way to the media, but due to the media's time and space constraints may have prevented them from giving the full picture.

First, we discuss misconceptions that have been generated regarding EFAs and then facts relating to EFAs that you may not be aware of, but we feel are important for you to understand.

PART I

Misconception 1:
Pyrrolizidine Alkaloids in Borage Oil

Throughout this book, we have discussed the amazing healing benefits of borage oil containing GLA, ranging from potent anti-inflammatory effects, resulting in decreased pain and stiffness in arthritis, to improvements in eczema symptoms and benefits for the heart. To understand why there would be any misconceptions about this powerful plant, you need to be aware of the plant constituents.

Borage (*borago officinalis*) is native to Europe, North Africa and Asia Minor and is widely grown in Europe and North America. Borage is an ancient herb first mentioned by Theophrastus as early as the third century BC. In the early centuries, borage had numerous uses, including steeping the leaves and flowers in wine, as a cooling accent to salads, pickles and vegetables, or as a garnish or put into candy, jam, jelly and syrup. Throughout the years the plant's leaves were found to have healing properties and were used to combat fevers, jaundice and sore throats.

Among GLA, the borage plant has been found to yield a variety of constituents, including potassium, calcium, vitamin C, glucose and galactose along with other sterols. Borage has also been shown to contain alkaloids. Alkaloids are organic compounds found mostly in seed-bearing plants. Some alkaloids are known to have profound effects on the human body. A few examples of alkaloids include nicotine, quinine, morphine, cocaine and strychnine. Large consumption of certain alkaloids could potentially put the user at risk of poisoning.

Pyrrolizidine alkaloids (PAs) are a group of more than 200 alkaloid compounds that are commonly found in such flowering plant families as fabacease, boraginaceae and asteraceae. These alkaloids share a common chemical structure that consists of a nitrogen containing double ring but are thought to function in the plant as a form of defense. Every plant organism produces a significant number of chemicals that are critical for survival. Without the production of these specific chemicals, which include toxins, the plant would be destroyed by elements of nature, such as insects and grazing.

Are PAs Harmful?

Of more than 200 PAs, approximately 100 are believed to display potentially harmful effects. These effects are attributed to the chemical structure of the PA. In general, saturated PAs (absence of double bonds in the double-ringed structure) are harmless; however, the unsaturated PAs are suspected to cause certain liver conditions. PAs can be converted by liver enzymes into potent agents that react very rapidly, resulting in cellular destruction or abnormal growth patterns. Accumulation of this cellular damage results in a syndrome known as hepatic veno-occlusive disease, a potentially life-threatening illness.

PAs in the Borage Plant

PAs have been detected in borage leaves, seeds and flower. Small amounts of the potentially toxic unsaturated lycopsamine and amabiline were found in the leaves and seeds, and the non-toxic, extremely rare saturated pyrrolizidine thesinine was found in the flowers. However, it is important to note that PAs have NEVER been found in borage seed oil. Due to the presence of nitrogen in the double-ring system, PAs are soluble in both water and alcohol, but are not soluble in the oil. Studies have shown that the total alkaloid amount in the plant, relative to dry weight, is less than 0.001%. Further studies have substantiated the absence of PAs in borage oil.

The bottom line is that borage oil is absolutely safe to consume because the alkaloids are not present.

Testing of PAs

The question of PAs in borage first arose with a publication by Larson, Roby and Stermitz in 1984, in which they found unsaturated PAs in the leaf tissue of borage plants. But this was not thought to be of major concern since many species of plants produce the alkaloids in their leaf tissue as a natural defense mechanism. That publication was followed by another in 1986 by Dodson and Stermitz which analyzed the flowers, seed and oil from borage plants. They found only saturated (non-toxic) PAs in the flowers. In one batch of seed they found only saturated PAs and in another batch of seed they found predominantly saturated with only a trace of unsaturated. In the oil samples no PAs were found at all.

In 1991 a study by de Smet pointed out that although no PAs had been identified in borage oil, the limit of detection on the testing method used was 5μg/g (micrograms per gram or 5 parts per million, ppm), while the German Federal Health Office recommended that intake of PAs should not exceed 1 μg per day (1 ppm). A testing method with a detection limit of 1 μg/g was required to ensure that borage oil was below this limit. The thin layer chromatography (TLC) method was developed with a detection limit of 0.1 ppm and again showed the absence of PAs in borage oil. The researchers stated that "it appears that the sample of borage seed oil under investigation does not contain any PAs."

A recent independent analysis undertaken by Chemisches Laboratorium in Hamburg Germany in 2002 has confirmed the absence of PAs in processed borage oil using a method with the most sensitive detection limit available in the world of 4 μg/kg, or 4 parts per billion (ppb), which is an impressive 250 times lower than the levels deemed safe by the German Health Office. These results would mean that a person would have to consume 250, 1,000 mg borage oil capsules per day for many years to experience any potentially harmful effects. However, low levels of PAs were detected in the borage seed and in the cake, which is left over after the seeds are pressed. This research was sponsored by Bioriginal Food & Science Corp., the leading manufacturer of borage and other essential fatty acid oils.

Some experts still recommend borage with caution because of the possible presence of toxic PAs; yet repeated tests that have been done and they do not detect the presence of these compounds in processed borage seed oil. It appears that there has been tendency to assume that because these compounds are found in the plant, they must therefore be in the oil, which is simply not the case. PAs are water-soluble and are therefore not found in the oil. Unfortunately, some of this information has been misinterpreted to consumers, and has led people to question the safety of borage oil.

The health benefits of borage oil as nature's richest source of GLA and a valuable dietary supplement have been documented numerous times in clinical research, and we should not avoid borage because of misinformation about PAs.

Misconception 2:
Is Fish Better Than Flax?

This is a question we get asked often. People have been told that fish oil is a superior source of omega-3s than flaxseed oil. The answer for this question isn't as black and white as it may seem. We agree that both flaxseed and fish have powerful health properties of their own, and therefore one cannot be substituted for the other.

Flax Facts

First let's look at flaxseed. By this point in the book, you know that flaxseed is recognized as a super food for many reasons. Flaxseed is a rich source of lignans that contains soluble and insoluble fiber (good for relieving constipation), protein, vitamins, minerals and, of course, the omega-3, alpha-linolenic acid (ALA). With all these powerful nutritional components combined, flaxseed has resulted in numerous health benefits. However, it is difficult for researchers to determine which components of flaxseed are providing the benefits and in what combination.

Although flaxseed has numerous nutritional components, flaxseed oil is also a popular dietary supplement because of its rich ALA content. Studies have shown the health benefits of ALA for many diseases, including cardiovascular protection and immune function. So regardless if you are taking the flaxseed or the oil, you will be receiving benefits from ALA, but the flaxseed oil will contain higher concentrations of ALA than the flaxseed.

Fish Facts

With that said, fish contains many nutritional properties as well, including protein, and the fat is a valuable source of the omega-3 fatty acids EPA and DHA. The consumption of fish has been well documented for heart health protection, and researchers are clearly able to say that the EPA and DHA are responsible for the beneficial health effects.

The Answer

If ALA, EPA and DHA are all omega-3s, what is the difference in their health effects? Remember in Chapter 1 we discussed the metabolic pathways of these fatty acids, and you will recall that ALA is the true 'essential' fatty acid because our body can't manufacture it and it must be received by the diet. Flaxseed and flaxseed oil are the richest sources of ALA in the North American diet. ALA is also found in walnuts, purslane, perilla seed and, in small amounts, in olive oil. It is also found in soybean oil and canola oil; however, we don't recommend canola and soybean oil because they are genetically modified.

Due to certain environmental and lifestyle factors, the conversion of ALA into EPA and DHA may be altered. Humans convert a small amount (research studies have shown various ranges from 0.2–18.5%) of dietary ALA into the longer chain omega-3s EPA and DHA, and an even lower conversion rate will be observed in the presence of a high linoleic acid diet (refined sunflower, safflower, canola, soybean, margarines that we don't recommend). EPA and DHA are known as "conditionally" essential because they can be made in our body by ALA; however, most EPA and DHA comes from our intake of fatty, cold-water fish, such as mackerel, salmon, herring, anchovy and tuna. They can also come from supplementing with a fish oil source that will provide your body with a direct source of EPA and DHA and will not need to rely on the metabolic conversion from ALA.

EPA is responsible for the production of beneficial prostaglandins of the 3 series, PGE3, which have anti-inflammatory properties that are useful in cardiovascular disease and arthritis. EPA will be converted into DHA, which has proven essential for infant brain development, visual acuity, mental health and numerous other diseases. Because ALA is not directly responsible for the production of prostaglandins, some researchers have concluded that ALA is not useful, as the conversion into EPA and DHA is limited and these are the two fatty acids that provide the beneficial effects. Therefore, many feel that taking a source of ALA from flaxseed or oil is not necessary. However, this is simply not true!

ALA has numerous health benefits by itself, without being converted into EPA and DHA, although their conversion is still an important nutritional consideration. These benefits have been documented by clinical studies and large population studies. If you recall in Chapter 4, we discussed how ALA has been shown to reduce blood cholesterol, triglyceride levels and the risk of stroke. The "Mediterranean diet" consisting of high amounts of tomatoes, olive oil, veggies, and fish has been shown as the ideal diet to help prevent heart disease.

In the Lyon Diet Heart Study, 300 patients who had survived a first coronary heart attack were instructed to consume a "Mediterranean diet" consisting of more fruit, vegetables, bread, chicken, and fish, and less cheese, meat, ham and sausage. Over the course of close to four years, the Mediterranean diet reduced the risk of a second heart attack and the overall death rate by as much as 70%. Among dietary constituents, only ALA was significantly related to a reduction in heart attacks. The researchers concluded that simple dietary changes, such as a reduction in total intake of saturated fatty acids and an increase in intake of ALA from flaxseed, flaxseed oil and olive oil, can led to significant reductions in coronary heart disease mortality.

Clinical studies have shown that elevated levels of blood cholesterol and increased risk for heart disease are associated with higher intakes of saturated fatty acids. As indicated earlier, the saturated fatty acid level of flaxseed oil is very low, only 7% of total fatty acids. A study published in *The American Journal of Clinical Nutrition* in 1991 showed that ALA in flaxseed oil is effective at reducing blood cholesterol levels as well as the "bad" cholesterol, LDL. The same study showed that ALA from flaxseed oil also lowers triglycerides, another blood fat fraction, which, when elevated, increases heart disease risk

Flaxseed oil may also protect against strokes by reducing blood-clotting and platelet aggregation. In a study published in *Stroke* in 1995, omega-3 fatty acids, including ALA, were shown to be associated with a lower risk of stroke in middle-aged men at high risk for coronary heart disease.

Although these studies mentioned here have focused upon the role of ALA in heart disease, increasing research is showing that other conditions, such as high blood pressure, cancer, skin diseases, and immune system disorders, such as renal failure, rheumatoid arthritis and multiple sclerosis, may be prevented and treated by supplementing the diet with ALA and other omega-3 fatty acids.

The American Heart Association (AHA) has recommended two servings of fish per week for the prevention of cardiovascular disease. However, some researchers and organizations have expressed concern with the dosages of EPA and DHA used in clinical studies. For example, to achieve the same levels of EPA and DHA used in one particular study, you would have to eat about six 3-ounce servings of salmon, or 26 servings of canned tuna, which goes far beyond the AHA recommendations. In consuming such high levels, a person may expose themselves to potentially high levels of environmental contaminants and heavy metals (such as mercury) found in fish (see Fact 2 on environmental toxins a little later in this chapter). To achieve these levels, fairly high doses of high quality fish oil capsules would need to be consumed.

Is fish oil superior to flax oil in its health effects? We feel that both fish oil and flax oil offer valuable fatty acids and that one should not be substituted for the other. Consuming both fish and flax will ensure you are receiving the essential fats that your body needs to defend against modern day diseases.

Misconception 3:
Golden Flax Seed is Superior to Brown Flax Seed

Does color indicate nutritional value of food? The research we have seen on this subject would lead us to believe that the color of food does not affect its nutritional value. Promoters of golden flax are causing confusion by claiming that golden flax is nutritionally superior to brown flax. But is there really a nutritional difference between the two flax varieties?

The Flax Council of Canada confirms that the color of the seed coat has little to do with the nutritional value of the flaxseed. Color is a trait that can be manipulated by conventional plant breeding methods.

The percentage of oil produced from the seed does not differ significantly between brown and golden seed varieties; as well, the omega-3, alpha-linolenic acid (ALA) levels between both are similar, and small differences may arise due to the growing conditions for that year. In fact, The Flax Council of Canada reports on samples that were analyzed by the Canadian Grain Commission in 2001 showed that the brown seed surpasses the "Dakota Gold" seed in ALA content, exactly the opposite of what the golden flaxseed promoters are marketing. The brown flaxseed samples contained about 8% more omega-3 than the "Dakota Gold" samples.

The majority of brown flaxseed available on the market is grown in western Canada where the cooler summers provide ideal growing conditions. Cooler post flowering temperatures (10 to 25 days following flowering) can increase both the oil content and the levels of ALA. The Canadian Grain Commission has compared agronomic data on flax quality and has found that the further south flax is grown, the lower the oil and ALA content. Golden flax is typically grown south of Saskatchewan in North and South Dakota, whereas brown flax is grown in the Canadian prairies, giving it an edge in quality over the flax grown in other climates.

Mucilage content (also known as soluble fiber) is slightly higher (2%) in the brown seed in comparison to the golden seeds. The mucilage is the coating of the seed, which gives the high shine and causes the seed to become sticky when wet. Most of the soluble fiber in flaxseed is mucilage. Soluble fiber has been linked to lowering blood sugar levels in people suffering from diabetes, reducing coronary heart disease risk by lowering cholesterol levels, preventing colon and rectal cancer and also reducing the risk of obesity.

Flaxseed, whether brown or golden in color, is packed with powerful nutritional components. Protein, dietary fiber, lignans and ALA are natural properties of flaxseed, which provide many health benefits. The components of flaxseed are known to help prevent certain types of cancer, protect the heart from cardiovascular disease, and help treat menopausal and premenstrual symptoms.

The effect of color on flaxseed nutrition is minor. Some people enjoy golden seeds when baking because of the lighter color; however, brown seeds have been shown to add a different texture to food because of the higher mucilage content. Despite certain marketing strategies promoting the superiority of golden flax, brown flax is nutritionally equal or superior to golden flax.

Misconception 4:
Evening Primrose Oil Causes Breast Cancer

As you will recall from Chapter 8 on breast cancer, much research has been done on the impact of diet on the risk of breast cancer. In fact, over the last few decades, we have learned that changes to diet can play a large role in the prevention and treatment of the disease. Recent dietary recommendations developed by the American Institute for Cancer Research (AICR) focus on increasing the fruits, vegetables, and fiber in the diet. These nutrients have a well-established role in the prevention of cancers. As well, bad fat in the diet (from red meat and dairy products) has been shown to increase the risk of all cancers, including breast cancer.

In their 1997 report *Food, Nutrition and the Prevention of Cancer*, the AICR provides a comprehensive review of the data surrounding the intake of fats and cancer risk. They state that diets high in total fats, particularly saturated fat, may increase the risk of breast cancer. When they examined the role of polyunsaturated fats (including linoleic acid, or LA), they found no relationship to breast cancer, other than the contribution that these fats make to total fat intake.

Nevertheless, some published articles have raised concerns about whether or not omega-6 oils, containing LA, are safe for women who are either at risk for breast cancer or who are breast cancer patients. Oils commonly referred to as "omega-6 oils" include corn oil, soybean oil, canola oil, sunflower oil, safflower oil, evening primrose oil, black currant oil, and borage oil. But these oils are not created equal in terms of their fatty acid content. They all contain differing amounts of LA, a polyunsaturated omega-6 fatty acid. As well, they contain differing amounts of other fatty acids, some of which are very beneficial for the body. The different fatty acid profiles of these oils are shown in the following table, Selected Fatty Acid Composition of Common Omega-6 Oils.

It is important to note that studies which linked intake of LA to breast cancer did not consider the total amount of fat or the type of fat in the diet. In animal studies where LA was linked to cancer, the link was the strongest when the diet was high in total fat. Furthermore, other studies have shown that omega-6 oils, such as evening primrose oil, can actually help reduce pain and tenderness of benign breast disease associated with cyclic breast pain (a risk factor for breast cancer.) Both evening primrose and borage oils contain GLA, which is responsible for these beneficial effects.

In fact, researchers have found that women with breast pain may have unusually low levels of GLA and the beneficial hormones it produces. When patients receive evening primrose oil supplements, the concentration of GLA and its hormones increases and the concentration of saturated fats in the breast decreases. Saturated fat in the breast is linked to a high saturated fat diet; therefore, by changing the types of fats and oils you consume to good, healthy fats like olive oil and flaxseed oil, they will help improve the fatty profile in the breast and other tissues by increasing the good fat and decreasing the bad.

In fact, GLA has been consistently shown to have anti-cancer activity in cell culture studies, as well as in animal and human studies. A British study published in 2000 found that women with breast cancer who received GLA from borage along with Tamoxifen demonstrated faster clinical response than those on Tamoxifen alone. Patients received about 3 g of GLA. Tamoxifen by itself is associated with significantly improved survival rates in postmenopausal breast cancer patients whose breast cancer is estrogen receptor positive.

Other essential fatty acid oils are also useful for reducing the risk of breast cancer (for example, omega-3 fatty acids from fish oils). The protective effect of omega-3 fatty acids was first observed in Greenland Inuit women who seemed to have a strikingly low rate of breast cancer. These women have a diet that is probably the highest in omega-3 fats of any population to date.

Another oil that has been associated with a lower incidence of breast cancer is olive oil, which is high in oleic acid, a healthy monounsaturated fat. A study published in 1995 demonstrated that increased olive oil consumption was associated with a 25% lower risk of breast cancer in Greek women.

It is impossible to draw strong conclusions from the research done to date. However, with the evidence we have so far, experts in the field of cancer and nutrition, such as the AICR, do not deem it necessary to restrict dietary omega-6s.

Recommendations

We recommend that women with breast cancer limit their intake of bad fat, particularly saturated fats and refined oils, such as corn, soybean, canola, safflower and sunflower. It is our opinion that GLA supplementation from borage and evening primrose oil is an effective tool for reducing the risk of breast cancer. The table, Selected Fatty Acid Composition of Common Omega-6 Oils, highlights how different the content of various fatty acids can be in oils commonly lumped together as "omega-6."

There is no evidence to suggest that linoleic acid intake affects the risk of breast cancer in healthy women. However, we do caution that the typical North American diet contains an excess of linoleic acid from refined oils, as mentioned above, which may lead to an overall imbalance of essential fatty acids, in the body. It is a healthy practice for all people to increase the intake of other fatty acids, such as GLA and the omega-3s. This can be achieved through a combination of food sources and the use of supplement oils, such as borage, evening primrose, black currant, flax and fish.

Misconception 5: Flax Oil Causes Prostate Cancer

Consumers and media people are hearing that flax oil can cause prostate cancer, but flax oil is the richest source of ALA, which has many health benefits. How can flax have such positive health effects and such harmful ones?

Udo Erasmus, author of *Fats That Heal, Fats That Kill*, gives a very detailed discussion of this issue on his website, www.udoerasmus.com. He feels that the relationship between ALA and prostate cancer is not as simple and straight forward as some organizations like the Prostate Forum would have us believe. The Prostate Forum recommends against the use of flax oil by men with prostate cancer because flax oil is the richest source of ALA. Udo feels there are many factors contributing to the development of prostate cancer. In fact, authors of published studies have been clear that the correlation of ALA with increased prostate cancer is not proof that ALA causes prostate cancer, and point out that the mechanisms involved in this finding remain unknown. We are going to give you an overview of some of this research.

ALA and Prostate Cancer – Link or No Link?

Data from the Health Professionals follow-up study, a group of about 51,500 American men age 40 to 75 years, was examined. These people filled a food frequency questionnaire in 1986. In 1988 and 1990, the food frequency questionnaire was sent to these people again to document new cases of various diseases. Of these people, 300 new cases of prostate cancer were diagnosed. Of these 300 patients, 126 men had advanced-stage cancer of prostate. Various food ingredients consumed by these people were analyzed from their food frequency questionnaire. This method is being used in various studies. The limitation of this

Selected Fatty Acid Composition of Common Omega-6 Oils

Fatty Acids	Corn	Soybean	Canola	Olive	Sunflower	Safflower	Evening Primrose	Black Currant	Borage
Palmitic	10.7 - 16.5	9.7 - 13.3	3.3 - 6.0	7.5 - 20.0	5.0 - 8.0	5.3 - 8.0	6.0 - 10.0	6.0 - 8.0	9.4 - 11.9
Stearic	1.6 - 3.3	3.0 - 5.4	1.1 - 2.5	0.5 - 5.0	2.5 - 7.0	1.9 - 2.9	1.5 - 3.5	1.0 - 2.0	2.6 - 5.0
Oleic	24.6 - 42.2	17.7 - 25.1	52.0 - 66.9	55.0 - 83.0	13.0 - 40.0	8.4 - 21.3	5.0 - 12.0	9.0 - 13.0	14.6 - 21.3
Linoleic	39.4 - 60.4	49.8 - 57.1	16.1 - 24.8	3.5 - 27.0	40.0 - 74.0	67.8 - 83.2	65.0 - 80.0	45.0 - 50.0	36.5 - 40.1
Gamma Linolenic	0	0	0	0	0	0	8.0 - 14.0	14.0 - 20.0	17.1 - 25.4

This table illustrates that, when it comes to omega-6 oils, not all are created equal.

method is that the changes in dietary habit are not recorded, which may have a significant impact on the outcome.

In this study there was a relationship between total fat intake and advanced stage prostate cancer, and the relationship was due primarily to animal fat (from red meat) and not vegetable fat. Red meat had the strongest positive association with advanced stage prostate cancer, and ALA had a positive relationship as well. However, red meat is a rich source of ALA in the North American diet. But ALA is not the only factor that can be directly associated with prostate cancer. Other interactions between various nutrients and changes taking place in the red meat during cooking were not discussed and yet they are potential causes.

As we discussed in Chapter 8, well-done meat produces heterocyclic amines that may be linked to increased cancer risk. Also researchers need to take into consideration the oxidation of fats during cooking. Because ALA is a polyunsaturated fatty acid that is highly unstable in the presence of oxygen and heat, during cooking of the meat, the ALA may become altered and become cancer causing. Red meat is a rich source of zinc, calcium and iron, oxidants that may enhance the rate at which ALA is damaged and oxidized, thus leading to cancer causing effects.

However, other studies have shown no link between ALA and prostate cancer. Researchers from Laval University in Quebec, Canada studied the association between fat intake and prostate cancer survival. Nutritionists interviewed 384 men with prostate cancer on their diet history. The researchers found that men who had a higher saturated fat diet had a three times greater risk of dying from prostate cancer than did the group with the lower saturated fat intake, and found no link between ALA and aggressive cancers.

Balancing The Omegas

We would not recommend that anyone consume only one of the omega family of fats. As we discussed in Chapter 1, a balance of the omega-3 and omega-6 is what is important to prevent and treat disease. As Udo Erasmus points out on his website, flax is very rich in omega-3 and low in omega-6. Exclusive use of flax oil can lead to an omega-6 deficiency within 2–8 months. Eczema, thinning hair, stiff joints and dry eyes are just a few of the symptoms that may be noticed when suffering from an omega-6 deficiency. (See Chapter 1 for more information on EFA deficiencies). As Udo reminds us again, EFAs are required for vital functions in all cells and tissues. We cannot live without them. They must be provided by foods and supplements. The body cannot make them.

Omega-3s Essential For Life

The big question that needs to be answered is, how could substances that are absolutely required for health give you cancer at the same time? It doesn't make sense. Omega-3s, in particular, have a long history of anti-cancer benefits. If they have anti-cancer properties, why are they causing cancer? Essential nutrients, which the body must have for life and for health, cannot easily be both pro-cancer and anti-cancer at the same time. As we learned in Chapter 11, recent research in 2002 has confirmed the healing properties of flaxseed for prostate cancer. Animals with prostate cancer that consumed a flaxseed rich diet had reduced size, aggressiveness and severity of their tumors.

So the question that must be answered is, what other issues are being overlooked when medical professionals (such as those from the Prostate Forum) issue edicts against the use of essential nutrients?

The Cause of the Increase in Prostate Cancer

According to Udo Erasmus, researchers have suggested that several possibilities need to be explored. These include:

1. Oxidation products of ALA formed during cooking of meat. Red meat is rich in iron, which has strong pro-oxidant action that can speed up the damage done to EFAs by light, oxygen, and heat. Because of ALA's far higher fragility, we should expect ALA to be damaged far more extensively than LA. As a result, far more toxicity should come from diets with higher ALA intake in association with pro-oxidants that lead to free radical formation and oxidation products.

2. Damage done to ALA molecules during processing. ALA, the most fragile of essential nutrients, must be considered as a possible cause of increased prostate cancer. As ALA consumption increases, so does the amount of damaged, toxic breakdown products of ALA resulting from careless treatment of this essential nutrient. Unless care is taken to protect ALA from being damaged and thereby being made toxic by light, air, and heat, health problems based on the toxicity of altered molecules of ALA should be expected.

3. Lack of balancing antioxidants, which are found in seeds, but are removed or damaged during processing and cooking practices. Research has consistently shown that increased intake of EFAs increases the need for antioxidants.

4. Free radical formation from fatty acid oxidation in meat. Free radicals damage tissues and cause cancer.

5. ALA-based free radicals (products of processing) that can damage genetic material (DNA) and lead to tumor formation.

6. Too low a ratio of LA to ALA (or too high a ratio of ALA to LA).

7. Alterations in the synthesis of hormones produced from EFAs—too many bad and not enough good being produced.

What Should You Believe?

With conflicting research studies and varying opinions, what should you believe? Just as we would recommend for any disease condition, too much of one substance is not a good thing. It is a balance of all the essential nutrients that is required to maintain good health. We wouldn't recommend getting rid of walnuts, flaxseed oil and other foods that contain omega-3s since a healthy diet containing these foods has been linked to reductions in heart disease risk, conditions which kill more people than any other disease, including cancer.

If you are someone who has prostate cancer, or who is at increased risk for developing prostate cancer, you will want to limit your intake of flax oil by itself. Be sure to have a varied diet, containing both omega-6 and omega-3, that is lower in saturated fat. As you can see by the list of seven "other considerations" listed above, there are other factors to take into account other than just ALA intake. Increasing your antioxidant consumption to prevent against free radical damage is very important. We agree with research and Udo Erasmus that ALA is essential for life and for health.

Misconception 6:
Evening Primrose Oil Is Contraindicated for Pregnancy

Like numerous other herbs and dietary supplements, safety data in pregnancy is often lacking. More women are starting to use complementary therapies to treat many of their conditions due to lack of effect from their conventional treatment options. But women who start taking these supplements want to know if they are safe in the case of pregnancy. Midwives have been recommending evening primrose oil for years as a natural way to promote cervical ripening in pregnancy (an unripe cervix may be responsible for prolonging labor).

Prostaglandins (hormones created from essential fats) are believed to play a major role in the cervical ripening process.

As we have learned throughout the book, evening primrose oil is a source of GLA, which is responsible for the production of beneficial prostaglandins. For this reason, evening primrose oil has been recommended in the alternative midwifery literature as an option to prevent long labor and post-date pregnancy. However, other studies have shown conflicting results in that evening primrose oil did not shorten gestation or decrease the overall length of labor. Furthermore, one study found that evening primrose oil may increase the risk of complications, including incidence of ruptured membranes, oxytocin augmentation, arrest of descent (when the baby does not move down the birth canal) and vacuum extraction (when a vacuum needs to be used to help move the baby down the birth canal because the birth is not progressing)

It is well known that essential fatty acids are critical for the proper development of the mammary gland, placenta and uterus during pregnancy, and, most importantly, for development of the fetus. Numerous research publications have expressed the importance for pregnant women to increase their consumption of polyunsaturated fatty acids, such as GLA, arachidonic acid, and DHA. This is because the EFAs are passed via the placenta to the fetus for their development. As well, lactating women require additional EFAs to meet the increased requirements of the infants, and deficiencies of omega-6s can result in cradle cap in infants. Human breast milk fatty acid composition depends largely upon the mother's diet, and a diet deficient in omega-6 fatty acids, such as GLA, will result in deficient breast milk.

Safety data, especially during pregnancy and lactation, is largely lacking because research is not performed on pregnant and nursing moms for many herbal supplements and drugs. The importance of GLA for pregnancy and infant development is undisputed.

Misconception 7:
Is Evening Primrose Oil Superior to Borage Oil?
This issue made its appearance when borage oil first started to be known as a competitive GLA product to evening primrose oil. Borage oil contains between 20–24% GLA, and evening primrose oil contains between 8–10% GLA. Both have been extensively studied as therapeutic agents in numerous conditions. Controversy has been generated by some evening primrose oil companies over the

clinical efficacy of evening primrose oil versus borage oil. Their argument is that although borage oil contains a higher amount of total GLA, it is not as readily converted in the body and therefore is less effective.

One other study conducted at the Texas A&M University showed that "Evening primrose oil supports the production of good prostaglandins and borage oil does not." This statement was a complete misrepresentation of the results of other research; in fact, borage oil produces very favorable effects on prostaglandin synthesis. This misquote was based on research conducted by Fan and Chapkin and published in the *Journal of Nutrition*.

In this study, after mice were fed diets containing either corn oil, borage oil, evening primrose oil or borage and fish oil, it was found that the highest ratio of PGE1/PGE2 was found following the borage oil diets containing the highest levels of GLA. They concluded that feeding GLA-rich oils, such as borage and evening primrose oil, will increase the production of beneficial prostaglandins such as PGE1.

Other arguments have been based on the premise that in evening primrose oil the GLA is found in the sn-1 and sn-3 position on the triglyceride molecule (natural form that fats are found in the diet) where it is most available, whereas in borage it is found primarily in the sn-2. Since the first publication of this research, it has largely been refuted and, if anything, it is considered that the fatty acid in sn-2 position (i.e., GLA in borage) is more bioavailable.

In one study published in the *American Journal of Clinical Nutrition* in 1995, they examined the absorption of infant formulas containing different concentrations of fat. Infants fed triglycerides that are predominantly in the sn-2 position (as is with borage) rather than the sn-1,3 position (as is with evening primrose oil) had enhanced absorption.

Other researchers have concluded that GLA is GLA regardless of the dietary source. The effect of different levels and sources of GLA (evening primrose oil and borage) have found that increases in tissue GLA and PGE1 production in rats were the same in both the borage and evening primrose oil enriched diets. The authors of this study concluded that borage oil and evening primrose oil are identical in regard to their absorption and metabolism of GLA. It is the amount of GLA independent of the source that results in higher levels of tissue GLA and PGE1 synthesis.

It can be concluded that GLA is GLA regardless of the source, and clinical research with both evening primrose and borage oils has yielded positive results in the treatment of rheumatoid arthritis, eczema, hypertension, and diabetes.

PART II

Fact 1:
Toxins in Evening Primrose Oil? Don't Worry

Environmental toxins are everywhere. At work, in the air, in the water we drink, and in the food we eat. We may not be able to get rid of all environmental contaminants, but we can certainly minimize our exposure. One such group of environmental toxins are known as polycyclic aromatic hydrocarbons (PAHs), which have been shown to exhibit potentially cancer-causing effects and are linked to certain cancers, including breast cancer in animals and humans.

Everyone has some exposure to PAHs on a daily basis. PAHs are a group of compounds most commonly derived from burning of hydrocarbon fuels (particularly diesel oil). The main sources of exposure are from breathing in PAHs that are found in second-hand smoke, traffic exhaust and other contaminated air. Studies have shown that cigarette smoking increases personal exposure to PAHs by thirty-fold. Other sources of PAHs in our everyday life may come from the food we eat that is grown in contaminated soil. Charbroiled meat, fish and smoked cheeses also have higher levels of PAHs. Water can become contaminated with PAHs from runoff, and waste water in certain industrial areas, for example, aluminum smelting. Water treatment plants are able to reduce the content of PAHs in the water we drink, but untreated water may contain up to five times the amount of PAHs found in refined water.

Concern has been generated in Europe over the presence of PAHs in evening primrose oil. Following routine product sampling tests for the presence of environmental contaminants in olive oil and fish oil, the Food Safety Authority of Ireland (FSAI) in 2002 conducted the same tests on evening primrose oil capsules for the presence of one of the PAHs, benzo (a) pyrene levels. The FSAI has received reports that two of the evening primrose oil brands tested had exceeded the guideline limits (2μg/kg) for the presence of benzo (a) pyrene. In view of the results, the FSAI is proposing a survey of all evening primrose oil capsules to determine the extent of the problem. The risk of carcinogenesis to consumers is very small at the levels of benzo (a) pyrene found in the evening primrose oil capsules, but the FSAI feels that this issue should not be ignored.

The History of PAHs in Evening Primrose Oil

PAHs first came to the attention of the edible oil industry a few years ago when high levels (3,000 µg/kg) were discovered in crude coconut oil, and their source was traced back to the use of diesel to dry the raw copra from which the oil is then extracted. The industry dealt with this by developing specific refining procedures to remove PAH, and through its trade association adopted a set of standards, defining maximum acceptable limits for these compounds in edible oils. Statutory limits have not been set, although there is now a European Union recommended guideline limit of 2 µg/kg maximum.

Since then PAHs have also been found in a range of other vegetable oils (rapeseed, sunflower, olive), although not at the levels identified in coconut oil, and it has become apparent that although diesel fired seed dryers are the most common source, general environmental contamination can also be responsible.

Current Proposed Limits

In the 1990s the following maximum levels for PAH in refined oils were adopted by the industry:

Total PAH	less than 25 ppb
Heavy PAH	less than 5 ppb
Benzo-a-pyrene	less than 1 ppb

The above limits were accepted as a code of conduct by the European trade association for edible oil producers (Fediol). However, it was recognized that the toxicity of the individual PAH varied, and so a system of calculating toxic equivalence based on the toxicity of benzo-a-pyrene was developed.

In 1999, Unilever proposed maximum limits of 2 µg/kg BaP equivalents and 1 µg/kg BaP. B-a-P equivalence was derived from a calculation based upon factoring the content of the six individual PAHs considered most carcinogenic.

Later, major European infant formula manufacturers proposed for their specific application maximum limits of 1.0 µg/kg BaP equivalents and 0.5 µg/kg BaP. Their formulation of equivalence was based upon the content of 10 individual PAH compounds.

Levels of PAH in evening primrose oils from all sources for several years have been analyzed by one major European supplier, of which they made the following conclusions:

- Results vary considerably from batch to batch and are unrelated to geographic origin.

- Significantly high levels of PAHs have been found in unrefined oils.

- PAHs do not result from the use of solvent extraction and are as likely to be found in cold pressed oils as solvent extracted.

This European supplier modified their refining procedures in 2000 to ensure removal of heavy PAHs. Over the past two years they have analyzed a total of 65 batches of oil, and since the introduction of the revised refining procedures, all batches of refined evening primrose oil have met the most stringent specifications outlined above. Crude or virgin oils, however, do continue to carry a risk of significant levels of contamination with PAHs: approximately 30% of crude oils would fall outside the limits proposed by the FSAI.

Both unrefined and conventionally refined oils can exhibit levels of PAH above that specified by the FSAI. Refining, according to certain procedures, ensures removal of PAH and compliance with all guidelines and specifications. However, not all manufacturers refine their oil to these specifications; there-fore, the same quality cannot be guaranteed for all suppliers.

Should You Be Concerned about PAHs in EPO?

No! Although the presence of PAHs in evening primrose oil is being investigated by the FSAI, it is important to remember that evening primrose oil has been used for decades with no adverse or toxic effects recorded. We are exposed to more PAHs from daily life in breathing automobile exhaust and consuming smoked meats and cheese than we would be from consuming evening primrose oil.

While animal studies have shown that PAHs can induce breast cancer, the types of PAHs used in these studies are mostly individual synthetic chemicals used only in laboratory experiment animals. Humans are not exposed to the same type of synthetic PAHs, and instead have exposure to a mixture of PAHs (which are thought to be less toxic) and environmental toxins, which have different effects on the body. As mentioned, there are numerous sources of PAHs that we are exposed to on a daily basis. For example, if you walk to work, you may be exposed to PAHs from the exhaust of the car passing by you.

We should not avoid evening primrose oil because of the potential presence of PAHs, although it is important to look for evening primrose oil that has been refined to remove environmental contaminants, such as PAHs. The fact still remains that evening primrose oil is a valuable source of the omega-6 fatty acid GLA that has numerous health benefits, and should be incorporated into our daily diet.

Fact 2:
Fish Oil Quality – Dioxins, PCBs and Heavy Metals

In 2002, FSAI released details of a study on the potential dioxin contamination of fish and fish oil capsules. Since 1999 there has been increased awareness in the European Union of the potential dangers posed by dioxins, furans and PCBs. The European Commission has published legislation to achieve a reduction in exposure to dioxins and PCBs.

The FSAI conducted a study in response to the pending levels set by the European Union to examine how dioxins in fish and fish oil capsules on the Irish market compared to this new maximum limit. The results of the study show that the levels of dioxins in Irish farmed trout and salmon are well below the maximum levels set by the European Union. Although some fish oil and fish liver oil capsules were found to exceed maximum limits, the FSAI has stated the levels of dioxins detected pose no health risk if consumers use the supplements by following the directions on the labels.

The Council for Responsible Nutrition, which is the science-based trade association for the dietary supplement industry, has published a voluntary monograph for suppliers and manufacturers that establishes more stringent quality standards for fish oils similar to the FSAI. The European Union is far more advanced over North America when it comes to testing for dioxins, PCBs and other contaminants.

Key Group of Environmental Toxins

Environmental toxins include many different substances. Some of these are designed to be toxic, such as herbicides and pesticides, while others are by-products from industry, including dioxins.

Environmental toxins make their way into the air or water where they may be transported long distances. They are incorporated into the fat of small animals low in the food chain. Today environmental toxins are mostly found in animal fats, including fish, exposing us to minute amounts of these substances from milk, meat, fish and oils. Because of this process, all types of fish contain environmental toxins that are accumulated through their lives. Consumption of dioxins above safe levels over a lifetime may result in an increased risk of cancer. However, the fish oil industry is aware of the risk associated with toxins and has procedures in place to ensure their products are safe for human consumption.

Through modern technology, environmental toxin levels are reduced during the refining of oils by temperature as well as specific processing steps. The levels in the final product are monitored to ensure that they are within acceptable ranges.

Dioxins and furans naturally occur in the environment and originate from various sources, including waste incinerators, waste water from the pulp and paper industry and as by-products of some industrial processes. Dioxins include 75 polychlorinated dibenzo-p-dioxin (PCDD) and 135 polychlorinated dibenzofuran (PCDF) substances. Of these, 17 are toxic in very small amounts. Dioxins are expressed in World Health Organization's (WHO) Toxic Equivalents (TEQ). Maximum levels are 2 pg TEQ/g, set by the European Union as well as the Council for Responsible Nutrition voluntary monograph.

PCBs (polychlorinated biphenyls) have been used for many years in transformers and capacitors. They are not produced today, but substantial amounts still exist in such products as sealed windows and can enter the environment through careless disposal practices. PCB limits include the sum of four individual non-ortho PCBs and eight mono-ortho PCBs and are expressed on a weight/weight basis. Levels for total PCBs are less than 0.09 µg/day set by European Union and Council for Responsible Nutrition.

Heavy metals are naturally occurring elements that are present throughout the environment and in plants and animals. In excess, these heavy metals can lead to potentially harmful health effects. Acceptable levels for heavy metals set by the European Union and the Council for Responsible Nutrition include:

Lead (Pb): Less than 0.1 mg/kg
Cadmium (Cd): Less than 0.1 mg/kg
Mercury (Hg): Less than 0.1 mg/kg
Arsenic (As): Less than 0.1 mg/kg

What Are The Health Risks From Environmental Toxins?

The effects of environmental toxins differ by substance, but the main concerns are effects on the immune system, on reproduction and as a cause of various types of cancer, while the list of conditions believed to be associated with environmental contaminants is extensive. The intensity or severity of the effects depend on many factors—the quantity of toxin someone has been exposed to, how long the exposure lasts, exposure frequency and the stage of life at which it occurs.

Testing and Analysis

When choosing a fish oil supplement, it is important to purchase only those that have been tested for dioxins, PCBs and heavy metals, in order to reduce your exposure to these potentially toxic compounds. The health food retailer you deal with should have access to certificates of analysis that lists these quality standards.

In the last chapter we provide you with the knowledge and the key questions to ask your healthfood store retailer when choosing a quality supplement.

Chapter 13

WHAT TO LOOK FOR IN A QUALITY EFA PRODUCT

N ow that you know all about the health benefits of EFAs, we want to make sure that you know how to choose a quality EFA product. The dietary supplement industry has been accused of not supplying quality products, not selling what the label claims to be selling, and offering non-efficacious products. However, this charge is not valid, as Kelley C. Fitzpatrick, President of the Saskatchewan Nutraceutical Network, explains:

Quality is important. In an industry that must answer to consumers, we are witnessing a greater commitment to the marketing of trustworthy products.

In addition to scientific efforts to validate the positive health effects of fats and oils, the industry has committed itself to excel in the area of high quality assurance. Over the almost twenty years that I have been involved in fats and oils research and communication activities, I have seen an evolution within the manufacturing sector to higher and higher standards of safety and quality control. This includes unique vertical integration, whereby every aspect of the supply chain (from sourcing of seed to processing through distribution and responsible marketing) is carefully monitored and controlled. The sophistication of some companies in this regard is truly extraordinary; even involving the ability to offer traceability of all seed procured back to the original location of its production at the farm level.

Strict testing of seed is undertaken to assure that raw materials are of the cleanest and purest possible. Some companies are able to offer processing that is conducted under pharmaceutical-level good manufacturing practices (GMPs), which require much more stringent quality standards, controls and operating procedures than food-level GMP. Third party laboratories are often used to test for a variety of quality parameters, the results of which are documented on the "Certificate of Analysis" that should accompany every shipment of product. Testing for purity and quality is a given in the fats and oils industry and great improvements have been made in analytical methods to detect both wanted and unwanted constituents. Many of the current methods now utilized have become so sophisticated that near "trace" levels of minor compounds can now be detected and recorded.

In my role as President of the Saskatchewan Nutraceutical Network, I have given over 200 invited presentations nationally and internationally to all groups interested in natural health products, from consumers through to retailers as well as scientists and the healthcare community. I am proud to speak on the health benefits of specialty fatty acids as I am confident in the ability of the industry to provide consumers with high quality, safe and very effective products. It is also gratifying, as a nutritionist who is looked upon to provide health-related recommendations, to have witnessed the evolution of the industry and the tremendous burst of science and clinical trials which has accompanied this growth.

In 1998, the SNN was established, the first fully funded and operational information resource for the nutraceutical and functional food sector in Canada. The SNN is the only such industry-focused organization in the country. Kelley has been an invited speaker in the areas of nutrition, food science and processing, oilseed genetics, nutraceuticals and functional foods at a variety of provincial, national and international events.

Consumer education is extremely important in determining how to pick out the best products on the health food store shelf. We want to ensure that you are supplementing your diet with EFAs that have gone through rigorous quality assurance tests, have been manufactured according to the methods we have discussed in this book and are free of toxins such as PCBs, dioxins and heavy metals. There are many excellent suppliers of EFAs in both Canada and in the U.S. and we have provided the brand names and suppliers of a few of those companies at the end of the book. Knowledge is the key to choosing quality EFAs.

NOT ALL FLAX IS CREATED EQUAL

Not all flax is equal in terms of its quality, but fortunately most health food retailers have the knowledge to answer questions related to the quality of flax. Consumers should utilize the expertise and value a health food store staff can bring.

Flax Quality Made Easy

There are many different things to consider when choosing a quality flax product, including where and how it is grown, processed and stored, whether it has organic certification, and what quality control measures have been taken to ensure freshness and quality. The following are some of the questions that could be asked of the health food retailer when purchasing flax.

Where is this flax grown?

The Canadian prairies offer a pristine growing environment for such oilseed crops as flax. The cooler northern climate results in higher levels of the beneficial omega-3, alpha-linolenic acid (ALA). ALA should be tested on every lot of flax and should then be reported on the certificate of analysis. When a customer specifies they want 55% ALA in their flax oil, they can be assured they are getting that level by what is reported on the certificate of analysis. Temperature, moisture conditions and planting and harvest times can all affect quality.

How were the flaxseeds selected?

Physical seed examination is very important in selecting the highest quality seed. Examining the seed purity identifies contaminants, such as wrong plant species, including wild oat seeds, mustard seeds and extraneous material like chaff. The seed should be cleaned to a minimum of 99% purity prior to use. The cleaned seed is conditioned by gently warming it. The conditioning dries the seed to ensure optimal moisture levels are attained prior to the storage of seed.

Is this flaxseed oil cold-pressed?

The terms cold-pressed and expeller-pressed can be used interchangeably. Expeller pressing is a mechanical process that does not utilize solvents, such as hexane or other harsh chemicals, or high levels of external heat (hence the term "cold" pressed). This results in a higher quality, more stable oil. Natural expeller pressing is an important criterion for judging flax quality.

What affects the flavor of the oil?

Generally, the more 'green' the flax oil tastes, the less processed and refined the oil is. There are many compounds in flaxseed that may contribute to the oil flavor, including phenolic compounds and free fatty acids. The quality of the flaxseed may also affect the desired taste of the finished oil. Seeds that have been frozen, cracked and diseased or were improperly stored may also negatively affect the flavor of the oil.

Is this flax certified organic?

Organically grown refers to farming that does not use chemical pesticides, herbicides and fertilizers which are commonly employed in conventional farming. The farmers employ different agriculture methods for soil fertility, and instead of using chemicals to kill weeds, they rely on crop rotation, cultivation and manure spreading. Certified organic really stands for no synthetic pesticides, herbicides, no chemical fertilizers and no irradiation.

There are numerous organic certifying bodies that ensure every step in the planting, growing, processing, storing, packaging and transporting of organic flax is done in accordance with organic standards. A laboratory can't tell whether or not a product is organic, so documenting every step is essential. This organic certification "paper trail" proves that the flax has met all the standards of the certifying organization.

According to the National Organics Program in the U.S., all packaged goods claiming to be organic must meet strict standards. Under their standards, labeling of foods or supplements are based on a specific definition of the percentage of ingredients that are organic. A manufacturer labeling their product as "organic" when it only contains 25% organic ingredients will be in violation of this regulation that was passed in October of 2002.

If you see the following organic claims on a flax label, you can be assured that the product meets the following criteria:

100% Organic – must contain 100% organically produced ingredients. This category would include milled flaxseed and defatted ground flaxseed (meal).

Organic – must contain not less than 95% organically-produced raw or processed agricultural products. Any remaining product ingredients must be organically produced, unless not commercially available in organic form. Nonagricultural substances or non-organically produced agricultural products produced in accordance with the National List of acceptable materials are also allowed in this category. Bottled organic flax oil would be included in this category because the antioxidant used is non-organic.

Made with Organic – must contain at least 70% organically-produced ingredients. This category would include organic flaxseed oil softgels, as the ingredients utilized in the manufacture of the shell are not available organically at this time.

Can this flax be traced?

What this refers to is tracing the flaxseed back to the original farm gate, which is often referred to as vertical integration. With this system the flax supplier controls every step of the process from seed selection, planting the seed, harvest, storage, processing and then ultimately selling to the end consumer. Any supplier who can offer a traceability system shows a real commitment to a quality end product. This traceability aspect for suppliers will help them in respect to the new "bioterrorism" legislation recently implemented in the U.S. This new law, inspired by terrorism, will change the way that food companies are regulated.

Was this flax processed in a GMP-certified facility?

Good manufacturing practices (GMPs) certification is given to manufacturers by Health Canada, or by the FDA in the U.S. after stringent quality checks and inspections are performed on the processing and manufacturing facility. GMPs are measures that ensure an effective overall approach to product quality control and risk management. They do so by setting appropriate standards and practices regarding product testing, manufacturing, storage, handling and distribution. The goal of GMPs is to provide safe, quality products. GMP certification gives the consumer confidence in the manufacturing facility, which ultimately affects the quality of the end product. GMP processing is important for all EFA oils, including fish, borage and evening primrose.

Is this flax genetically-modified?

A genetically-modified strain of flax has been developed, so it is important to confirm that the flax being purchased is truly not genetically-modified. A test developed by the Saskatchewan Research Council (SRC) in Canada can determine the genetically-modified status of flax. The test is done using a probe that has DNA markers from the genetically modified flax. The test can confirm that these DNA markers are not present in the non-genetically modified variety. Very few suppliers utilize DNA testing, so being knowledgeable about the flax supplier will confirm whether or not it can be scientifically proven that the flax variety is truly non-genetically modified.

Has this flax been tested for quality parameters?
A third party laboratory should be testing flax for a variety of quality parameters, to determine microbial levels, the presence or absence of pesticides, herbicides and heavy metals, which are natural elements that exist in the environment and are commonly found in plants and animals. Peroxide value is tested as an indicator of oil freshness and quality. Acceptable levels are below 10 meq/kg. High peroxide values are an indicator of oxidation. Acid value as a measure of free fatty acids in the oil is tested and acceptable levels should be below 4 mg KOH/g. Acid value levels higher than this are an indication of poor quality oil with a high content of free fatty acids being undesirable for plant and marine based oils.

Anisidine levels indicate secondary oxidation products, including ketones and aldehydes, that are undesirable. Someone purchasing oil with a high anisidine level should question what kind of processing the oil has been subjected to, as high levels usually indicate harsh or excessive processing. For plant-based oils, such as borage, evening primrose and flax, guidelines/recommendations for anisidine levels do not exist; however, some suppliers will test for anisidine as sort of a "double check" for oxidation even though peroxide may have already been tested. Ideal levels are generally zero to five. Heavy metals are tested with acceptable levels being less than 10 ppm. Pesticide and herbicide levels are also tested with acceptable levels ranging from 0.05–2 ppm.

The test results are reported in a certificate of analysis that should be sent to the manufacturer with every shipment for their records. Testing for these quality control measures ensures a more stable product with a longer shelf life and ensures that no harmful toxins are present. The same quality control tests mentioned above are also performed on borage and evening primrose oil.

Should my flaxseed be in a vacuum-sealed pack?
Because of the difficulty of digesting whole flax, it is often milled before packaging. Milled flaxseeds should be vacuum-sealed to prevent exposure to oxygen (oxygen

will cause the oil in the seed to turn rancid). The package should have a zip-lock closure so it can be resealed after opening to preserve the flavor and nutritional components. You can also keep milled flaxseed in the refrigerator or freezer in between use to slow down the oxidation.

Can I buy Kosher Certified Flax?

Yes! The Hebrew word kosher means fit or proper as it is related to dietary (kosher) laws. Kosher-certified foods are important for the Jewish community, and this is a marker showing the food has been permitted or accepted by a rabbi. Although the term Kosher dates back thousands of years for traditional foods, it has come to be considered an indicator of quality for products sold in health food stores. Many consumers look for the kosher seal of approval for this reason.

How Well Do You Know Your Fish Oil?

Fish oil has a poor reputation among consumers. You may have heard your parents describe horror stories about when they were kids and had to take teaspoons of cod liver oil that tasted terrible; there is the burping and aftertaste experienced; and the latest news on mercury poisoning and dioxins in the fish oil supply is disturbing. Like other EFA sources, it is extremely important to take a high quality fish oil product to ensure you aren't getting more than you bargained for. The following will answer your questions to ensure you can select a high quality fish oil.

Where does fish oil originate?

That depends on the type of fish oil you are buying! Norway is the world's largest exporter of salmon and trout. Atlantic salmon is actually the driving force behind the Norwegian aquaculture (fish farming) industry and is exported to more than 100 countries. Cod liver oil also comes from cod fish caught in the Atlantic; however, today there is scarcely enough cod available to meet the demand of the world market. Different strategies to deal with this shortage are being addressed by the Norwegian aquaculture industry.

Chances are if you are taking salmon or cod liver oil supplement, it originated in the cold waters of the Atlantic Ocean. Other fish oils, such as those derived from sardines, anchovies, and mackerel, are usually caught off the coast of Chile and Peru in the cold, deep waters of the South Pacific Ocean.

There are only a few high quality fish oil manufacturers in the world, and one of them is located in Norway. They process fish that is caught either in the Atlantic or South Pacific, and is then sold into the health and nutrition industry all around the world.

How is fish oil processed?

Once the fish is caught, it goes through a process called rendering, in which the oil is gently pressed from the fish body. Once the oil is obtained, it goes through processing techniques known as neutralization and winterization. In these steps you remove water-soluble components like free fatty acids, the majority of the saturated fatty acid and other contaminants. The oil is then bleached to reduce the odor, taste and color.

The final stage the oil will go through is a purifying process known as deodorization and/or distillation. This can either be done through steam or through vacuum/molecular distillation techniques. Either method will help ensure that contaminants, such as PCBs, dioxins and other volatile components like pesticides, are removed from the fish oil.

Distillation is a process of heating a liquid, in this case fish oil, until its more volatile components pass into the vapor phase, and then cooling the vapor to recover the constituents in liquid form. Distillation separates several components in a mixture by taking advantage of their different volatilities or the separation of volatile materials from non-volatile materials. The principle objective is to obtain more volatile constituents in pure form.

Deodorization is a process in which steam is passed into the mixture that is to be deodorized. The liquid will then vaporize. Such a mixture always boils at a temperature lower than that of either constituent; and the percentage of each constituent in the vapor depends only on its vapor pressure at this temperature.

Deodorization and distillation removes substances at temperatures below their normal boiling points because of the reduction of pressure, called a vacuum. Air is evacuated from the apparatus with a vacuum pump, and the vacuum formed causes the materials being heated to boil at a temperature lower than they would under normal atmospheric pressure. The greater the degree of vacuum, the lower the distillation temperature.

In molecular distillation the substance is placed on a plate in an evacuated space and heated. The condenser is a cold plate, placed as close to the first as possible. Most of the material passes across the space between the two plates, and therefore very little is lost. Molecular distillation is as effective as steam distillation; however, the only real difference is the cost of the final product, and generally fish oils distilled with molecular distillation are more costly.

After distillation, the fish oil has additional antioxidants, vitamins and flavor added to it. It will then be packaged under the presence of a nitrogen blanket to ensure that no oxygen is present to cause the oil to go rancid. This is an extremely important stage as fish oil contains high levels of long chain omega-3 fatty acids that are extremely sensitive to oxygen.

What quality assurance tests are usually performed on fish oil?
As discussed in Chapter 12, fish oils have been found to contain environmental toxins, including PCBs, dioxins, as well as heavy metals. If the processing methods described above are not employed, for example if the oil is not distilled properly, then there is a chance that the fish oil may contain fairly high levels of these contaminants. Therefore, to be on the safe side, and to prove the absence of these toxins, most manufacturers test their fish oil for the presence of dioxins, PCBs and heavy metals.

These test results get reported on a certificate of analysis, which is then sent to the manufacturer as a confirmation that the oil has been tested and that the levels of heavy metals and toxins meet certain guidelines that have been established for the fish oil industry.

The following are tests that may be performed on fish oil:

Acid Value is a measure of the free fatty acids in the oil. Normally fatty acids are found in the triglyceride form, however during processing, there is a possibility that the fatty acids may get hydrolyzed into what is known as free fatty acid form. The higher the acid value found, the higher the level of free fatty acids in the oil, which corresponds into decreased oil quality. The Council for Responsible Nutrition's omega-3 monograph has recommended acid value to be less than 3 mg KOH/g (measured in potassium hydroxide per gram).

Peroxide Value (PV) is an important indicator of quality oil and freshness. If the oil has been exposed to oxygen, the peroxide value will go up as an indication of rancidity. The Council for Responsible Nutrition recommends PV to be less than 5 meq/kg (measured in milli equivalents per kilogram).

Anisidine Value (AV) is another important indicator of oil quality, and it measures secondary oxidation products. The Council for Responsible Nutrition recommends AV be less than 20.

TOTOX is the result of a calculation that takes (2 x PV) + AV. The purpose of this measure is to avoid selling fish oil that has the maximum possible quantity for both the PV and the AV. The Council for Responsible Nutrition believes that a product with maximized levels for both measures will be unacceptably oxidized. The TOTOX measure provides some flexibility with either PV or AV, yet limits total oxidation. The Council for Responsible Nutrition recommends TOTOX to be below 26.

Dioxins, naturally occur in the environment and originate from various sources, including waste incinerators, waste water from the pulp and paper industry and as by-products of some industrial processes. Dioxins include the sum of 75 poly-chlorinated di-benzo-p-dioxin (PCDD) and 135 polychlorinated di-benzofuran (PCDF) substances. Of these, 17 are toxic in very small amounts. Dioxins are expressed in World Health Organization's (WHO) Toxic Equivalents Factors (TEQ). Maximum levels are 2 pg TEQ/g as set by the European Union and the Council for Responsible Nutrition.

PCBs have been used for many years in transformers and capacitors. They are not produced today, but substantial amounts still exist in such products as sealed windows and can enter the environment through careless disposal practices. PCB limits include the sum of four individual non-ortho PCBs and eight mono-ortho PCBs and are expressed on a weight/weight basis. Levels for total polychlorinated biphenyls (PCBs) are less than 0.09 μg/day as set by Council for Responsible Nutrition.

Heavy Metals are naturally occurring elements that are present throughout the environment and in plants and animals. In excess these heavy metals can lead to potentially harmful health effects. Acceptable levels for heavy metals in fish oil set by European Union and Council for Responsible Nutrition include:

Lead (Pb): Less than 0.1 mg/kg
Cadmium (Cd): Less than 0.1 mg/kg
Mercury (Hg): Less than 0.1 mg/kg
Arsenic (As): Less than 0.1 mg/kg

The media has paid considerable attention to mercury levels in fish oil and the risk of mercury poisoning from consumption of fish. The U.S. Environmental Protection Agency (EPA) and the Food and Drug Administration (FDA) has released statements recommending that pregnant women, nursing mothers and young children limit their fish consumption to one meal per week and that mercury levels should be less than 1 part per million (the recommendations of the Council for Responsible Nutrition are below this level). This would be the equivalent of 6 ounces of cooked fish, and 8 ounces of uncooked fish per week. This recommendation was made to raise the awareness of the potential harm that high levels of methyl mercury can cause to a baby's developing brain and nervous system.

It is important to note that not all types of fish contain high levels of mercury. Tilefish, swordfish, king mackerel and shark (tuna is also very suspect) tend to be the largest, longest living kind of fish, with the greatest exposure to mercury. Despite cautions about these four fish, the FDA maintains their position that seafood is an important part of a balanced diet and that eating a variety of fish, including shellfish, and smaller ocean fish will not pose the same risk.

This is why fish oil supplements are ideal for maintaining your levels of the healthy omega-3s EPA and DHA. Fish oil supplements generally consist of oil from cod, salmon, tuna, sardines, mackerel and anchovies—none of which are listed in the FDA's warning. Also, what most people don't realize is that methyl mercury is stored in the muscle of the fish, rather than the fat, significantly reducing the amount of mercury found in fish oil supplements as compared to whole fish.

With the Council for Responsible Nutrition's recommendations for heavy metal testing, it is important to find a supplier that tests for these heavy metals, allowing you to take fish oil supplements safely, without the risk of contamination.

What is the difference between "pure" and blended fish oil products?
Buyers beware! It is very common for fish oil manufacturers to label their product as pure salmon oil 18/12, or something to make the consumer believe that they are getting a pure product at the level of EPA and DHA described. However, what needs to be understood is that each fish oil source contains different levels of natural EPA and DHA. For example, what is meant by 18/12 is that 18% of the oil contains EPA, and 12% contains DHA. This is expressed in the ratio of EPA/DHA.

The only fish oil products that result in a natural level of 18/12 is a blend of mackerel, sardines and anchovies. There is no such thing as salmon 18/12. Salmon's EPA and DHA level is 6/9, meaning 6% EPA and 9% DHA. The content of EPA and DHA varies, but is never as high as 18/12. To achieve a level of 18/12, manufacturers must fortify the salmon with a more concentrated source of EPA and DHA.

Certain fish oil suppliers want to stop the sale of these salmon 18/12 products, as it is misleading to consumers. It is important to recognize that for an oil to contain 18% EPA and 12% DHA, you will not likely be getting salmon oil, and it will be a blend of other fish oils. When purchasing pure salmon oil, make sure you look for 6% EPA and 9% DHA.

How does concentrate processing differ from regular fish oil?
As we discussed in the processing section for regular fish oil, concentrates are processed in much the same way, except they have additional distillation steps added for concentrating the EPA and DHA. Just as for regular fish oil, it is important that concentrates are packaged under nitrogen to ensure the absence of oxygen. Marine oil concentrates will be required to meet the same quality assurance measures that regular fish oil does.

Borage Oil – Quality Counts

Just as with flax oil, borage oil should be subjected to many of the same procedures and quality control measures. Borage cultivation has traditionally centered in northern Europe on small farms; however, as with flax, the Canadian prairies offer unique growing environments friendly to borage plant growth. The flowers of the borage plant are star shaped and bright blue.

Commercial seed production of borage presents unique challenges because of seed shattering, the indeterminate vegetative growth habit, the lack of concentrated flowering and seed set, and the non-uniform seed maturation. Although considerable natural variation exists within the species, no plants with a non-shattering habit have been identified. Plant breeding research is needed to overcome production problems, especially those related to seed shattering.

What happens to the borage seed after harvest?
Following harvesting the seed is dried to less than 10% moisture, followed by cleaning of the seed and removal of impurities prior to processing. Physical seed examination is very important in selecting the highest quality seed. Examining the seed purity identifies contaminants, such as wrong plant species, including wild oat seeds, mustard seeds and extraneous material like chaff. In preparing the oil, the borage seed is selected and then dried. Drying of the seed ensures optimal moisture levels for storage.

How is borage oil processed?

In the manufacturing process for borage, consistent quality, safety and stability can be maintained or assured by establishing, documenting and monitoring critical control points through each process, as in GMP. Proper documentation systems should be in place to ensure seed traceability.

Oil can be extracted by following standard techniques of solvent extraction or expeller/cold press, although cold-pressed borage oil is more desirable in the health and nutrition industry.

Cold Press/Expeller Pressed: In this process, the seeds are gently warmed and pressed using a screw press. The pressure built in the press expresses the oil, which is collected in nitrogen-purged tanks. The presses are maintained under nitrogen atmosphere to protect the oil from oxidation. The crude oil is filtered and collected in a nitrogen purged stainless steel storage tank. Processing can be used to remove the volatile components, including free fatty acids and oxidation products.

Solvent Extraction: This is not the kind of oil processing we recommend. This is the standard process for toxic oils sold in your grocery store shelf. In this process the seeds are cracked using a screw press/roller mill. The cracked seeds are then extracted with food grade solvent (hexane/alcohol) in a sealed container to prevent evaporation of solvent into the atmosphere. The oil/solvent mixture is then transferred to a distillation still where the solvent is removed under reduced pressure. The process known as deodorization further purifies the oil where the volatile components (oxidation products, free fatty acids, and traces of solvents) are removed.

What quality control tests are performed on borage oil?

Very similar to flax oil, borage oil is tested for various quality parameters.
- Peroxide value – Acceptable levels are below 10 meq/kg.
- Acid value – Acceptable levels should be below 4 mg KOH/g.
- Heavy metals – Acceptable levels being less than 10 ppm.
- Pesticides and herbicides – Acceptable levels ranging from 0.05-2 ppm.
- PAs – Acceptable levels less than 4 parts per billion

How is borage oil stored?

The oil should be purged with nitrogen and stored in a cool place away from direct sunlight. The oil usually has an expiry date after one year under optimal storage conditions. Antioxidants may be added to the oil to protect against oxidation. The oil is commonly encapsulated into softgels for sale in the health and nutrition dietary supplement industry.

Is there a traceability system in place for borage?
As with flax, a high quality borage oil supplier should be able to trace the borage oil back to its original farm gate, in which the borage supplier controls every step of the process from seed selection, planting the seed, harvest, storage, processing, and then ultimately selling to the end consumer. Any supplier who can offer a traceability system shows a real commitment to a quality end product. As with flax, this traceability aspect for suppliers will help them in respect to the new "bioterrorism" legislation recently implemented in the U.S.

Evening Primrose Oil Quality: From Seed to Oil

Like other EFA oils, evening primrose oil should be of highest quality. Evening primrose seed, unlike borage and flax, is not usually grown in Canada. While some evening primrose oil is grown in various parts of Europe, the greatest production originates in China with local farmers who go to great lengths to hand harvest the seed.

While the majority of evening primrose oil available on the market is not 'certified organic', it would likely be considered organic by North American standards because the Chinese do not have access to economical synthetic pesticides and herbicides commonly employed by conventional agriculture in North America. Evening primrose oil that is grown and processed in China is sold into various markets, including the health and nutrition supplement industry, around the world.

How is evening primrose oil processed?
In preparation for oil processing, the seeds are conditioned by gently warming them. The conditioning dries the seed to ensure optimal moisture levels for processing. Just as with other EFA oils, evening primrose oil can be processed by one of two methods, expeller-/cold-pressed or solvent extracted. As previously mentioned, expeller-pressed is more desirable in the health and nutrition industry.

How is evening primrose oil packaged and stored?
The oil should be purged with nitrogen and stored in a cool place away from direct sunlight. The oil usually has an expiry date after one year under optimal storage conditions. Antioxidants may be added to the oil to protect against oxidation. The oil is commonly encapsulated into soft gels for sale in the dietary supplement industry.

What quality control tests are performed on evening primrose oil?
Very similar to flax oil and borage oil, evening primrose oil is tested for various quality parameters.
- Peroxide value – Acceptable levels are below 10 meq/kg.
- Acid value – Acceptable levels should be below 4 mg KOH/g.
- Heavy metals – Acceptable levels being less than 10 ppm.
- Pesticides and herbicides – Acceptable levels 0.05 to 2 ppm.
- PAHs – Acceptable levels 2µg/kg.

EFA Quality Solved

Not all EFAs are created equal, so having the right information is vital for choosing the best product. Educated consumers asking the right questions will keep manufacturers and suppliers accountable and have a positive impact on the quality of EFAs available on the market.

GLOSSARY OF TERMS

Alpha-linolenic acid (ALA)—is the parent omega-3 polyunsaturated essential fatty acid. ALA is the precursor to eicosapentaenoic acid (EPA) docosahexaenoic acid (DHA) and some hormones, including prostaglandins of series 3 and leukotrienes of series 5.

Arachidonic acid (AA)—is an omega-6 polyunsaturated fatty acid. Arachidonic acid is abundant in the diet, being found in eggs as well as animal and fish fats. AA is the precursor to hormones, including prostaglandins of series 2 and leukotrienes of series 4. Arachidonic acid has varied effects, including blood vessel constriction and pro-inflammatory effects.

Cold-pressed—a method of gentle crushing and squeezing the seed to release the nutritional oil. Cold pressing is also known as "expeller pressing." This gentle low temperature process will increase stability and preserve nutritional components of the oil. It does not use solvent extraction, where higher temperatures and solvents are used.

Conjugated linoleic acid (CLA)—is a polyunsaturated fatty acid with one of the double bonds in the cis position and the other in the trans configuration. The most common natural CLA is the cis-9, trans-11. CLA is converted through a patented process from linoleic acid that is found in high concentrations in sunflower and safflower oil.

Conditionally essential fatty acids—are fatty acids such as GLA, EPA and DHA that are manufactured in the body from the essential fatty acids LA and ALA. Due to the limitations that can occur in the metabolism of LA and ALA, GLA, EPA and DHA may become "conditionally essential."

Delta 6-desaturase enzyme (D6D)—this enzyme is critical for the metabolic conversion of LA into GLA and ALA into EPA and DHA. This enzyme is often considered the "rate limiting" step, meaning it is the slowest step in the reaction of the metabolic pathway. The D6D enzyme functions at different rates in individuals based on certain environmental and lifestyle factors. For example, smoking and aging may reduce the activity of the D6D enzyme, resulting in EFA deficiency.

Dihomogamma-linolenic acid (DGLA)—is an omega-6 fatty acid formed from GLA, and is the precursor to the series 1 hormones.

Docosahexaenoic acid (DHA)—is an omega-3 polyunsaturated fatty acid. DHA is a very long chain fatty acid formed in the body through a series of steps, starting with ALA. DHA is used in membranes, especially in the brain and the eye.

Eicosanoids—are a family of powerful, hormone-like compounds produced from EFAs. Eicosanoids include prostaglandins, leukotrienes and thromboxanes which are responsible for many of the beneficial effects of EFAs. Eicosanoids control numerous body processes (e.g., inflammation, blood clotting, blood pressure, immune response) and are formed in the body from essential fatty acids.

Eicosapentaenoic acid (EPA)—is an omega-3 polyunsaturated fatty acid. EPA is a very long chain fatty acid formed from ALA through a series of steps. EPA is the immediate precursor to some hormones with anti-inflammatory and blood-thinning effects.

Essential fatty acids (EFAs)—are fatty acids that the human body cannot make and that must be obtained in the diet because they are required for essential activities in the body, including cell membrane structure and function, hormone formation, brain development and growth. There are two families of essential fatty acids that are polyunsaturated: the omega-6 fatty acid linoleic acid and its by-products GLA and AA; and the omega-3 fatty acid alpha-linolenic acid and its by-products EPA and DHA.

Fatty acid—a carboxylic acid with a carbon chain.

Gamma-linolenic acid (GLA)—is an omega-6 polyunsaturated fatty acid that can be formed from LA by the action of the delta-6-desaturase enzyme and is the precursor to anti-inflammatory and vasodilatory hormones. It is not common in the diet, but is found in its highest concentrations in borage, evening primrose and black currant oils.

High density lipoprotein (HDL)—is the blood lipoprotein that contains high levels of protein and low levels of cholesterol, and is the most dense of the lipoproteins. Synthesized primarily in the liver and small intestine, HDL picks up cholesterol and transfers it to other lipoproteins. HDL cholesterol sometimes is called "good cholesterol" as high levels of HDL correlate with decreased coronary heart disease risk.

Hydrogenation—is the process by which liquid oil is converted into solid. Total hydrogenation would turn any unsaturated fatty acid into a saturated fatty acid. Partial hydrogenation turns polyunsaturated fatty acids into less unsaturated fatty acids, but not necessarily into saturated fatty acids. Partial hydrogenation creates transfatty acids.

Lignans—are naturally-occurring substances found in plants and are classified as phytoestrogens. Flaxseed is nature's most abundant source of lignans, containing a concentration more than 100 times greater than other lignan-containing foods, such as grains, fruits and vegetables.

Linoleic acid (LA)—is an omega-6 polyunsaturated essential fatty acid found abundantly in the average diet (in vegetable oils, margarine and processed foods). Ideally, the body converts some LA to GLA, but many people cannot adequately convert LA.

Lipids—is a scientific term for fats.

Lipoproteins—are produced in the blood when lipids are bound to proteins as a transport mechanism for cholesterol and triglycerides. They are categorized by their density, such as HDL, LDL and VLDL.

Low density lipoprotein (LDL)—is the blood lipoprotein that contains low levels of protein and high levels of cholesterol. As LDL circulates in the blood it can slowly build up in the walls of the arteries that feed the heart and brain and may result in hardening of the arteries. LDL is often referred to as "bad cholesterol" because increased levels are associated with an increased risk of heart disease.

Monounsaturated fatty acid—is a chemical term for fatty acids that contain a carbon chain with one double bond.

Oleic acid (OA)—is an omega-9 monounsaturated fatty acid that is not considered essential as it can be manufactured from other fats in the body. Oleic acid is a healthy type of fat found primarily in olive oil, avocados and nuts.

Omega—is a scientific term for different "families" of fatty acids.

Omega-3—is the term for polyunsaturated fatty acids, including ALA and its derivatives EPA and DHA.

Omega-6—is the term for polyunsaturated fatty acids, including LA and its derivatives GLA, DGLA and AA.

Omega-9s—are monounsaturated fatty acids including oleic acid. Omega-9s are not essential like the 3s and 6s, although they are considered "good" fatty acids.

Polyunsaturated fatty acid—is a chemical term for fatty acids that contain a carbon chain with two or more double bonds. Polyunsaturated fatty acids are liquid at room temperature and are considered healthy fats. The higher degree of unsaturation (the more double bonds), the healthier the fat is considered to be.

Prostaglandins—are hormone-like by-products with important metabolic roles. They are formed from essential fatty acids. There are three families, including series 1, series 2 and series 3. Series 1 and 2 are formed from the omega-6 fatty acids and series 3 are formed from the omega-3 fatty acids.

Saturated fats—are dense fats that are solid at room temperature and structurally contain no double bonds. Saturated fats are found in animal products, such as meat, lard, butter and other dairy products, as well as in processed foods. They are generally considered "bad fats" because they can contribute to cardiovascular disease.

Transfatty acids—are man-made unnatural fats created through hydrogenation and/or when fats are subjected to high temperatures or chemically altered. They are difficult for the body to process and interfere with the body's ability to process other good fats. Small amounts of certain transfatty acids (such as CLA) occur naturally in milk and dairy products. These naturally-occuring transfats function different in the body, and are not the same as transfats found in processed and convenience foods. However, the majority of transfats are found in high amounts in partially hydrogenated vegetable oils, shortenings and hard margarines.

Triglycerides—are composed of three fatty acids attached to a glycerol backbone. Most dietary fats are consumed in the form of triglycerides. Triglycerides are also the predominant storage form of fat in the body.

Unsaturated fats—is a chemical term for fatty acids that contain a carbon chain with one or more double bonds, and are fluid at room temperature.

Very low density lipoprotein (VLDL)—is the blood lipoprotein that contains very low levels of protein and high levels of cholesterol. VLDL deposits cholesterol on the walls of arteries and increased levels are associated with hardening of the arteries and coronary heart disease.

REFERENCES

Chapter 1

Burr G, Burr M. "A new deficiency diseased produced by a rigid exclusion of fat from the diet." *Journal of Biological Chemistry* 82, no.2 (1930):345-367.

Das UN. Horrobin D.F., et al. "Clinical Significance of essential fatty acids." *Nutrition* 4 (1998):337.

Enig M. *Know Your Fats: The Complete Primer for Understanding the Nutrition of Fats, Oils and Cholesterol.* Silver Spring, MD: Bethesda Press, 2000, pp. 65,68,127-133,134,177-181,193,200.

Erasmus, Udo. *Fats that Heal, Fats that Kill.* Burnaby, BC: Alive Books, 1993, pp. 11-73,100,242.

Fan YY, RS Chapkin. "Importance of dietary gamma-linolenic acid in human health and nutrition." *Journal of Nutrition* 128 (1998):1411.

Horrobin DF "The importance of gamma-linolenic acid and prostaglandin E1 in human nutrition and medicine." *Journal of Holistic Medicine* 7, no. 9 (1981 Sept):1211-1220.

Jump D, Clarke S. "Regulation of Gene Expression by Dietary Fat", *Annu Rev Nutr* 19 (1999):63-90

Shils, et.al. *Modern Nutrition in Health and Disease.* New York, NY: Williams and Wilkins, 1999, pp. 81-88

Vanderhaeghe, Lorna R. *Healthy Immunity.* Toronto, ON: Macmillan Canada, 2001, pp. 73-75, 377-381.

Chapter 2

American Chemical Society National Meeting News. "CLA could help control weight, fat, diabetes, and muscle loss." August 20, 2000.

Birmingham, CL, JL Muller, A Palepu, JJ Spinelli and AH Anis. "The cost of obesity in Canada." *Canadian Medical Association Journal* 160 (1999):483-488.

Blankson, H, JA Stakkestad, H Fagertun, E Thom, J Wadstein, and O Gudmundsen. "Conjugated linoleic acid reduces body fat mass in overweight and obese humans." *Journal of Nutrition* 130 (2000):2943-2948.

Chalon S, S Delion-Vancassel, C Belzung, D Guilloteau, A-M Leguisquet, J-C Besnard, G Durang. "Dietary fish oil affects monoaminergic neurotransmission and behavior in rats." *Journal of Nutrition* 128 (1998):2512-2519.

Gnadig S, R Rickert, JL Sebedio and H Steinhart. "Conjugated linoleic acid: physiological effects and production." *European Journal of Lipid Science Technology* 103 (2001):56.

Keys A, F Fidanza, MJ Karvonen, N Kimura and HL Taylor. "Indices of relative weight and obesity." *J Chronic Dis* 25 (1972):329-43.

Kriketos AD, RM Robertson, TA Sharp, H Drougas, GW Reed, LH Storlien and JO Hill. "Role of weight loss and polyunsaturated fatty acids in improving metabolic fitness in moderately obese, moderately hypertensive subjects." *J Hypertens* no. 10 (Oct 19, 2001):1745-54.

Pariza MW, Y Park, and ME Cook. "Mechanisms of action of conjugated linoleic acid: evidence and speculation." *Proceedings of the Society for Experimental Biology and Medicine* 2000;223:8-13.

Pariza MW, Y Park, and ME Cook. "Conjugated linoleic acid and the control of cancer and obesity." *Toxicological Sciences* 52 (supplement) (1999):107-110.

Pariza MW. "The biological activities of conjugated linoleic acid." *Advances in Conjugated Linoleic Acid Research*, vol. 1 (1999). Champaign, IL: AOCS, pp. 12-20.

Thom E, J Wadstein, and O Gudmundsen. "Conjugated Linoleic Acid Reduces Body Fat in Health Exercising Humans." *The Journal of International Medical Research* 29 (2001):392-396.

Chapter 3

Belury MA. "Role of conjugated linoleic acid (CLA) in the management of type 2 diabetes: evidence from Zucker diabetic (fa/fa) rats and human subjects." Presented at the American Chemical Society National Meeting, Aug 21, 2000.

Cameron, Norman and Mary Cotter. "Metabolic and Vascular Factors in the Pathogenesis of Diabetic Neuropathy." *Diabetes* 46, Supplement 2 (1997):S31-S37.

Colditz GA, WC Willett, A Rotnitzky, and JE Manson. "Weight gain as a risk factor for clinical diabetes mellitus in women." *Ann Intern Med.* 122 (1995):481-486.

Horrobin DF. "Essential Fatty acids in the management of impaired nerve function in diabetes." *Diabetes* 46, Supplement 2 (1997):S90-3.

Jamal GA et al. "Gamma Linolenic acid in diabetic neuropathy." *The Lancet* 10 (1986):1098.

Keen H, Payan J, Allawi J, Walker J, Jamal GA, et al The Gamma Linolenic Acid Multicenter Trial Group. "Treatment of Diabetic Neuropathy with Gamma Linolenic Acid." *Diabetes Care* 16, no. 1 (1993):8-15.

Mokdad, AH, BA Bowman, ES Ford, F Vinicor, JS Marks and JP Koplan. "The Continuing Epidemics of Obesity and Diabetes in the United States." *JAMA* 286, no. 10 (September 12, 2001):1195-1200.

Montori V, Farmur A, Wollan P, Dinneen S. "Fish Oil Supplementation in Type 2 Diabetes." *Diabetes Care* 23, no.9 (2000): 1407-15.

Petersen M, Pedersen H, Major-Pedersen A et al. "Effect of Fish Oil versus Corn Oil Supplementation on LDL and HDL subclasses in Type 2 Diabetic Patients." *Diabetes Care* 25, no. 10 (2002):1704-8.

The Gamma Linolenic Acid Multicenter Trial Group. "Treatment of Diabetic Neuropathy with Gamma Linolenic Acid." *Diabetes Care* 16, no. 1 (1993):8-15.

Chapter 4

Albert CM, H Campos, M Stampfer et al. "Blood Levels of Long-Chain n-3 Fatty Acids and the Risk of Sudden Death." *New England Journal of Medicine* 2002;346(15):1113-1118.

Cunnane SC, LU Thompson, *Flaxseed in Human Nutrition*. Champaign, IL: AOCS Press, 1995.

Djousse L, J Pankow, J Edkfeldt et al. "Relation between dietary linolenic acid and coronary arter disease in the National Heart, Lung, and Blood Institute Family Heart Study." *Am J Clin Nutr* 2001;74:612-9.

Dyerberg J, HO Bang, E Stoffersen, S Moncada, and JR Vane. "Eicosapentaenoic acid and prevention of thrombosis and atherosclerosis?" *The Lancet* 2 (8081) (July 15, 1978):117-119.

Hirai A, T Terano, Y Tamura, and S Yoshida. "Eicosapentaenoic acid and adult diseases in Japan: epdimeological and clinical aspects." *J Intern Med* 225 (731) (Supplement 1989):69-75.

Hu F, L Bronner, W Willett, M Stampfer, K Rexrode, C Albert, D Hunter, and J Manson. "Fish and Omega-3 Fatty Acid Intake and Risk of Coronary Heart Disease in Women." *JAMA* 2002;287(14):1815-1821.

Hu et al. "Dietary intake of alpha-linolenic acid and risk of fatal ischemic heart disease among women." *Am J Clin Nutr.* 1999;69:890-7.

Iso H, K Rexrode, M Stampfer, JE Manson, G Colditz, F Speizer, C Hennekens, and W Willett. "Intake of Fish and Omega-3 Fatty Acids and Risk of Stroke in Women." *JAMA* 2001;285:304-312.

Kris-Etherton P, W Harris, L Appel. "Fish Consumption, Fish Oil, Omega-3 Fatty Acids, and Cardiovascular Disease." *Circulation* 2002;106:2747-2757.

Kromhout D, EJ Feskens, CH Bowles. "The protective effect of a small amount of fish on coronary heart disease mortality in an elderly population." *Int J Epidemiol.* 1995;24:340-345.

Mills D. et al. "Dietary fatty acid supplementation alters stress reactivity and performance in man." *Journal of Human Hypertension* 1989;3:111-16.

Mori TA, LF Beilin, V Burke, et al. "Interactions between dietary fat, fish, and fish oils and their effects on platelet function in men at risk of cardiovascular disease." *Arterioscler Thrombo Vasc Biol.* 1997;17:279-286.

Sears B. *The Omega Rx Zone.* "Who Wants to Die of a Heart Attack?" Regan Books: New York, NY, pp. 131-135.

Chapter 5

Behan P, WMH Behan, and D Horrobin. "Effect of high doses of essential fatty acids on the postviral fatigue syndrome." *Acta Neruol Scan* 82 (1990):209-216.

Birch EE, S Garfield, DR Hoffman, R Uauy and DG Birch. "A randomized controlled trial of early dietary supply of long-chain polyunsaturated fatty acids and mental development in term infants." *Developmental Medicine and Child Neurology* 42 (2000):174-181.

Filburn C. "Dietary supplementation with phospholipids and docosahexaenoic acid for age-related cognitive impairment." *JAMA* 3, no. 3 (2000):45-55.

Gray JB, and AM Martinovic. "Eicosanoids and essential fatty acid modulation in chronic disease and the chronic fatigue syndrome." *Medical Hypothesis* 43 (1994):31-42.

Hamazaki T, et. al. "The effect of docosahexaenoic acid on aggression in young adults: a placebo-controlled double-blind study." *J Clin. Invest* 97 (1996):1129-33.

Hibbein J. "Fish consumption and major depression." *The Lancet* 351(1998):1213.

Kapoor R, A Klimaczewski, and J McColl. "Essential Fatty Acids and Stress." *International Journal of Integrated Medicine* 3, no. 1 (2001):18-21.

Kalmijn S, L Launer, A Ott, J Witteman, A Hofman, and M Breteler. "Dietary fat intake and the risk of incident dementia in the Rotterdam Study." *Ann Neruol* 42 (1997):776-782.

Nemets B, Z Stahl, and R Belmaker. "Addition of Omega-3 Fatty Acid to Maintenance Medication Treatment for Recurrent Unipolar Depressive Disorder." *Am J Psychiatry* 159 (2002):477-479.

Sawazaki S, T Hamazaki, K Yazawa, and M Kobayashi. "The effect of docosahexaenoic acid on plasma catecholamine concentrations and glucose tolerance during long-lasting psychological stress: A double-blind placebo-controlled study." *J Nutr Sci Vitaminol* 45 (1999):655-665.

Stoll A, E Severus, et al. "Omega-3 fatty acids in bipolar disease." *Archives of General Psychiatry* 56 (1999):407-412.

Stoll A. *The Omega-3 Connection.* New York, NY: Simon & Schuster, 2001.

Yehuda S, S Rabinovitz, RL Carasso, and DI Mostofsky. "Fatty acid mixture counters stress changes in cortisol, cholesterol and impaired learning." *Int J Neurosci* 101, nos. 1–4 (2000):73-87.

Chapter 6

Anderson G.L. "Docosahexaenoic acid is the preferred dietary n-3 fatty acid for the development of the brain and retina." *Pediatric Research* 27, no. 1 (1990):89-97.

Birch EE, D Birch, D Hoffman et al. "Breast-feeding and optimal visual development." *J Pediatr Opthalmol and Strabismus* 30 (1993):33-38.

Burgess J, L Steven, W Zhang, and L Peck. "Long-chain polyunsaturated fatty acids in children with attention-deficit hyperactivity disorder." *Am J Clin Nutr* 71 Supplement (2000):327S-30S.

Cheruku S, H Montgomery-Downs, S Farkas, E Thoman, and C Lammi-Keefe. "Higher maternal plasma docosahexaenoic acid during pregnancy is associated with more mature neonatal sleep-state patterning." *The American Journal of Clinical Nutrition* 76, no. 3 (2002):608-613.

Gazella K. "Essential Fatty Acids and Learning Disorders." *International Journal of Integrative Medicine* 1, no. 4 (1999):27-33.

Hansen AE, HF Wiese, AN Boelsche, et al. "Role of linoleic acid in infant nutrition: Clinical and chemical study of 428 infants on milk mixtures varying in kind and amount of fat." *Pediatrics* 31 (1963):171-192.

"Recommendation for the Essential Fatty Acid Requirements of Infant Formula." *ISSFAL Newsletter* 1 (1994):4.

Mitchell EA, MG Aman, SH Turbott, and M Manku. "Clinial characteristics and serum essential fatty acid levels in hyperactive children." *Clin Pediatr* 26 (1987):406-11.

Nelson GJ, PC Schmidt, G Bartolini, DS Kelley, and D Kyle. "Dietary docosahexaenoic acid lowers plasma triglycerides in the absence of dietary eicosapentaenoic acid in human males." *Prost Leuk Essen Fatty Acids* 57 (1997):187.

Olsen S, and N Secher. "Low consumption of seafood in early pregnancy as a risk factor for preterm delivery: prospective cohort study." *British Medical Journal* 324 (2002):447-50.

Richardson A, and B Puri. "A randomized double-blind, placebo-controlled study of the effects of supplementation with highly unsaturated fatty acids on ADHD-related symptoms in children with specific learning difficulties." *Progress in Neuro Psychopharmacology & Biological Psychiatry* 26 (2002):233-239.

Stevens LJ, SS Zentall, JL Deck, ML Abate, BA Watkins, et al. "Essential fatty acid metabolism in boys with attention-deficit hyperactivity disorder." *Am J Clin Nutr* 62 (1995):761-8.

Stordy J. "Dark adaptation, motor skills, docosahexaenoic acid, and dyslexia." *Am J Clin Nutr* 71 Supplement (2000):323S-6S.

Werkman SH, and SE Carlson. "A randomized trial of visual attention of preterm infants fed docosahexaenoic acid until nine months." *Lipids* 31 (1996):91-7.

Chapter 7

Arjmandi B, D Khan, S Juma, et al. "Whole flaxseed consumption lowers serum LDL-cholesterol and lipoprotein concentrations in postmenopausal women." *Nutrition Research* 18, no. 7 (1998):1203-1214.

Brush MG, SJ Watson, DF Horrobin, and MS Manku. "Abnormal essential fatty acid levels in plasma of women with premenstrual syndrome." *Am J Obstet Gynecol* 150 (1984):363-366.

Chenoy R, S Hussain, Y Tayob, PM O'Brien, MY Moss, and PF Morse. "Effect of oral gammalinolenic acid from evening primrose oil on menopausal flushing." *British Medical Journal* 308, no. 6927 (1994):501-503.

Deutch B, EB Jorgensen, and JC Hansen. "Menstrual discomfort in Danish women reduced by dietary supplements of omega-3 PUFA and B12." *Nutrition Research* 20 (2000):621-631.

Deutch B. "Painful menstruation and low intake of n-3 fatty acids." *Ugeskr Laeger* 158, no. 29 (July 15, 1996):4195-4198.

Gianetto-Berruti A, Feyles V. "Effects of a Herbal Formulation on Premenstrual Symptoms: A Randomized Controlled Trial." *Journal of Obstetrics and Gynaecology Canada* 23, no. 9 (2001):817-24.

Haggans CJ, et al. "Effects of flaxseed consumption on urinary estrogen metabolites in postmenopausal women." *Nutrition and Cancer* 33, no. 2 (1999):188-95.

Harel Z, FM Biro, RK Kottenhahn, and SL Rosenthal SL. "Supplementation with omega-3 polyunsaturated fatty acids in the management of dysmenorrhea in adolescents." *Am J Obstet Gynecol* 174, no. 4 (April 1996):1335-1338.

Horrobin DF. "The role of essential fatty acid and prostaglandins in the premenstrual syndrome." *J Reprod Med* 28 (1983):465-468.

Horrobin DK, and MS Manku. "Premenstrual syndrome and premenstrual breast pain (cyclical mastalgia):disorders of essential fatty acid (EFA) metabolism." *Prostaglandins Leukotrienes and Essential Fatty Acids* 37, no. 4 (September 1989):255-261.

Lemay A, S Dodin, N Kadri, H Jacques, JC Forest. "Flaxseed Dietary Supplement Versus Hormone Replacement Therapy in Hypercholesterolemic Menopausal Women" *Obstetrics & Gynecology* 100, no. 3 (2002):495-504.

National Center for Complementary and Alternative Medicine. "Alternative Therapies for Managing Menopausal Symptoms." www.nccam.nih.gov/ August 2, 2002.

NIH News Release. "NHLBI Stops Trial of Estrogen Plus Progestin Due to Increased Breast Cancer Risk, Lack of Overall Benefit." July 9, 2002 www.nih.gov

Ockerman PA, I Bachrack, S Glans, and S Rassner. "Evening primrose oil as a treatment of the premenstrual syndrome." *Recent Adv Clin Nutr* 2 (1986):404-405.

Puolakka J, L Makarainen, L Viinikka, and O Ylikorkala. "Biochemical and clinical effects of treating the premenstrual syndrome with prostaglandin synthesis precursors." *J Reprod Med* 30, no. 3 (1985):149-153.

Taylor N. *25 Natural Ways to Relieve PMS*. New York, NY: Contemporary Books 2002, pp. XV- XXV and 39-47.

Jensen K, Vanderhaeghe L. *No More HRT: Menopause Treat the Cause*. Hillsburg, ON: Health Venture Publications, 2002, and Kingston, ON: Quarry Press, 2003, pp. 247-256.

Chapter 8

Aro A, S Mannisto, I Salminen, ML Ovaskainen, V Kataja, M Uusitupa. "Inverse association between dietary and serum conjugated linoleic acid and risk of breast cancer in postmenopausal women." *Nutrition and Cancer* 2000;38(2):151-7.

Bagga D, KH Anders, HJ Wang, JA Glaspy. "Long-chain n-3-to-n-6 polyunsaturated fatty acid ratios in breast adipose tissue from women with and without breast cancer." *Nutr Cancer* 2002;42(2):180-5.

Brooks J, W Ward, J Hilditch, J Lewis, L Nickell et al. "Flaxseed, but not soy, significantly altered urinary estrogen metabolite excretion in healthy post-menopausal women." *The FASEB Journal*, 2002;16(5):A1005.

Caygill CP, A Charlett, MJ Hill. "Fat, fish, fish oil and cancer." *Br J Cancer* 1996;74:159-164.

Djuric Z, V Uhley, J Depper, K Brooks, S Lababidi, L Heilbrum. "A Clinical Trial to Selectively Change Dietary Fat and/or Energy Intake in Women: The Women's Diet Study." *Nutrition and Cancer* 1999;34(1):27-35.

Erickson K. "Is there a relation between dietary linoleic acid and cancer of the breast, colon or prostate?" *Am J Clin Nutr* 1998;68:5-7.

Gonzalez, Carlos, et al. "Borage consumption as a possible gastric cancer protective factor." *Cancer Epidemiology, Biomarkers & Prevention*, Vol. 2, pp. 157-158 (1993).

Goss PE, T Li, M Theriault, S Pinto, L Thompson. University Health Network/Princess Margaret Hospital, Toronto, ON, Canada; University of Toronto, Toronto, ON, Canada. Data Presented at the 23rd Annual San Antonio Breast Cancer Symposium. Dec 6-9, 2000.

Hardman WE. "Omega-3 fatty acids to augment cancer therapy." *Journal of Nutrition* 2002 Nov; 132(11 suppl):3508S-3512S.

Holmes M, D Hunter, G Colditz, M Stampfer et al. "Association of dietary intake of fat and fatty acids with risk of breast cancer." *JAMA* 1999;281:914-920.

Hutchins A, M Martini, B Olson, W Thomas, J Slavin. "Flaxseed influences urinary lignan excretion in a dose-dependent manner in postmenopausal women." *Cancer, Epidemiology, Biomarkers and Prevention* 2000;9:1113-1118.

Hutchins A, C Martini, A Olson, W Thomas, J Slavin. "Flaxseed consumption infuences endogenous hormone concentrations in postmenopausal women." *Nutrition and Cancer* 2001;39(1):58-65.

Kenny F, S Pinder, IO Ellis, J Gee, R Nicholson, R Bryce and J Roberston. "Gamma linolenic acid with tamoxifen as primary therapy in breast cancer." *Int J Cancer* 2000;85:643-648.

Klein V, V Chajes, E Germain, G Schulgen, M Pinault et al. "Low alpha-linolenic acid content of adipose breast tissue is associated with an increased risk of breast cancer." *Eur J Cancer* 2000 Feb;36(3):335-40

Maillard V, P Bougnoux, P Ferrari, ML Jourdan, M Pinault et al. "N-3 and N-6 fatty acids in breast adipose tissue and relative risk of breast cancer in a case-control study in Tours, France." *Int J Cancer* 2002 Mar 1;98(1):78-83.

Phipps W, M Martini, J Lampe, J Slavin and M Kurzer. "Effect of flax seed ingestion on the menstrual cycle." *Journal of Clincial Endocrinology and Metabolism*. 1993;77:1215-1219.

Thompson LU, T Li, J Chen and PE Goss. Nutritional Sciences, University of Toronto, Toronto, ON, Canada; Medical Oncology, Princess Margaret Hospital, Toronto, ON. Canada. "Biological Effects of Dietary Flaxseed in Patients with Breast Cancer." Data Presented at the 23rd Annual San Antonio Breast Cancer Symposium. Dec 6-9, 2000.

Zheng W, D Gustafson, R Sinha, J Cerhan, D Moore et al. "Well-Done Meat Intake and the Risk of Breast Cancer." *Journal of the National Cancer Institute* 1998;90(22):1724-1729.

Chapter 9

Andreassi, M., et al. "Efficacy of Gamma Linolenic Acid in the Treatment of Patients with Atopic Dermatitis." *The Journal of International Medical Research* 1997; 25:266-74.

Bosche T, D Platt. "Effect of borage oil consumption on fatty acid metabolism, transepidermal water loss and skin parameters in elderly people." *Archives of Gerontology and Geriatrics*, 2001; 30:139-150.

Businco L, Ioppi M, Morse NL, Nisini R, Wright S. "Breast milk from mothers of children with newly developed atopic eczema has low levels of long chain polyunsaturated fatty acids." *J Allergy Clin Immunol* 1993;91:1134.

Downing DT, Stewart ME, Wertz PW. "Essential fatty acids and acne." *Journal of the American Academy of Dermatology* 1986;14:221-5.

Hansen TM, A Lerche, V Kassis, I Lorenzen and J Sondergaard. "Treatment of rheumatoid arthritis with prostaglandin E1 precursors cis-linoleic acid and gamma-linolenic acid." *Scandinavian Journal of Rheumathology* 1983; 12(2):85-8

Henz, BM. "Double-blind, multicentre analysis of the efficacy of borage oil in patients with atopic eczema." *British Journal of Dermatology*, 1999;Vol. 140:685-88.

Horrobin DF. "Essential fatty acid metabolism and its modification in atopic eczema." *Am J Clin Nutr.* 2000; 71(suppl):367S-372S.

Nissen HP, H Blitz, R Muggli. "The effect of gamma linolenic acid on skin smoothness, humidity and TEWL—A clinical study." *Inform* 1995;6 (4):519.

Orengo IF, HS Black, AH Kettler, JE Wolf. "Influence of dietary menhaden oil upon carcinogenesis and various cutaneous responses to ultraviolet radiation." *Photochemistry and Photobiology* 1989;49(1): 71-77.

Rhodes LE, BH Durham, WD Fraser and PS Friedmann. "Dietary fish oil reduces basal and ultraviolet B-generated PGE2 levels in skin and increases the threshold to provocation of polymorphic light eruption." *J Invest Dermatol* 105:532-535, 1995

Tollesson A, and A Frithz. "Borage oil: An effective new treatment for infantile seborrhoiec dermatitis." *Br J Dermatol* 1993;129:95

Tollesson A, and A Frithz. "Transepidemral water loss and water content in the stratum corneum in infantile seborrhoeic dermatitis." *Acta Derm Venereol* 1993;73:18.

Yoon S, J Lee and S Lee. "The Therapeutic Effect of Evening Primrose Oil in Atopic Dermatitis Patients with Dry Scaly Skin Lesions is Associated with the Normalization of Serum Gamma-Interferon Levels." *Skin Pharmacol Appl Skin Physiol* 2002;15:20–25.

Chapter 10

Anbalagan K, and Sadique "Wighania somnifera (Ashwagandha), a rejuvenating herbal drug which controls alpha-2 macroglobulin synthesis during inflammation." *Int J Crude Drug Res* 1985;23:177-83.

Barham J, M Edens, A Fonteh, M Johnson, L Easter and F Chilton. "Addition of Eicosapentaenoic Acid to Alpha-Linolenic Acid-Supplemented Diets Prevents Serum Arachidonic Acid Accumulation in Humans." *J Nutr* 2000;130(8):1925-1931.

Belch JJ, et al. "Effects of altering dietary essential fatty acids on requirements for non-steroidal anti-inflammatory drugs in patients with rheumatoid arthritis: a double blind placebo controlled study." *Annals of Rheumatoic Disease*, 1988; 47: 96-104.

Belch JJ, A Muir. "N-6 and n-3 Essential fatty acids in rheumatoid arthritis and other conditions." *Proceedings of the Nutrition Society* 1998;57:563-569.

Belch JJ, Hill A. "Evening primrose oil and borage oil in rheumatologic conditions." *Am J Clin Nutr* 2000;71(suppl):352S-6S.

Curtis CL, SG Rees, J Cramp, CR Flannery, CE Hughes and et al. "Effects of n-3 fatty acids on cartilage metabolism." *Proc Nutr Soc* 2002 Aug;61(3):381-9.

Curtis C, SG Rees et al. "Pathologic indicators of degradation and inflammation in human osteoarthritic cartilage are abrogated by exposure to n-3 fatty acids." *Arthritis & Rheumatis*, 2002;46(6):1544-1553.

DeLuca P, D Rothman, and R Zurier. "Marine and Botanical Lipids as Immunomodulatory and Therapeutic Agents in the Treatment of Rheumatoid Arhtritis." *Rheumatoid Arthritis* 1995;21(3):759-776. *Rheum Dis Clin North Am* 2000;26 (1):1-11.

Guillermo T, et al. "Suppression of Acute and Chronic Inflammation by Dietary Gamma-linolenic Acid." *Journal of Rheumatology*, Vol. 16, pp 729-33 (1989).

Kremer J. "N-3 supplements in rheumatoid arthritis." *Am J Clin Nutr* 2000 Jan 71 (1):349S-3451S.

Kruger MC, DF Horrobin. "Calcium Metabolism, osteoporosis and essential fatty acids: A review." *Prog Lipid Res* 1997;36(2.3):131-151.

Kruger MC, H Coetzer, R de Winter, G Gericke, DH van Papendorp. "Calcium, gammalinolenic acid and eicosapentaenoic acid supplementation in senile osteoporosis." *Aging Clin Exp Res* 1998;10:385-394.

Lane NE. "Pain management in osteoarthritis: the role of COX-2 inhibitors." *J Rheumatology* 1997;24 Suppl 49:20-24.

Lau CS, KD Morleu, JJ Belch. "Effects of fish oil supplementation on nonsteroidal antiinflammatory drugs requirement in patients with mild rheumatic arthritis-a double blind placebo controlled study." *Br J Rheumatol* 1993;32:982-989.

Leventhal LJ, et al. "Treatment of Rheumatoid Arthritis with Gamma-linolenic Acid." *Annals of Internal Medicine* 1993; 119: pp. 867-73.

Navarro E, M Esteve, A Olive, J Klassen, et al. "Abnormal fatty acid pattern in rheumatoid arthritis. A rationale for treatment with marine and botanical lipids." *The Journal of Rheumatology* 2000;27:298-303.

Pejovic M, A Stankovic, DR Mitrovic. "Determination of the apparent synovial permeability in the knee joint of patients suffering from oseoarthritis and rheumatoid arthritis." *Br J Rheumatol* 1995;34:520-524.

Pullman-Mooar S, M Laposata, D Lem, RT Holman, LJ Leventhal, D DeMarco et al. "Alteration of the cellular fatty acid profile and the production of eicosanoids in human monocytes by gamma-linolenic acid." *Arthritis Rheum* 1990;33:1526-35.

Volker D, P Fitzgerald, G Major and M Garg M. "Efficacy of Fish Oil Concentrate in the Treatment of Rheumatoid Arthritis." *J Rheumatol* 2000; 27:2343-6.

Watkins BA, and MF Seifert. "Conjugated linoleic acid and bone biology." *J Am Coll Nutr* 2000 Aug;19(4):478S-486S.

Chapter 11

Aronson WJ et al. "Modulation of omega-3/omega-6 polyunsaturated ratios with dietary fish oils in men with prostate cancer." *Urology* 2001 Aug;58(2):283-8.

Berges RR, J Windeler, HJ Trampisch, T Senge. "Randomised, placebo-controlled, double-blind clinical trial of ß- sitosterol in patients with benign prostatic hyperplasia." *The Lancet* 1995;345:1529-32.

Conquer JA et al. "Effect of DHA supplementation on DHA status and sperm motility in astheno-zoospermic males." *Lipids* 2000;35:149-154.

Denmark-Wahnefried W, DT Price, TJ Polascik, CN Roberston, and EE Anderson et al. "Pilot study of dietary fat restriction and flaxseed supplementation in men with prostate cancer before surgery: exploring the effects on hormonal levels, prostate-specific antigen, and histopathologic features." *Urology.* 2001 Jul;58(1):47-52.

Motaung E, et al. "Cytotoxicity of combined essential fatty acids on a human prostate cancer cell line." *Prostaglandins Leukot Essent Fatty Acids* 1999 Nov;61(5):331-7.

Norrish AE, CM Skeaff, GL Arribas, SJ Sharpe and RT Jackson. "Prostate cancer risk and consumption of fish oils: a dietary biomarker-based case-control study." *British Journal of Cancer* 1999 Dec;81(7):1238-42.

Palombo JD, A Ganguly, BR Bistrian and MP Menard. "The antiproliferative effects of biologically active isomers of conjugated linoleic acid on human colorectal and prostatic cancer cells." *Cancer Letters* 2002 Mar 28;177(2):163-72

Schuurman AG, PA van den Brandt, E Dorant, HA Brants, et al. "Association of energy and fat intake with prostate carcinoma risk: results from The Netherlands Cohort Study." *Cancer* 1999;Sep 15;86(6):1019-27.

Wynder EL, et al. "Nutrition and prostate cancer: a proposal for dietary intervention." *Nutr Cancer* 1994;22(1):1-10.

Chapter 12

Awang D. "Borage." *CPJ-RPC.* 1990;123:121-126.

Carnielli VP, IH Luijenkijk, RH van Beek, GJ Boerma and HJ Degenhart et al. "Effect of dietary tria-cylglycerol fatty acid positional distribution of plasma lipid classes and their fatty acid composition in preterm infants." *Am J Clin Nutr* 1995;62(4):776-81.

Code of Practice on Polycyclic Aromatic Hydrocarbons (PAH), FEDIOL, Brussels.

Cornell University, Program on Breast Cancer and Environmental Risk Factors in New York State. (BCERF), www.cfe.cornell.edu

Council for Responsible Nutrition, Voluntary Omega 3 Monograph, September 2002.

de Smet. "Safety of borage seed oil." *CPJ-RPC* January 1991, p.5

Dodson, Stermitz. "Pyrrolizidine Alkaloids from Borage seeds and Flowers." *Journal of Natural Products* 1986;49(4):727-728.

Dove D, and P Johnson. "Oral Evening Primrose Oil: Its effect on length of pregnancy and selected intrapartum outcomes in low-risk nulliparous women." *Journal of Nurse-Midwifery* 1999;44(3):320-324.

Food Safety Authority of Ireland. "Summary of Investigation of Dioxins, Furans and PCBs in Farmed Salmon, Wild Salmon, Farmed Trout and Fish Oil Capsules, March 2002." www.fsai.ie/industry/dioxins3.htm

Gerster H. "Can adults adequately convert a-linolenic acid (18:3n-3) to Eicosapentaenoic Acid (20:5n-3) and Docosahexaenoic Acid (22:6n-3)?" *International Journal of Vitamin Research* 1998;68:15-173.

Giovannucci E, E Rimm, G Colditz, M Stampfer et al. "A Prospective Study of Dietary Fat and Risk of Prostate Cancer." *Journal of the National Cancer Institute* 1993;85(19):1571-1579.

Larson, Roby and Stermitz. "Unsaturated Pyrrolizidines from Borage." *Journal of Natural Products*. 1984;47(4): pp.747-748.

Parvais, et al. "TLC detection of pyrrolizidine alkaloids in oil extracted from the seeds of borage offici-nalis." *Journal of Planar Chromatogrpahy*. 1994;7: pp.80-82.

Ramirez M, L Amate and A Gil. "Absorption and distribution of dietary fatty acids from different sources." *Early Hum Dev* 2001 Nov;65 Suppl:S95-S101.

Simon JA, J Fong, JT Bernert and WS Browner. "Serum fatty acids and the risk of stroke." *Stroke* 1995; 26(5):778.

World Health Organization. "Dioxins and Their Effects On Human Health." *Fact Sheet* no. 225, June 1999. www.who.int/inf-fs/en/fact225.html

Chapter 13

Beaubaire NA, and JE Simon. "Production of Borago officinalis L." *Acta Hort* 1987;208:101-113.

Council for Responsible Nutrition. *Voluntary Omega-3 Monograph*. September 2002.

Enironmental Protection Agency, "EPA National Advice on Mercury in Freshwater Fish for Women Who Are or May Become Pregnant, Nursing Mothers, and Young Children." www.epa.gov/ost/fish.

Fell KR, Peck JM. "Anatomy of the Leaf and Flower of Borago officinalis." *Planta Med* 1968; 16:29-42.

Food and Drug Administration, Mercury in Fish: Cause for Concern? *FDA Consumer Magazine*, September 1994, www.fda.gov/fdac/reprints/mercury

National Organics Program, www.usda.gov/nop/regtext.htm, October 2002.

Norwegian Fish Farmers Association, NFF. *Aquaculture in Norway*. July 2001.

U.S. Food and Drug Administration, Center for Food Safety and Applied Nutrition. *Guidance for Industry Importers and Filers: Food Security Preventive Measures Guidance*. Jan 9, 2002, www.cfsan.fda.gov

RESOURCE GUIDE

Manufacturers

Arkopharma, LLC
19 Crosby Drive, Bedford, Massachusetts, U.S.A.
01730
Phone: (781) 276-0505
Fax: (781) 276-7335
Toll-free: 1-800-477-2249
E-mail: efa@hfts.com
Website: www.healthfromthesun.com
Brand Name: Health From The Sun
Distributed in the U.S. through health/natural food stores.

Health From The Sun is the leader in essential fatty acid nutritional products, offering value and experience you can trust. Health From The Sun provides unbiased and comprehensive information on the benefits of all essential fatty acid (EFA) oils. They offer EFA oils in over 50 varieties and sizes, more than
three times their nearest competitor. Health From The Sun delivers optimal product quality at reasonable
prices. In 1979, Health From The Sun was founded with the goal of becoming a leader in EFA nutritional products through innovation. In March 1999, Health From The Sun was acquired by Arkopharma
Laboratories, France's largest nutritional supplements manufacturer. Health From The Sun is proud of
this pairing because Arkopharma's commitment to research, education and innovation matches their
own.

Health From The Sun offers a complete range of EFA products, including borage, black currant, evening
primrose, organic flax, fish, perilla, The Woman's Oil and The Total EFA™ in softgel form. For those who
prefer to take EFAs by the spoonful or incorporate them into their daily diet, Health From The Sun
offers bottled liquid borage, evening primrose, fish, organic flax, organic flax with lignans, The Woman's
Oil and The Total EFA™. Milled flaxseed and a combination of milled flax and fermented soy (Super
FiproFLAX™) offer great nutrition and can be used in baking and other foods. Health From The Sun also
offers condition-specific formulas, designed to support specific areas of the body. These combinations of
EFA oils with other vitamins, minerals and herbs offer maximum health benefits. Health From The Sun
condition-specific formulas are available for PMS, heart, brain, skin, blood sugar, bones and joints.

Puresource Inc.
R.R. #7
Guelph, Ontario, Canada
N1H 6J4
Phone: 1-519-837-2141
Fax: 1-519-826-9142
Toll-Free: 1-888-313-3369
E-mail: Sylvia.Finlay@puresource.ca
Website: www.puresource.ca
Brand Name: Herbal Select™
www.herbalselect.com

Distributed primarily in Canada through health food, drug and grocery stores under the Herbal Select™
and NOW brands.

Puresource has more than 10 years of specialized experience responding to the unique natural health concerns of Canadians. Herbal Select™ is an extensive line of herbal and nutritional supplements that provide consistent quality, potency, selection and value. Puresource is proud of their reputation for excellence and is committed to making quality products that deliver the consistently effective therapeutic results needed to satisfy customers and cultivate loyalty. Herbal Select™ supplements are formulated using only the world's finest medicinal herbs and ingredients containing a high level of active components or key biological markers.

The Herbal Select™ brand includes a full range of EFA liquids and soft gels including multi-EFA (Essential 3-6-9), borage, evening primrose, organic flax, pumpkin, and fish oil supplements. Organic whole and milled flaxseeds by Herbal Select™ are also great additions to your daily diet. Herbal Select™ offers condition-specific formulas specifically targeted towards women's health concerns such as PMS and menopause. Alphea™ is a clinically proven formula combining EFAs, vitamins, minerals and herbs that are effective in treating symptoms of PMS, including bloating, cramping, headaches and irritability. Alphea 50+™ offers a unique combination of EFAs, vitamins, minerals and herbs designed to help women with their menopausal symptoms. Trust Herbal Select™ essential fatty acids for your mind, body and soul.

Swanson Health Products
P.O. Box 2803
Fargo, North Dakota, U.S.A.
58108-2803
Toll-free: 1-800-451-9304
Fax: 1-800-726-7691
E-mail: customercare@swansonvitamins.com
Website: www.swansonvitamins.com
Brand: Swanson OmegaTru™
Distributed by mail order in the U.S.A. and Canada.

Swanson Health Products is an independently owned and operated company based in Fargo, North Dakota. Founded by Leland Swanson in 1969, today they are one of the largest and most successful privately-owned health product companies in America.

The seed of Swanson Health Products was planted when Mr. Swanson placed his first newspaper ad for vitamin E over 30 years ago. Today, under the direction of his son, Lee Swanson, the company remains true to its original vision of bringing wellness to the world through high-quality, affordable natural health aids.

Swanson offers a range of EFA oils under the OmegaTru™ brand, including black currant, flax, perilla, borage, and evening primrose oil in softgel form. Swanson's bottled organic flax oil, high lignan flax oil, and flaxseed concentrate should also be part of your daily diet.

Preferred Nutrition Inc.
153 Perth St.
Acton, Ontario, Canada
L7J 1C9
Phone: 1-888-284-9920
Fax: 1-888-773-7069
E-mail: Retailer@preferrednutritiononline.com
Website: www.preferrednutritiononline.com or www.hormonehelp.com
Brand: Preferred Nutrition's FemmEssentials™, EstroSense™, MenoSense™, BodySense™
Distributed exclusively through health food stores across Canada.

Preferred Nutrition Inc. sells natural nutritional products exclusively to health food stores and has developed a line of women's products formulated by Lorna R. Vanderhaeghe. Key products in this line include EstroSense™ for balancing hormones and breast cancer protection, MenoSense™ to relieve the symptoms of menopause, FemmEssentials™, a women's daily multi-nutrient formula that contains organic flaxseed oil and evening primrose oil and The BodySense™ Diet for fat burning and weight loss.

Preferred Nutrition also sells Dr. Julian Whitaker products exclusively through health food stores. For more information, visit www.hormonehelp.com , www.drwhitaker.com or call 1-888-284-9920.

Great American Health Products
P.O. Box 248
Mapleton, North Dakota, U.S.A.
58059
Toll-free: 1-800-437-2733 (retailers only please)
Fax: 1-800-450-5047 (retailers only please)
Website: www.doctorsa-z.com
Brand: Doctor's A–Z™
Distributed nationally.

National wholesale distributors of Doctor's A–Z™ brand dietary supplements. Doctor's A–Z™—Quality uncompromised. Value beyond compare.

Raw Material Suppliers

Bioriginal Food & Science Corp.
102 Melville St.
Saskatoon, Saskatchewan,Canada
S7J 0R1
Phone: 306-975-1166
Fax: 306-242-3829
Website: www.bioriginal.com
E-mail: business@bioriginal.com

Bioriginal Food & Science Corp. is the world's leading supplier of essential fatty acid (EFA) oils, including flax, evening primrose, borage (starflower), black currant, and fish, as well as CLA. Delivery systems range from bulk oil and capsules, to the finished packaged product. In addition to the standard oil or seed formats, Bioriginal has the capability of supplying highly concentrated EFA oils and water-soluble EFA powders.

Located in the pristine growing region of Western Canada, Bioriginal provides nutritional supplements and other EFA products that offer unmatched quality and potency. Their quality assurance measures include: manufacturing to Canadian GMPs; in-house testing/quality control; complete ingredient disclosure; independent raw material and product testing; participation in clinical trials, education and research; and sending a Certificate of Analysis with every shipment.

Bioriginal serves wholesale customers in five key product categories: nutritional supplements, cosmetics, pet and veterinary, over-the-counter pharmaceuticals and functional foods.

Denofa
PO Box 1214
N-1610 Gamle Fredrikstad
Norway
Website: www.denofa.no

Denofa, a member of the Orkla Group, is a leading global player within fish oils for a wide range of applications. They supply fish and vegetable oils to fish feed, animal feed and pet food producers in Europe. Denofa processes approximately 20% of the global fish oil production. The Company's marine lipids, vegetable oils and lecithin are used in dietary supplements, functional foods, clinical nutrition and pet food.

Denofa offers non-GMO soya backed by an IP program.

Croda Chemicals Europe Ltd
Cowick Hall
Snaith
Goole
East Yorkshire
DN14 9AA
UK
Website: www.croda.com/europe/hc

Croda is one of the world's leading producers of specialty chemicals. With its unequalled expertise in lipid concentration and purification technologies, Croda is well placed to meet the stringent demands of the healthcare market. High purity lipids and omega-3/omega-6 essential fatty acid derivatives—so called because they are essential to good health—are a major growth area for Croda, particularly for dietary supplements and pharmaceutical applications.

Websites

www.fatsforhealth.com—Comprehensive consumer EFA information site
www.supplementinfo.org—Dietary Supplement Education Alliance
www.crnusa.org—Council for Responsible Nutrition
www.flaxcouncil.ca—Flax Council of Canada
www.omega3ri.org—Omega-3 Research Institute
www.wisc.edu/fri/clarefs.htm—University of Wisconsin CLA information site
www.ameriflax.com—AmeriFlax
www.saskflax.com—Saskatchewan Flax Development Commission
www.healthyimmunity.com—Lorna R. Vanderhaeghe
www.fatflush.com—Ann Louise Gittleman

Books

Dietary Fat Requirements in Health and Development
by Joyce Beare-Rogers, Editor for the American Oil Chemists' Society
Bureau/Nutraceutical Health Protection Branch Department of Health & Welfare
Ottawa, ON (1988)

Eat Fat, Lose Weight
by Ann Louise Gittleman, N.D., C.N.S.
Keats Publishing, Lincolnwood, IL (1999)

Fats That Heal, Fats That Kill: The Complete Guide to Fats, Oils, Cholesterol and Human Health
by Udo Erasmus
Alive Books, Burnaby, BC (1993)

Flax Your Way to Better Health
by Jane Reinhardt-Martin, R.D., L.D.
TSA Press, Moline, IL (2001)

Flaxseed in Human Nutrition
by S.C. Cunnane and L.U. Thompson, Editors
AOCS Press, Champaign, IL (1995)

Healthy Immunity, Scientifically Proven Natural Treatments for Conditions from A–Z
by Lorna R. Vanderhaeghe, B.Sc
Wiley & Sons, Toronto, ON (2002)

Know Your Fats: The Complete Primer for Understanding the Nutrition of Fats, Oils and Cholesterol
by Mary G. Enig, Ph.D.
Bethesda Press, Silver Spring, MD (2000)

No More HRT: Menopause Treat the Cause
by Karen Jensen, N.D. and Lorna R. Vanderhaeghe, B.Sc
Health Venture Publications, Hillsburg, ON (2002) and Quarry Health Books, Kingston, ON (2003)

Omega 3 Oils: To Improve Mental Health, Fight Degenerative Diseases, and Extend Your Life
by Donald O. Rudin, et al
Avery Penguin Putnam, New York, NY (1996)

The Fat Flush Plan
by Ann Louise Gittleman, M.S., C.N.S.
McGraw Hill, New York, NY (2002)

The Omega Plan
by Artemis P. Simopoulos, M.D.
Harper Collins Publishers, New York, NY (1997)

INDEX

mind

EVERY DAY, IN SILENT WAYS,

YOUR BODY MAY BE CRAVING

THE NUTRIENTS YOU NEED FOR

OPTIMAL HEALTH AND WELL-BEING.

REPLENISH YOUR BODY WITH

ESSENTIAL FATTY ACIDS,

SCIENTIFICALLY PROVEN TO BE

ESSENTIAL FOR LIFE.

body

soul

OFF BALANCE?

TAKE CONTROL OF YOUR HORMONES NATURALLY

Count on Alphea™, a clinically proven formula to relieve PMS or try Alphea™50+ to relieve the daily burden of menopausal symptoms.

1-888-313-3369 • www.alphea.ca

 Alphea
Take control of PMS - naturally

 Alphea 50+
Take control of menopause - naturally